Ernie In Kovacsland

From the Collection of Josh Mills & the Kovacs Estate

Compiled and Edited by
Josh Mills, Ben Model, and Pat Thomas

Contents

All selections by Ernie Kovacs except as noted

"He saw
laughter as
a means of
survival,

**and created
a television
of the absurd
as a fallout
shelter.''**

ERNIE KOVACS:
TOO HIP FOR THE ROOM
Ann Magnuson

WITH GREAT ANTICIPATION AND EXCITEMENT, WE ENTERED THE MUSEUM OF Broadcasting for our appointment with the past. It was 1982, and I was with my good friend and fellow punk rock/theater enthusiast Kestutis Nakas. He was about to launch *Your Program of Programs*, his very own public access show on Manhattan Cable.

The title was a play on the famous Sid Caesar comedy classic *Your Show of Shows*, and Kestutis wanted his program to have the 1950s look and feel from The Golden Age of Television. He had enlisted me to be part of it, so together we trekked uptown to 53rd Street to the TV museum for some inspiration.

In those days, there was no easy way to access the past. There was no internet, no Google, no online archives or 24-hour streaming services, and only a select few owned a VCR. Conventional TV often ran old movies, but it ended at midnight and began at dawn and was under the tight control of rich conservative white men who owned the networks.

But there was a time when the medium was so young, so new, so uncharted and full of possibilities that NO ONE was in control of it. Which meant that someone out-of-control could slip in and make history.

The museum archivist brought us the tapes we'd requested, and soon the screen lit up, transforming our viewing booth into a black-and-white wonderland. The opening credits rolled, a mystical door was unlocked, and we entered a magical kingdom ruled by a sharply dressed court jester smoking a cigar.

What we watched Ernie Kovacs do onscreen was raw and exciting and almost entirely unscripted. Even 30 years on, it felt fresh. Supremely charming, this man with the Clark Gable mustache had a flair for the debonair as well as the ridiculous. He took improvisation to a surreal level of nuttiness. Quirky and whip smart, Ernie Kovacs was a man clearly too hip for any room, but he gleefully invited us to join his never-ending party. We were bedazzled! His magnetism was spellbinding, his confidence supreme, and we were thoroughly seduced.

As baby boomers, we shared our infancy with this newfangled medium called television. We knew we had seen Ernie when he was first broadcasting, but our toddler brains were still forming, and the abstractions on the family TV set didn't come into clearer focus until around 1962 — the year Kovacs tragically died in a car accident.

However, I very clearly recall seeing Edie Adams, Kovacs's widow, doing her sexy Muriel cigar ads (earning the money needed to pay off her husband's massive tax debt). She was unforgettable, and by 1982, Edie Adams had become a goddess of retro sexiness. Her pizzazz was recreated by many of us young women in downtown New York's theatrical playground at clubs like Mudd and Club 57. Of course, we were aided and abetted by the luscious outfits found in local thrift stores (no doubt discarded by the stars and showgirls who appeared on those old TV shows).

But Ernie? Our memories of Ernie came in and out — like a static-filled transmission from another dimension.

By the time Kestutis and I first met at CBGBs in 1978, we knew enough about Ernie to discuss how he was an innovator — a wild "madman" and showbiz legend whose creative

energy influenced renegade comics and shows like *Laugh-In* and *Saturday Night Live.*

I'm pretty damn sure we had both seen the 1968 ABC special, *The Comedy of Ernie Kovacs.* And there was a PBS program about him in the mid-'70s. I do remember how hard my dad laughed while watching Kovacs clips whenever they were shown (which was always evidence of comic excellence in our household). And although the details of Ernie's work were still hazy, we knew these truths to be self-evident: he brought wacky chaos to the staid conservative world of 1950s conformity, and he was hip, kind of crazy, and kind of punk rock!

Even in our simpler toddler minds, Ernie Kovacs made an impression. And unlike memory, which is prone to obfuscation (thanks to an overwhelmed brain navigating a media-drenched world), an impression runs much deeper. Memories come and go, but an impression becomes embedded in our DNA.

The name "Ernie Kovacs" was always invoked with admiration and awe. Like when Chevy Chase thanked him at the 1976 Emmys. Ernie's name even became a kind of hipster "code." When you found out somebody knew who Ernie Kovacs was ... well then, you knew without a doubt that that someone was "with it" and could immediately be your friend!

When Kestutis and I saw the archival tape of Ernie in his

glorious prime, we were whisked back in Time and felt the radioactive charge of meeting a kindred spirit!

This man was doing "DIY" before there was a name for it, and as we made our way back to the grimy East Village, we were on fire with ideas and confidence, ready to create fun TV on no budget "just like Ernie!"

The creative anarchy that we experienced in '80s downtown New York was so reminiscent of everything that Ernie Kovacs had been up to that we all have a debt of gratitude to pay him.

In fact, The Golden Age of Television shared a lot in common with our artistic scene. We, too, harnessed our unbridled imagination and ingenuity to get around the fact that nobody had any money. We didn't really know what we were doing, but we did it anyway, and the creative chaos of punk rock, New Wave, and hip-hop eventually infiltrated the worlds of music, art, fashion, journalism, cinema — you name it!

Public access TV was having its own kind of "golden age" at the time. Writer and Andy Warhol cohort Glenn O'Brien had premiered his ultra-hip *TV Party* on Manhattan Cable in 1978, with the soon-to-be mega-famous artist Jean-Michel Basquiat acting as cameraman. Basquiat was doing all kinds of crazy camera work, adding surreal non-sequitur text to the screen with the studio's Chyron generator, as well as other hijinks that were extremely reminiscent of Ernie Kovacs's visual experimentations with the medium.

And Ernie would certainly have been proud of guerilla filmmakers Pat Ivers and Emily Armstrong who secretly "borrowed" Manhattan Public Access studio equipment overnight to film seminal punk bands in the clubs — footage which ended up as their own public access TV show called *Nightclubbing*. (Those tapes have since been exhibited in museums and are now archived at NYU Fales Library.)

All the new "video art" that was exploding onto the scene, especially the goofier output by Keith Haring and Kenny Scharf, was continuing an experiment that Kovacs pioneered. And it's not too much of a stretch to see Ernie's influence on "No Wave" Super-8 filmmakers like John Lurie (who recreated a Gemini space flight in his East Village apartment for the underground classic *Men in Orbit*) and Jamie Nares (whose *Rome '78*

starred New York punk rockers in a largely improvised re-creation of ancient Rome).

I also remember how my fellow mischief-making performer Joey Arias and I would take our crazy characters outside to improvise with store owners and unsuspecting passersby. Of course, we had grown up watching similar antics on the 1960s TV show *Candid Camera*, but Ernie Kovacs was the first to take a TV camera out of the studio to create playful mayhem on the streets of Manhattan.

MTV soon co-opted our downtown '80s ethos which altered, once again, the landscape of pop culture. And when that eventually became stale, a new generation took over the internet with their own brand of DIY craziness on YouTube and TikTok. There's no telling what kind of new technologies will next be coming down the pike. But you can bet your sweet bippy that when some young wisenheimer who is too hip for those futuristic rooms gets ahold of the latest medium, the subversive scent of Ernie Kovacs's cigars will be all over it. ☉

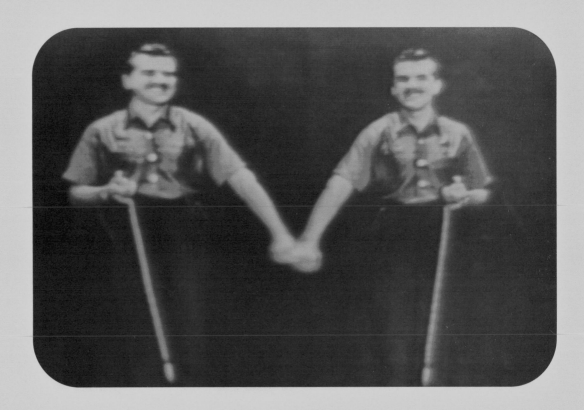

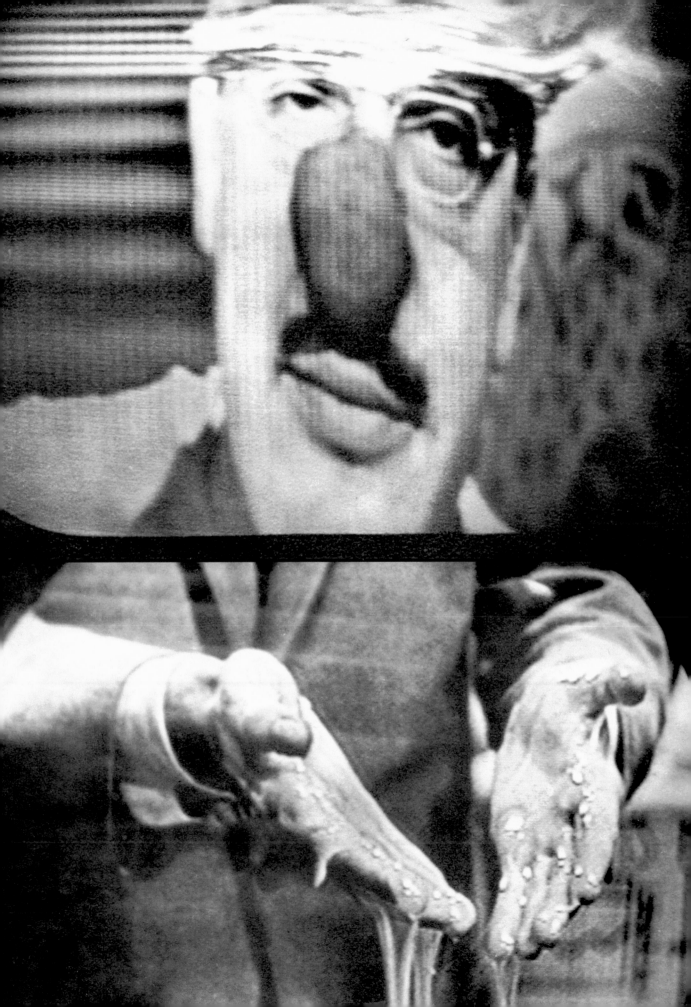

STUDIO NOTEBOOK

In the field of television, where the idiosyncrasies of a performer are often accentuated, Comedian Ernie Kovacs, who begins a new program this week at 2:15 p.m. over WNBK, will probably be a sure hit. According to the NBC publicity department, Ernie will fill his 15-minute program with such antics as getting out puppets to act out a song recording; arguing with a big stuffed dummy-girl who has the voice of Bugs Bunny or whoever else happens to be in the transcription file, giving pantomimes of songs and talking to a film of a cowboy badman as he rides over a hill and perhaps shooting the cowboy with a cap pistol.

Guild Player Show Will Open Tonight

Tonight and Friday night, at 8:30 in The Contemporary auditorium, the Trenton Guild Players will present Thornton Wilder's Broadway hit, "Our Town." The play is being directed by Ernest Kovacs who will also assume the part of Mr. Gibbs.

The cast includes Robert Green, stage manager; Beverly Zarling, Emily Webb; Joseph Vine, George Gibbs; Edna Medved, Mrs. Webb; Kermit Klagg, Mr. Webb; Dorothy Tress, Mrs. Gibbs; Carmela Di Stasi, Rebecca Gibbs; Robert Garvis, Simon Stimson; Adele Wilson, Mrs. Soames; Robert Rence, Joe Stoddard; Otto Lohmann, Howie Newsome; Gordon Latella, Constable Warren; Sam Craig, Norman Downing; Phyllis Sherman, Si Crowell; Joseph Behm, Farmer McCarthy, and Wally Webb will be played by Charles Wilson.

Norman Downing is taking charge of the lighting effects and Frank Huff is the soundman. Tickets may be purchased at the box office which will be opened at 7.

Director Named For Rider Play

Kovacs Long Identified With Amateur Dramatic Groups Here

Ernest Kovacs, widely known in dramatic circles in this vicinity, is acting as director for the Rider College Paint and Powder Players' production, "Pursuit of Happiness," to be presented in Junior 3 auditorium on February 17.

Kovacs was associated with the Community Players and the Spring Street Players as director. He also headed the Theatre Guild which produced plays for several Summer seasons in Morrisville.

As an actor, he is noted for his

PLAY ON, NAIROBI TRIO!

Ron Mael

LONG, LONG AGO, WHEN I WAS A YOUNG LAD GROWING UP IN VENICE, California, I had one Sunday evening ritual in the summer of 1956, which was to watch the weekly performance of The Nairobi Trio. *The Ernie Kovacs Show*, on which The Nairobi Trio performed and which, I would later find out, included Kovacs as the cigar-smoking ape, was a summer replacement for Sid Caesar's *Caesar's Hour*, and for this brief time, I gained what could only be called an addiction to this sketch (to call The Nairobi Trio performances "sketches" is hugely belittling, but I can't think of another term). It was, to me, funny beyond anything I found funny at the time, but there was something also so elemental about it that it reached me very deeply. Of course, the musical theme "Solfeggio" was perfect and irresistible. I'm sure I loved the rest of the show, but The Nairobi Trio eclipsed everything else for me at the time. It was my religion.

Since that time, terms such as surrealism, reinvention of the television medium, breaking the fourth wall, etc., etc., were added, for better or worse, to my vocabulary and are applicable to everything Kovacs did. I almost miss the days when I just thought he was really funny.

I, of course, still find him hilarious, but I've grown to appreciate how special his humor and his use of the rather new medium of television was. There wasn't then and there hasn't been since anything to compare to *The Ernie Kovacs Show*.

One final comment about Ernie Kovacs — I find that his humor shares one thing with Buster Keaton's in the sense of the artist's lack of telegraphing to the audience how great what they're doing is. I find this quality to be a large part of why I find Keaton to be the greatest silent comedian, but it is also equally present in Ernie Kovacs's humor. What a genius Ernie Kovacs was, and what a funny person. Long live The Nairobi Trio! Play on! ⊙

RON MAEL

Kovacs created the infamous "Nairobi Trio" during the first month of DuMont's *The Ernie Kovacs Show*. Those ape masks were lying around, possibly part of his costume trousseau that he took from network to network, when he heard the record of "Solfeggio" for the first time.

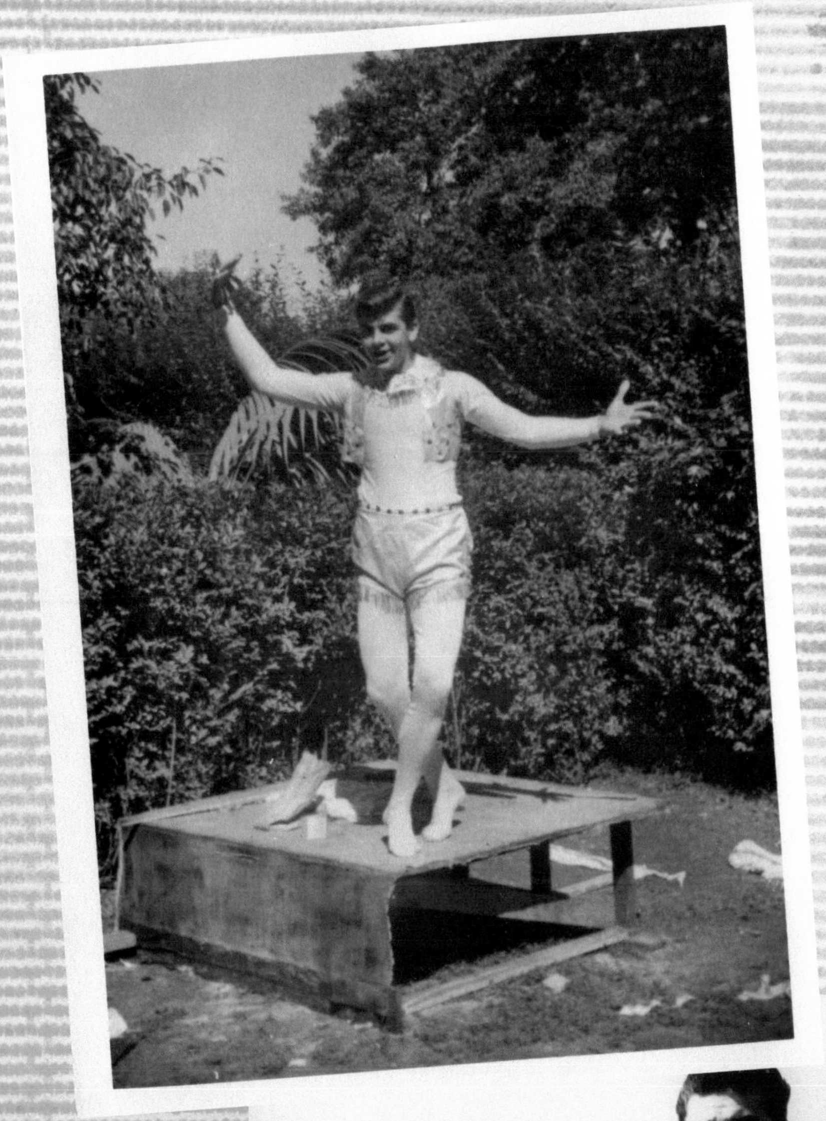

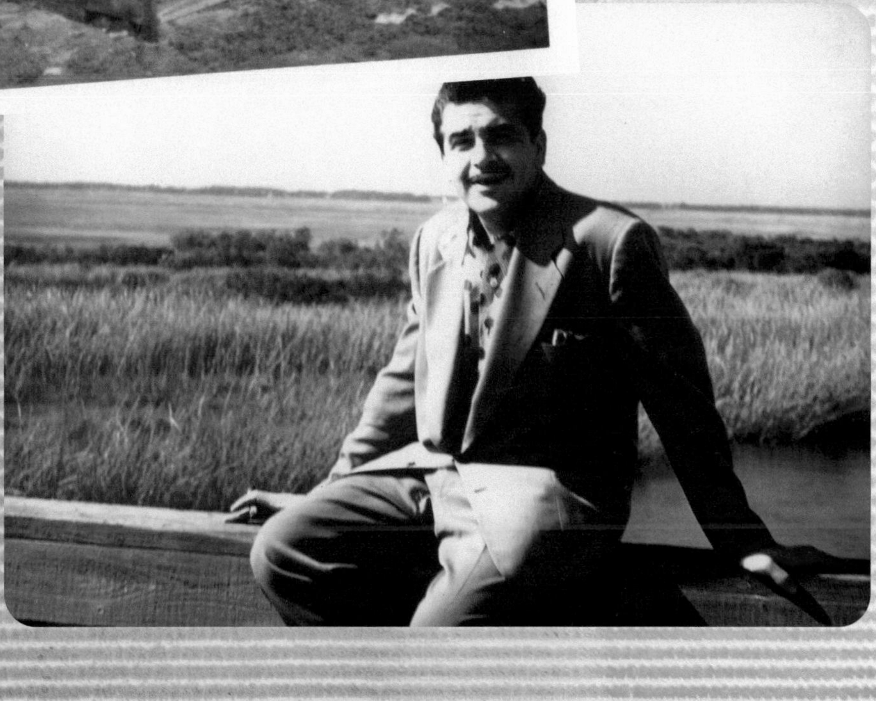

OMNIPRESENT KOVACS

Joshua Mills

IT'S BEEN MORE THAN A DECADE SINCE MY MOTHER, EDIE ADAMS, PASSED away, and I'm still finding treasures she saved from her life, including her life with her first husband, comedian Ernie Kovacs.

Poring over the artifacts in her collection, it's obvious that she lived many lives, and not just with Ernie, either. There are still boxes that I have not looked into. Not because it's emotionally draining, but because there is so damn much of it. I've found photographs, genealogy records, contracts, gifts from friends (dating back to the 1950s), personal and professional documents, clothing, cash register receipts, magazines, press clippings, scripts, memos, medical records, personal writings, government records, and on and on. I could curate a museum on both of their lives. My mom saved so many things from her early childhood to the very end of her life that it would take me a lifetime to discover it all.

The most shocking thing about this collection is how anyone could keep it all. But she did. She wasn't a hoarder. She wasn't keeping decades of old newspapers or used tinfoil, although there were an inordinate number of taper candles to coincide with every major holiday on her shelves. She kept things because they were a part of history. Her history. Ernie's history. Hollywood history. How do I know this? Because when I asked her why she bought back Ernie's kinescope and videotape archive (the first part in 1963 and the rest in 1968 when the networks began taping over and scrapping Kovacs shows to save on storage space and money), she told me, "Because I knew what he was doing was special."

I did find weird curios, though, such as 1978 Chinese restaurant receipts, a business card from a long-defunct Mobil gas station in Malibu, and countless photos of her beloved Welsh Corgis (three decades' worth).

But in this time capsule, I also found Ernie's paystubs from the early 1950s from NBC-TV in New York, Kodachrome slides from vacations she took with Ernie and his two daughters from his first marriage, Betty and Kippie (to Bermuda, Acapulco, Rome, Paris, Venice, Cuba, Lake Tahoe, San Francisco, Yosemite, Disneyland, et al.), and letters that Edie's father, Sheldon Enke, wrote to his soon-to-be wife Ada in 1918 during World War I. Sheldon was a balloonist for the U.S. armed forces in France, and Edie wanted to contact Ken Burns after *The War* (Burns's World War II documentary) premiered on PBS in 2007 to pitch him on doing a World War I prequel based on her father's letters. She was serious, too.

There were tax returns from the 1950s and 1960s which she kept after she and Ernie were audited by the IRS. They were in a 90% tax bracket, and Edie always maintained that an IRS agent who dealt with "Hollywood people" wanted a kickback in exchange for a guarantee they wouldn't be audited. They refused. And they were audited.

I found home movies on Super 8 film from our Bicentennial blowout in 1976 at our beach house in Malibu which featured Jack Lemmon, Sylvester Stallone, directors John Avildsen and Billy Wilder, and musical guests Tony Bennett and The Tonight Show Band. I found more than 1300 video and audio elements of television history stored in a temperature-controlled environment offsite. It might be one of the largest privately held collections of television history in existence. Edie paid for that storage from 1963 until her death in 2008. Even when she was broke, that bill was always paid.

She kept this stuff because she knew it deserved to be preserved, but it wouldn't be if she didn't do it. It was important to her that these things be saved from the dustbin of entertainment history because she and Ernie lived a full lifetime in just over a decade together. Which is why she was adamant in 1963 about buying all the Kovacs masters after his death. If that were the only thing she had saved, she still might be the patron saint of television preservation, as one television archivist told me. But she saved it *all* because it was not only her history, but Ernie Kovacs's history as well.

I think it's safe to say that Ernie Kovacs was clearly the love of my mom's life. It doesn't pain me to say that, even though Ernie Kovacs wasn't my father. My dad, Martin Mills, was my mom's second husband. They married in 1964, and while their marriage didn't last, they always got together for birthdays, holidays, Mother's Day, Father's Day, and the like. I know they did it for my sake, but still they sang songs together from The Great American Songbook over dessert at the now-shuttered Pacific Dining Car restaurant, reminisced about mutual friends who had come and gone, and generally got along for the two-plus hours we were together. Beginning each February on Valentine's Day and running through to my birthday in August, we usually got together at least every other week for some celebration. When you have a Jewish father and a Presbyterian mother, religious holidays, birthdays, American greeting card holidays, and the like meant that we saw each other a lot. That's the life I remember with my parents. But before all that, there was my mom's life with Ernie.

My parents married about two years after Ernie's tragic end in a single-car accident at Beverly Glen Boulevard and Little Santa Monica Boulevard on January 13, 1962. Who really knows if he was actually reaching for a cigar when he lost control of his Corvair on the rain-slicked Los Angeles roads that night? That was the story the police told the reporters covering the crash, or maybe one of the photojournalists on the scene made it up, but it's been part of his legend ever since. Edie guarded Ernie's legacy fiercely for the rest of her life because — as his wife and his partner/editor — she knew how special he was as a person and as a creative genius.

Thankfully, Edie lived in a 3500-square-foot home where she could store this vast collection. She converted bedrooms into closets to house her pristine stage-worn gowns and costumes through the years. The garments were meticulously preserved, and each was tagged with the year and the production she wore it in. There were so many that she had clothing racks made from metal plumbers' pipes so they wouldn't sag under the weight. She converted the garage into more storage for her gowns and for items like her massive "EDIE ADAMS" stenciled trunks that she transported everything in when she went on the road as a solo performer after Ernie's passing. The house was packed with items that summed up their lives together and her life after Ernie. She even built a cedar closet in the garage to house her stage-worn fur coats so they would remain in pristine condition. When fur was no longer in fashion and Jack Lemmon's wife, the actress Felicia Farr, suggested she give them to the homeless, Edie couldn't part with them.

My mom made a small cottage industry by archiving her and Ernie's past. She hired family friends and assistants to assemble her memories into boxes with attached envelopes and a table of contents with names like "1940s Personal" or "Kovacs Business Receipts 1950s." It was remarkable what she saved and documented. Still, she didn't get to everything, and her garage was filled with steamer trunks with "Wonderful Town" stickers, massive books of press clippings that spanned decades (and featured every mention of her life — from her stints opening her own branded "Edie Adams Cut-N-Curl" hair salon franchises in the 1960s and 1970s to her nightclub stints in San Juan, New Orleans, San Francisco, et al., as well as articles written about her film and TV career). The sheer volume was overwhelming. Don't ask about the 9,000 hardcover copies of her autobiography, *Sing a Pretty Song*, that she saved from being pulped in 1990.

Edie's collector's spirit and her own smarts are the foundation for the book you hold in your hands. If Edie had been a minimalist, we wouldn't have any of this. Much to my chagrin now, there were times I wondered if holding onto all this Kovacs stuff was worth it. There were many lean financial years for us — especially in the 1980s. In 1982, my mother lost her only child with Ernie, my half-sister Mia, in a car accident. Ernie and Mia's fatal injuries were exactly the same, and, eerily, father and daughter each died in single-car accidents — 20 years apart — each just days before their respective 43rd and 23rd birthdays. Mere months after my sister's death, my mother had to go to Birmingham, Michigan, to earn a living playing Miss Mona, the owner of the Chicken Ranch, in *The Best Little Whorehouse in Texas*. Every performance, she had to sing "Girl, You're a Woman Now" to a beautiful young blonde ingénue who looked a lot like Mia. I don't know how she managed that even once, but she did it, night in and night out.

A year later, in 1983, she found out that she might have colon cancer, and she didn't know whether she would live or die. The surgeon extracted a grapefruit-sized mass from her, but it turned out to be benign. Nonetheless, it weighed on her (and me) throughout much of that decade as she tried to fight off depression and earn a living. Somehow, she did it. I don't know if I've ever met a stronger woman than my mom.

It was in times like those that I often thought to myself that the sheer amount of "stuff" she had accumulated might be holding her back. Could it be that she was living in the past and wasn't able to move forward at the turn of the new decade? Perhaps. But I stopped thinking that way because Ernie saved her ass in the 1990s and the 2000s. All those three- and four-figure storage bills at a variety of "media asset management providers" in Southern California finally paid off.

With the help of her solid-as-a-rock publicist and de facto manager Henri Bollinger and businessman and friend Gordon Smith, Edie was finally able to turn her life around when she made deals with The Comedy Channel (now Comedy Central), Kultur/White Star Home Video, and the now-defunct Trio Network to bring Ernie Kovacs's vital career and legacy back into popular culture. The money mattered to Edie, but not as much as Ernie's legacy. She almost lost everything on more than one occasion. But she always made sure that the bills to save Ernie's television shows at Bekins and Bonded Services were paid.

So, *Ernie in Kovacsland* is honestly about Edie as much as it is Ernie. My mom guarded his professional career and their personal life together so closely that almost everything you will see in these pages is due to her — from the scans made from the 60 (!) boxes of material she donated to the UCLA Special Collections Library to the ephemera in an uncounted number of boxes in her house. The other 10% is stuff I found on eBay to help fill in the blanks.

It's immensely gratifying to share this Ernie Kovacs book with his fans because it's something my mom would be proud of. It's a book she herself would love to read. She really wanted people to know how much of a genius Ernie Kovacs was. He couldn't tell a joke to save his life, my mom told me. But he knew what made him laugh, and he translated that to the small screen in the 1950s before anyone had played with the medium of television like he did.

"How did he know it would work?" *Mystery Science Theater* creator Joel Hodgson asked my mom about Ernie's groundbreaking visual comedy when we were working on a Kovacs project together in the 1990s.

He just did.

Best,

JOSH MILLS

EDIE ADAMS   ERNIE KOVACS

INCH WORM

ERNIE KOVACS

PIANO CONDUCTOR

Arr. by PETER MATZ

KEEP FIGHTING, YOU EGGHEADS— HELP IS ON THE WAY!

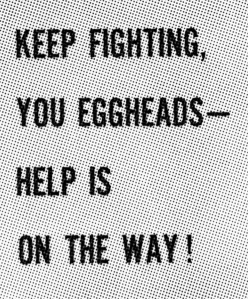

Ernie Kovacs
and
Edie Adams
offer some fresh ideas
to satisfy
intellectual appetites

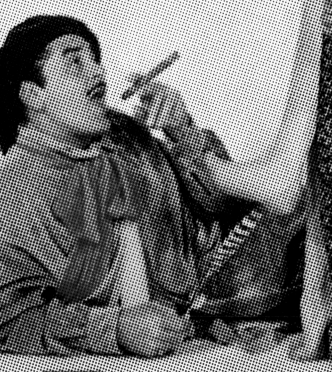

o the rescue of those who feel that television hasn't enough culture comes Ernie Kovacs, star of ABC's *Take a Good Look.* Assisted by his wife Edie Adams, Ernie offers some formats that might be defined as "cracked egghead." If the networks ignore this call to culture, don't blame Ernie and Edie. They tried.

● Mr. Kovacs is a staunch advocate of a less stuffy approach to the arts, including taxidermy. He has accordingly devised a TV series with a human approach to the great masterpieces. The episode above is titled 'Now, Say "Gorgonzola."' Irving Gauguin, postimpressionist, is at work in his Montmartre (Iowa) studio. Gauguin's impressions of posts are, of

course, treasured from the Uffizi Galleries in Florence to the Florence Galleries in Uffizi. Here he coaxes a shy smile from the only model available to struggling painters of his period—a Mrs. Charles Monalisa, his landlady. What gives Irving's achievement its lasting significance is that at this time he was six months behind in his rent. Soon thereafter Mr. Monalisa was found mysteriously drowned in a tube of burnt umber, the only clue being a half-smoked cigar near the body. Irving married the widow and they made a fortune peddling canned laughter.

● As a more candid documentary, the Kovacs recommend a series called *Good Evening, Ed.* Here, playwright Miller Arthur and his movie-star wife are captured in the spirit and in the flesh by Ed Marrow, a bony reporter. Mr. Arthur is the author of such psychoanalytical studies as 'Death of the Iceman' and 'All My Sons Are Boys.' About his wife, little has been known except the dimensions of her shoulder blades, the color of her irises and her unpublished Master's thesis on the Pittsburgh backfield. The look of satisfaction (left) and joy (right)

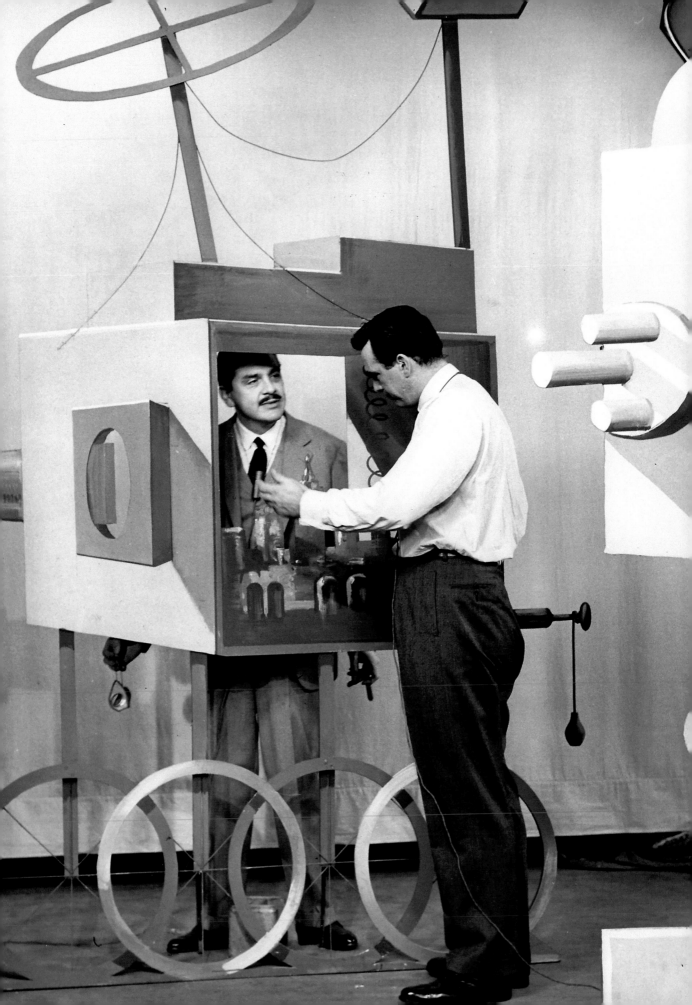

ERNIE KOVACS:
TELEVISION COMEDY'S FIRST AUTEUR

Ben Model

ERNIE KOVACS WAS NEVER A STAND-UP COMEDIAN. HE DIDN'T RATTLE OFF jokes with a punchline — the "water cooler" stuff that you'd share at the office the next day. It was the satirical or humorous *idea* behind his sketches that was "the funny."

And funny he was. Jack Lemmon put it best in the documentary *Television's Original Genius*: "To me, Ernie had what I call a true *sense* of humor … Ernie had the *sense* of humor, of seeing what is funny, and how to get to it."

I could list his famous characters, but if you don't know them in the context of the Kovacs comedy universe, they may not bring a smile to your face. Ernie's "Superclod," which sounds like an obvious spoof, wasn't so much a send-up of the Man of Steel (as so many have done) as it was a constant poke with the question, "Hey, how come nobody recognizes this guy just because he's wearing glasses?"

Kovacs was best known for his Nairobi Trio routine. Try explaining *that* one to somebody who's never seen it.

You could get laughs imitating Wolfgang von Sauerbraten, Percy Dovetonsils, or Miklos Molnar in the same way you might get laughs doing impressions of Bob Hope, Eddie Murphy, or Gilbert Gottfried, but there's really no way to do an impression of Ernie Kovacs. It was his unique sense of humor — that he fought against network suits to maintain — that you'd have to impersonate to "do" Kovacs. That's the legacy that has made his television comedy timeless, more so than many of his contemporaries.

For eleven solid years during television's (first) "golden age," Ernie Kovacs had his own show on one network or another. None of Ernie's shows were popular enough to be considered a hit, but they were popular enough for him to remain on the air — for about a year or so. Or for the next network to take a flier at giving Ernie a slot after he'd been released from his prior engagement over the orthicon tube.

From 1950 to 1952 he logged upwards of twelve hours a week of live and often impro-vised television on Philadelphia NBC affiliate WPTZ. From 1952 to 1954 he had a half-hour morning show on CBS. From 1954 to 1955, Ernie was pioneering late-night programming on the fledgling DuMont network. 1955 and 1956 found Kovacs doing another half-hour morning show on NBC, plus replacing *Caesar's Hour* in prime time, plus doing a three-hour morning drivetime dj show on New York City's WABC radio. When that all ended in the fall, he ran out the year tag-team hosting *Tonight*.

From 1957 to 1959, Ernie did guest shots while being a contract player at Columbia Pictures. From 1959 to the very end, in January 1962, Ernie had a half-hour comedy show on ABC that followed *The Untouchables* — first a weekly panel quiz show, and then a series of monthly specials. Nearly all his programs were called *The Ernie Kovacs Show*, and his theme song remained the same from 1951 all the way through.

It's not easy to describe Kovacs's comedy to someone who isn't familiar with it already. I've been wracking my brains, and there is just this "you had to be there" *je ne sais quoi* about his humor. How do you explain something delicious like Jell-O, collard greens, or paprikas to someone who's never heard of them?

But mention Kovacs to someone who does know Kovacs and watch their face light up in a knowing manner. Instantly, you both know you're fellow members of a secret club.

Case in point: when the first *Ernie Kovacs Collection* DVD box set came out in 2011, I was booked as a guest on a midday NPR show in New York City. While I was waiting in the green room, the show's producer introduced me to the guest who'd just been on, Alice Cooper. I said hello and shook hands, and Cooper politely did the same. How many people is Alice Cooper introduced to every day on press junkets? Then he was told I was there to promote the new Ernie Kovacs DVD set. His eyes lit up. Kovacs! It was like two strangers realizing both were Masons or Knights of Columbus. Apparently, when he was growing up, everything in the Cooper household stopped on Thursday nights so the family could gather around to watch Ernie Kovacs.

I'd discovered Ernie Kovacs the way most people of my generation did, through the *Best of Ernie Kovacs* series that aired on PBS in 1977. But I hadn't heard about it from friends at school, the way I had with Monty Python. My folks were fans from when Ernie was on the air. Knowing my passion for visual comedy and silent movies, they made sure I was in front of our black-and-white Zenith on Tuesday nights at 9:30. I was hooked. Kovacs hit me in my comedy solar plexus the way Buster Keaton had a couple of years earlier.

Kovacs never "tipped," the way Monty Python or Steve Martin or *Saturday Night Live* or SCTV did. They went from hilarious and offbeat shows only you and a small bunch of your friends watched to — *boom!* — movies and tours and TV specials and hit records. Suddenly, quoting bits you'd seen them do ceased to be a secret handshake. Ernie Kovacs should be much more widely known, but, so far, he remains an inside joke among his fans.

Ah, but that inside joke is spreading.

You're holding this book, aren't you?

That true sense of humor of Ernie's influenced the television comedy that followed. The DNA of Ernie's television comedy can be found in a great deal of television comedy that followed his — programs much better known than his are.

Laugh-In has the kitchen-sink variety and irreverence of the Kovacs shows, but tempo-wise, it runs in fifth gear instead of first. No surprise there. Jolene Brand, part of Ernie's

PATHETIC NEWS

VIDEO................ THE VIDEO MEN
AUDIO............. THE AUDIO MEN
LIGHTING........ THE LIGHTING MAN
MASTER CONTROL....MASTER CONTROL
FLOORS SWEPT.......KOVACS

WROTE AND PRODUCED BY

ensemble from 1960 to 1961, was *Laugh-In* producer George Schlatter's wife — and Schlatter himself was around the Kovacs set, hanging out and talking shop and comedy with Ernie. The early Letterman shows bear a striking resemblance in feel and format to Ernie's NBC daytime comedy-variety show. And why not? Letterman's writers were spending time at the fledgling Museum of Broadcasting (now the Paley Center for Media) watching kinescopes of Ernie's 1956 show.

Ernie's shows weren't broadcast in England until very recently, and so an influence on Monty Python might not be obvious, but the Kovacs comedy ethos is imbued in there somewhere. Minnesotan Terry Gilliam had been heavily influenced by Kovacs, and surely had the "What would Ernie Kovacs do?" mantra floating through his sensibilities when working on the series.

When *Saturday Night Live* won its first Emmy, Chevy Chase acknowledged his fellow cast members and said, "I also would like to thank Ernie Kovacs. I swear!" Some of the send-ups and commercial spoofs of cheap late-night television — like the ones for Bass-O-Matic and Shimmer Floor Polish — are Kovacsian. The darkly written Michael O'Donoghue pieces and the wordless cold open of "The Dead String Quartet" are pure Kovacs. *Mystery Science Theater 3000* and *The Kids in the Hall* carry the aesthetic through the turn of the current century.

With Kovacs, though, the inside joke was also between Ernie and you.

He'd cultivated his own personal sense of humor and style of writing over several years, post–high school and living in Trenton, New Jersey.

He did double duty writing a regular column for *The Trentonian* from 1945 to 1950 while also spinning records and doing patter and spoof commercials on the town's AM station, WTTM, where he'd been a host/announcer/deejay since 1941. That one-to-one connection between writer/performer and reader/listener was what Kovacs later referred to as "an intimate vacuum" in his television work.

That's the inside joke aspect to Kovacs's sense of humor.

Watching his shows feels like visits with him.

Some of his live programs, which only survive in audio form, have that feel. There's no opening monologue or jokes — again, Kovacs had never been a nightclub comic — and from the way it sounds, sometimes the start of episodes of *Kovacs Unlimited* (CBS, 1952–1954) sound like we just wandered into his rec room and found him there.

Of the handful of episodes that I've been able to listen to, after the opening title music, there is no opening monologue or formal greeting, as one might expect from a TV show host. Sometimes Ernie is chatting with the crew or with pianist Eddie Hatrak. Ernie then transitions from his on-set coffee klatch to include us in the goings-on. If someone with a headset connected to the control booth had been counting down from ten and then giving Ernie the "and — GO!" signal, you'd never know it.

Kovacs was prolific, and he was a fountain of ideas. His wife, Edie Adams, said Ernie woke up on a manic high and never came down, and that he brought his typewriter to his dressing room when he was on movie shoots so he could write. There are cartoons and doodle-ish drawings that survive. He answered his fan mail and was creative about it.

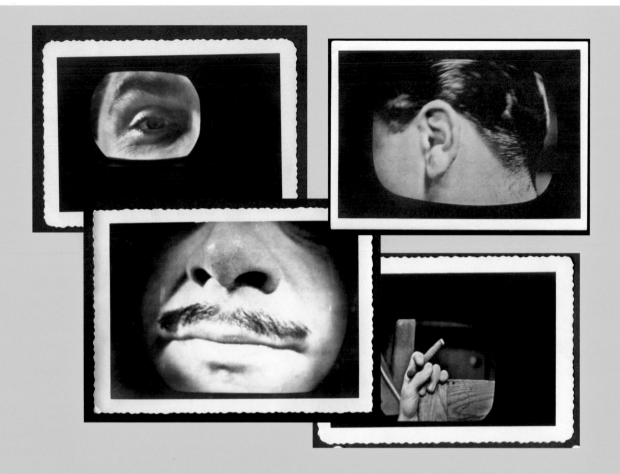

Ernie wrote for *Mad* magazine during the mid- to late-1950s. He'd fallen in love with the magazine at its start, and even had *Mad*'s publisher, William Gaines, and its founding editor, Harvey Kurtzman, on as guests on *Kovacs Unlimited* in 1954. He loved the satire and irreverent nature of the magazine's spoofs. He would read it everywhere, often tucked inside a more "establishment" magazine so as not to be seen reading a comic book in a fancy ristorante. Mostly what he wrote for *Mad* was "Strangely Believe It," a recurring feature illustrated by Wallace Wood that was his takeoff on *Ripley's Believe It or Not*. These were bits he'd written and performed on his ABC radio program in 1956 (which Kovacs called "Oddities in the News") or as newsreel spoofs on his NBC-TV show that same year ("Pathetic News — the Eyes, Ears, Nose, and Throat of the World").

There are no credits for the four-minute promotional film for Ernie's first film, *Operation Mad Ball* (1957), but the film and gags are pure Kovacs. The promo is basically Ernie, on a movie set of a suburban home's den, calmly delivering an irreverent comic monologue about the film and who's in it. This is punctuated throughout with sight gags, and the only glimpses of *Operation Mad Ball* itself are a few shots that are only on screen for two or three seconds.

He wrote and performed his own TV commercials for Dutch Masters cigars.

He didn't have to — there were conventional spots already made for the Consolidated Cigars product that was the sponsor of Ernie's 1959–1962 ABC-TV show. Ernie had a knack for publicity and cooked up his own wordless blackout gags to promote Dutch Masters. He was very proud of them, and when they were included in the body of his bizarro quiz panel show, *Take a Good Look* (1959–1961), he ran them for the studio audience during the show. One of the spots shows Kovacs in the audience of a classical music concert. We hear a well-known movement from a Haydn string quartet (now attributed to Roman Hofstetter) begin. Kovacs starts to noisily unwrap a cigar. The entire audience turns to glare at him, and he stops. The single take continues, and the camera slowly pans over to the stage, where we find the string quartet performing, all four members smoking cigars. We hold for a moment for this to register, then the camera tilts down to reveal an open box of Dutch Masters cigars, and the announcer reads the product's tagline. Blackout. The commercial won a Clio — the ad business equivalent of the Oscar — the first year Clios were given out.

It's clear from at least one TV interview — done in the summer of 1961 for the CBC — and several pages of notes and typed script that have just turned up, that Ernie had been planning to make a *Eugene* movie.

Eugene was Ernie's silent character who had been featured in two different half-hour shows — the *NBC Color Spectacular* in January 1957 and ABC's *The Ernie Kovacs Special* in November 1961. The former had put Kovacs on the map, and in the summer of 1961, he spoke in minute detail about scenes from the film he wanted to make, which would ideally have starred Alec Guinness. He discusses lens focal length, camera movements, detailed gags, and scenes.

Ernie did not like any creative interference.

He was used to doing things the way he did things, as his creative process had simply always gone that way since his Trenton years.

If some of the network suits poked their heads in the door with suggestions, Ernie would tell them to thread up a Western. (Westerns choked the airwaves during that era, and the easiest way to fill or kill airtime would be to grab a 16mm print of one off the racks.)

Kovacs's creative flow was already his "wheelhouse" when he entered the medium and fanned out to include all the visual possibilities in the TV toolbox. Matting, superimpositions, reverse-polarity (negative), split-screens, cutting or specific camera shots used for comic effect or timing — it was all possible from day one. Like Buster Keaton in cinema before him, Ernie Kovacs innately got what you could do, or what *else* you could do with television. Not just for visual humor, but for visual humor that happened in that intimate vacuum — the inside joke between him and us at home.

Up until the point Ernie entered the orthicon tube in 1951, television had been used for comedy as something to point three cameras at. Milton Berle's *Texaco Star Theater* (1948–1956) had its cameras at the back of the theater so the viewer at home was almost a fly on the wall of the auditorium for Berle's weekly live theatrical presentation of sketches, monologues, and big musical numbers. *The Colgate Comedy Hour* (1950–1955) was the same, with the technology being used to bring big-city comedy and variety entertainers — and their huge live-theater audiences' reactions — into American living rooms.

In 1951, Kovacs and his crew taped an empty orange juice container to the front of a camera's lens and stuck a kaleidoscope on it. They stuck empty tomato paste and soup cans together with a mirror or prism inside and attached *that* to the camera to make the image appear upside down — so Ernie could appear to be vacuuming the ceiling. Ernie's first network show, *Kovacs Unlimited* (CBS, 1952–1954), had no studio audience, and Ernie wanted it that way. Ernie employed the language of cinema in a medium whose visual language was used by everyone else just to make sure you were seeing everything important. He'd live-cut to a close-up reaction shot of himself registering dismay about something going amok the way you'd have seen Oliver Hardy reacting to Stan Laurel in one of their 1930s comedies. There was a deliberateness to the use of the kinds of shots and to the timing of cameras cutting from one to another that resembled what you'd see in movies. This traveled with Ernie from network to network regardless of who was getting directorial credit on the shows.

In 1956 when working for NBC and forced to have a live audience, he didn't play to them. He continued creating comedy sketches that worked on the small screen in people's homes. He'd tell the studio audience, on-air, "Watch the monitors, or you're not going to get any of this!" When viewing these 1956 NBC shows, you find yourself laughing and wondering why the audience isn't, only to realize that none of the comedy works in a proscenium stage setting — it only works on a screen.

Ernie's is also a body of work that has an astonishing survival rate, considering the body count of most television from the same era. This is thanks to Ernie's partner in crime — and in comedy and in life — Edie Adams. Not only did Edie make valiant efforts to secure the original 2-inch master videotapes before they were wiped by the network and the 16mm kinescopes before they were given cement shoes and tossed into the Hudson River, she was saving Kovacs shows while they were being broadcast.

What we are left with is an intense body of television work that Ernie Kovacs made from 1950 to 1962. This survives thanks to the efforts of Edie Adams, patron saint of television conservation. That body of work is television that utilized the technology and filmic language that was there from the beginning but which most comedians didn't employ in their humor. They were comedians *on* television, but Kovacs *was* television — at least more so than his contemporaries were.

More than 100 16-inch audio transcription discs survive out of the total Edie had had made during the run of *Kovacs Unlimited* (CBS) and during Ernie's DuMont show. Initially, she'd wanted to be able to hear herself singing, to improve her pop vocal techniques, but she continued to have them made because the shows weren't being kinescoped, and she knew what Ernie was doing was important and should be saved. Who was thinking about and actually *preserving* (live) TV in 1952?

And where did this come from, this notion of saving early television while it was actually being made? Edythe Adams, blonde, blue-eyed Pennsylvania Dutch gal, was only a couple of years out of Juilliard when she auditioned for *Ernie in Kovacsland* in mid-1951. Edie always claimed it was her conservatory background that informed her preservation of Ernie's work. But the idea of making audio transcription discs of the 1952–1954 Kovacs shows — long after the purpose of hearing herself sing pop tunes was outgrown — was forward-thinking, even revolutionary. As for kinescopes, only one survives out of that show's 21-month run. Were there others? We may never know.

Edie and Ernie were married in 1954, no surprise to fans of the show. The two of them had been in sketches together regularly ever since Edie joined up as a "girl singer," and in some ways the two were a comedy team. Their chemistry, timing, and shared sense of humor show in the surviving kinescopes from the 1950s. Edie's devotion to Ernie and his creative work is impressive, and she was still rounding up copies of his shows and the rights to them in the 1960s and 1970s.

Edie saved scripts, props, costumes, and other items. During the years of the early live shows in Philadelphia and on CBS, Ernie encouraged viewers and fans to take photos of their TV screen and mail them in. This was for a weekly "pikskers" contest, in which winners would be sent promotional items provided by sponsors. Edie kept several boxes of these "snepshots," as they were also referred to.

But there's also Ernie's *writing* and "illustrated profuselies" and all the other creativity in the margins of his television work that's survived. Drawings. Unfinished manuscripts. Short pieces of written humor, published posthumously in men's magazines. Songs he wrote. And on and on. Ernie was a fountain of comedy and creative ideas. So much, much more than Percy Dovetonsils odes and different iterations of The Nairobi Trio.

There's plenty more Kovacs that lies "outside the bookends," as Percy Dovetonsils would say in his sign-off. And that's what's served up here for you to savor and enjoy. Just the way Ernie would with a fine Cuban cigar or a chilled-to-just-right martini.

Best wishes,
BEN MODEL

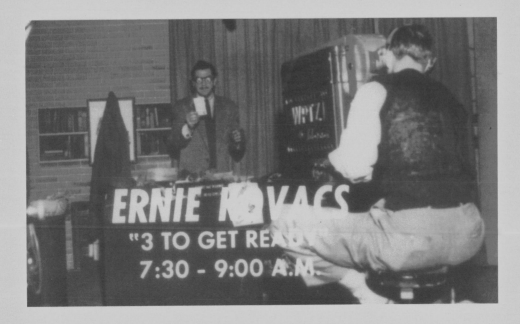

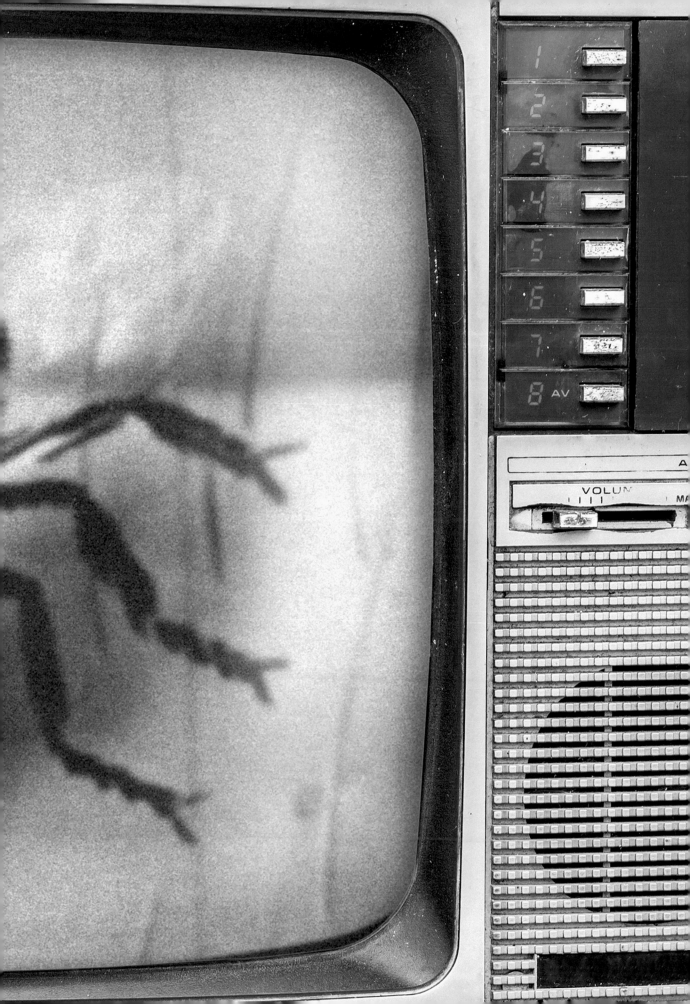

KOVACS & THE COUNTERCULTURE

Pat Thomas

JOSH MILLS AND I ARE SITTING WITH JERRY CASALE OF DEVO DISCUSSING
Ernie Kovacs's influence on the New Wave performance art mavericks when it occurs to me that Kovacs is like Jimi Hendrix — his professional career was short, but his influence was wide and lasting. Casale quickly agrees.

Later, I'm visiting with political satirist (and co-founder of The Yippies) Paul Krassner when I mention Kovacs to him. He fondly lights up hearing that name, contrasting Ernie against today's obnoxious late-night TV comedians who scream for effect and don't write much of their own material. He says, "Kovacs's show was never the same twice," going on to make the point that today's shows always follow a format [such as an opening monologue that *must* happen each evening]. "Ernie was relaxed," Krassner continued, "never shrieking, and he wrote all of his own skits and jokes. I liked his easy-going approach that didn't need a bunch of writers and producers to bring it to fruition."

While youngsters like David Letterman and Jay Leno were paying attention to Kovacs's M.O., they sadly overlooked the subtle persona of his delivery. But they borrowed at least one of his (and *Tonight Show* host Steve Allen's) ideas — go to the street with a camera and interview average joes walking by. That skit (no matter who does it) never fails to get a laugh.

As Edie Adams, Ernie's wife, points out in her 1990 memoir, *Sing a Pretty Song*, "Letterman's head writer, Steve O'Donnell, and his staff spent three months … studying Kovacs kinescopes, so I know they're fans." She also says, "Alan Zweibel, a former writer on *Saturday Night Live*, said that all the writers on that show 'had Kovacs at the core of everything we did … whenever there was a question, we said, 'What would Ernie have done?'"

Zweibel continues, noting Kovacs's interest in "the distortion of pictures and sound." Edie solidifies the SNL influence when she notes that when that group of "Not Ready for Prime Time Players" won their first Emmy, "Chevy Chase grabbed the mike and said a special thank-you to Ernie Kovacs. I'll never forget him for it."

While I was watching an old Ernie TV episode with vintage pop culture fan Kristin Leuschner, she pointed out how Kovacs pushed the boundaries of simple camera angles — Kovacs made the audience POV part of the eye-popping fun, be it putting his face right up into the lens or pulling way back to allow a different or a wide view not normally done in those early days of television.

And while Kovacs was a popular late 1950s/early1960s phenomenon, he posthumously inspired the late '60s counterculture. As writer Martin McClellan pointed out in *The Seattle*

Review of Books, "*Laugh-In* [took some] visual tricks straight out of Ernie Kovacs's playbook … fast zooms in on dancing girls, guitar-based twangy upbeat music, prop walls that opened and slid to reveal actors and comics delivering sharp one-liners."

Kovacs — along with Lenny Bruce, Jack Kerouac, Allen Ginsberg, *Mad* magazine, and others — fueled Krassner and his fellow Yippies Jerry Rubin and Abbie Hoffman. Jerry and Abbie revolutionized political activism in the 1960s. The stunts they pulled are infamous. They shut down the New York Stock Exchange by dropping dollar bills onto the floor, which traders fought over, and they turned a march on Washington into a psychedelic happening at the Pentagon in October '67. When Jerry was federally indicted as part of the Chicago 8 (later the Chicago 7) — for "The whole world is watching" riots that took place during the 1968 Chicago Democratic Convention, he described that moment as winning "the Academy Award of protest." Kovacs's comedy was apolitical, but his style helped inspire a later generation of leaders that led young people against the bogus Vietnam War.

Journalist Jack Newfield, in *The New York Times,* December 29, 1968, wrote, "Abbie Hoffman is a charming combination of Ernie Kovacs, Artaud, and Prince Kropotkin. He is a put-on artist, an acid head (over 70 trips), a mass-media guerrilla…"

In Hoffman's own 1968 tome, *Revolution for the Hell of It,* he interviewed himself:
Can you think of any people in theater that influence you? "W.C. Fields, Ernie Kovacs, Che Guevara, Antonin Artaud, Alfred Hitchcock, Lenny Bruce, the Marx Brothers."

1960s underground cartoonist Skip Williamson — described by *The New York Times* in a 2017 obituary as "a rambunctious creator of underground comics that merged his radical politics with his love of scatological humor" (the *Times* included a Williamson drawing of Jerry Rubin) — was another Kovacs devotee. In a March 2017 *ComicMix* article, editor/commentator Mike Gold wrote: "Skip's most revered character was Snappy Sammy Smoot, a hippie take on Ernie Kovacs's popular character Percy Dovetonsils, only — and incredibly — even more surreal."

In fact, Kovacs was a contributor to *Mad.* The magazine's founder Harvey Kurtzman enjoyed a mutual admiration relationship with Kovacs, and Ernie's own humor would pop up in various issues. Kovacs even wrote the introduction to the 1958 *Mad* anthology paperback, *Mad for Keeps.*

Arguably, early Kovacs musical skits cut a path for some of the surreal MTV videos produced by the likes of the Cars — check out the Cars' "You Might Think" for an example of Ernie's visual influence. As one Kovacs biographer pointed out, "the love-stricken singer turning into a fly and buzzing towards his beloved's nose is practically a mini-homage to Ernie's 1950 camera tricks."

Speaking of pop music, let's not forget Harry Nilsson's Kovacs-inspired moment — during a 1972 BBC TV live performance, Harry visually mimics Ernie's "Nairobi Trio" while singing his own song "Coconut" in a gorilla suit. Frankly, the wacky repetitive lyrics are a Kovacs pastiche as well.

I was drafted (by Josh Mills) to work on this collection of Kovacs material after the publication of my book that gathered up some of Yippie Jerry Rubin's ephemera — and while I worked on this Ernie book, I concurrently assembled a similar collection of writings, drawings, and photographs from Allen Ginsberg's personal archive. Halfway through the Kovacs/Ginsberg process (with the Chicago 8's theatrics in the back of my mind), I began to realize that a counterculture thread connected them.

I was too young to have lived the 1960s hippie journey as it was happening, but I felt validated by a book review penned by Frederic and Mary Ann Brussat. (I confess I haven't read the memoir written by Wes "Scoop" Nisker, which they describe as "recommended for those who are nostalgic for the wild experimentation of the 1960s and the ardent idealism of youth and would like to have a jaunty trip down memory lane.") But since Nisker lived during the era I'm attempting to encapsulate in this essay, this is what caught my eye:

"Born December 22, 1942, in Nebraska … Nisker says that his first guru was Alfred E. Neuman of *Mad* magazine. He felt connected to the youth culture that came alive in the 1950s with rebel James Dean on the screen and rock-and-roll on the radio. The author lionized Beat poets and writers — Jack Kerouac, Gary Snyder, and Allen Ginsberg. Nisker also fed his discontent with the status quo with the sarcasm of his favorite comedians — Sid Caesar, Ernie Kovacs, Lenny Bruce, and Mort Sahl."

Lastly, I recently discovered that the first-ever biography of Ernie, *Nothing in Moderation*, was written in 1975 by David Walley. I wasn't familiar with Walley, but I noted his previous book was a biography of Frank Zappa. In a 2020 Zappa documentary titled *Zappa*, there's a vintage clip of Zappa praising Ernie for inspiring his own "lifelong pursuit of utilizing the ordinary for a unique musical approach."

The director of the Zappa film, Alex Winter, told *Variety* in November 2020:

"And the thing that I liked about Zappa's humor was that it was not often the humor that he put into his records. The way he used humor in his records was almost like another musical instrument. The way, say, Ernie Kovacs would use it…"

I rest my case.

PAT THOMAS
in "Burbank, Home of Warner Bros. Records"

Celebrates Birthday

Club

eeting
f the
iation,
th the
Those
ander-
raasch.
White.
under.
nham,
elight-
s were

decor-
terest-
ng the

ief

Ernest Kovacs

Who is the son of Mr. and Mrs.
Andrew J. Kovacs, of Union Street.
celebrated his eighth birthday an-

t. Jos-
ion, a
ing in
Avenue.
renton.

Ode to Stanley's Pussycat

I was a strong child and considered quite manly,
I lived in the suburbs next door to Stanley.
I planned to be a fireman: he planned to be a doctor.
His mother taught psychiatry: honest! I could've socked her.

She taught her son to exert his mind on animal and friend.
What he did to his pussycat was just about the end.
Stanley's pussycat at first was just as nice as silk,
He purred like other pussycats and always drank his milk.

Then that awful Stanley put his pussycat on the couch
And psychoanalyzed poor pussycat and made him such a grouch.
That pussycat's personality slowly began to change.
His friendly purr became a snarl with an Yma Sumac range.

He'd sneak into the living room with steps as soft as satin,
Climb up on the cocktail bar and mix a strong manhattan.
He'd gulp it down and drop all shame and lose all sense of fear.
Then he'd drink a second one and spit the icecube at the mirror.

He'd drink till dawn, then down the street he'd stagger, round and fat.
Soon everyone was gossiping 'bout Stanley's pussycat.
His drinking went from bad to worse, 'twas really most disturbin' -
He'd catch the mice at any bar in trade for a shot of bourbon.

Stanley's pussycat became a drunk: he stole to purchase liquor.
When nice pussycats drank milk and cream, Stanley's would hiccup and
    snicker.
Soon he couldn't catch the mice at all, the bars refused to pay him,
The mice ran away when he sneaked upon them, 'cause his breath would
    always betray him.

Then doom did come as it comes to all. His pussycat went to the clinic.
The doctor sneered as he examined him, the doctor was a cynic.
His heartbeat was so awfully fast, and even more his pulse, sir.
Stanley's pussycat has switched to cream, he has a pussycat ulcer.

Takes Active Part in Outdoor Sports

Ernest Kovacs

Popular son, of Mr. and Mrs. Andrew Kovacs, of 366 Union Street, who recently celebrated his fourth birthday anniversary. Ernest is a general favorite with all who know him and is very fond of ponies.

Ernie Kovacs and Stogies To Do New TV Panel Show

NEW YORK (UPI)—Ernie Kovacs, the intelligently hilarious, overgrown Hungarian leprechaun of the airwaves, thinks he has found a television medium that will leave him free from worry about what those eternal bogies, the critics, will say.

"A panel show I'm going to like," he says, "because the next day you don't have to sit down and read the critics. After all, what can you do wrong with a panel show? Maybe they don't like the arrangement of the chairs? Maybe they could criticize poor block letters in the titles?"

Regardless of what the critics write, Ernie's upcoming panel show has one lovely item that many listeners will applaud: Silent commercials. He's going to do them himself.

The only noise will be the sweet strains of a string quartet playing a Haydn theme. However, there's a possibility he'll have the musicians puffing big cheroots. The sponsor is a cigar maker.

He should enjoy doing commercials (he'll write them and act in them) because he habitually smokes 10 to 20 cigars a day. And as a former radio news commentator, newspaper columnist and student of current history, he should enjoy the new show, which begins in October.

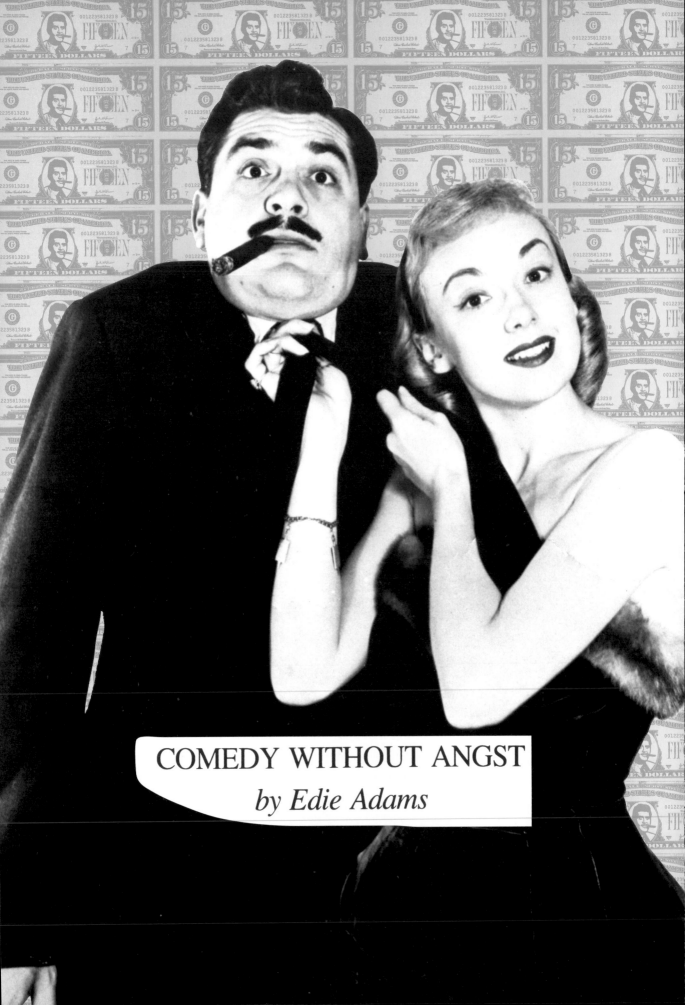

COMEDY WITHOUT ANGST

by Edie Adams

first met Ernie in 1951 when, fresh out of Juilliard and a recent "loser" on Arthur Godfrey's *Talent Scouts*, I went to Philadelphia to audition for a new television show called *Ernie in Kovacsland*. What I remember most from that first and fateful meeting is a man in a large, floppy hat, with a black moustache and an enormous cigar in his mouth. He was unlike anyone I had—or have—ever met, and a decided contrast to my very proper parents. Through the years, Ernie taught me a great deal about comedy and a lot about television but, most important, he taught me how to play.

At home, nothing was ever taken seriously. He was on a permanent manic high from the time he got up in the morning; at breakfast, the orange juice was *the best* orange juice, the eggs were *the best* eggs—everything in life was to be enjoyed to the fullest. Life for Ernie was recess and not, as my parents had taught me, the serious classroom of lessons on which one was to be graded. What Ernie taught me was, I think, what he also tried to teach the television audience: that life was a romp and anything too serious or too pretentious was to be shot down. His humor was what I call the "laughing in church" type and if some people still preferred the sermons, then so be it.

"Too erratic, his comedy is too extreme and too frequently he gets his punch line from the grisly side of life . . . man being torn apart by horses . . . trick golf expert missing the golf ball and bashing in his assistant's head." Such was the judgment rendered by nationally syndicated television columnist John Hope on the comedy of Ernie Kovacs.

In reality, it was Kovacs on Kovacs: Ernie wrote those words for Hope, a character who appears in his satiric novel, *Zoomar*, published in 1957. Always his own—and toughest—critic, Ernie would have been the first to admit that his comedy was sometimes too erratic and sometimes too extreme. But he would have

been the last to admit that he fashioned his humor from the grisly side of life; that statement was his jab at those he dismissed as the "don't you think, boys," the Monday morning quarterbacks of the television columns.

His ideas on humor were analogous to journalism's adage on what makes news: "Dog bites man," does not stop the presses; "Man bites dog" is worthy of a headline. Similarly, Ernie always said that "humor lies in the incongruity, in the unexpected" and much of his own work, particularly his famous blackouts and sight gags, evolved from his theory that the comic response emanated from "suppressed desire to logical ending."

been the last to admit that he fashioned his humor from the grisly side of life; that statement was his jab at those he dismissed as the "don't you think, boys," the Monday morning quarterbacks of the television columns.

His ideas on humor were analogous to journalism's adage on what makes news: "Dog bites man," does not stop the presses; "Man bites dog" is worthy of a headline. Similarly, Ernie always said that "humor lies in the incongruity, in the unexpected" and much of his own work, particularly his famous blackouts and sight gags, evolved from his theory that the comic response emanated from "suppressed desire to logical ending."

As a performer on all of Ernie's early shows broadcast from Philadelphia (*Ernie in Kovacsland*, *Kovacs Unlimited*, and *The Ernie Kovacs Show*) and many of his later shows broadcast from New York or Los Angeles, I was very often the "logical ending" of "suppressed desire"—the well-dressed, perfectly made-up girl who winds up with a cream pie in the face. It was an ending my training at the Juilliard School of Music had not prepared me for, but like the dog on the receiving end of a spurt of water from a fire hydrant or the wooden duck who fires back at his would-be attacker from a shooting gallery, it was an ending that was unexpected and funny—and pure Kovacs.

What was truly incongruous, of course, was that Ernie's comedic artistry was so highly advanced in what was then so highly primitive a medium. It is important, I think, to remember the context of the times in which these shows were produced. Live television in the early 1950s was a low budget, black-and-white visual "entertainment" without benefit of the video technology we now take for granted. All camera work, zoom, focus, etc., was performed manually by one cameraman (and in those days it was always a camera-*man*, not a cameraperson); if he took a break, I or another cast member filled in for him.

It is little wonder then that the majority of entrees on the fifties TV menu were the variety show, the drama, and the sitcom—video vaudeville and pictured proscenium. To Ernie, however, who was one of the very few comedians not to come to television via vaudeville or nightclub, these limitations were simply opportunities through which to explore and expand the potential of the medium; to make, in

McLuhan's terms, the medium the message, a message in which effects took precedence over "meaning." With a budget of only fifteen dollars per week for props on his Philadelphia productions, Ernie invited his viewers to send in items, and these donations—a hodgepodge "Salvation Army" property closet—provided the fodder for some of his most famous and spontaneous bits. As one of us threw these curios of the audience's family histories to him, he would improvise. Thus a pair of trick glasses became the basis for Percy Dovetonsils, and a thirty-nine-cent toy kaleidoscope taped to an orange juice can and then attached to the camera lens emerged as a footnote to small screen history as the first psychedelic image ever to appear on television, fifteen years before the era of psychedelic "art."

Many times, of course, the spontaneity was fully scripted, for Ernie was essentially a writer. Perhaps this was a carry-over from his days as a newspaper columnist in Trenton, New Jersey, where he was a deadline writer, fast and concise. Once as we were leaving the house for a month-long European vacation, our secretary came running out to the car saying that the ad agency was on the phone from New York and needed a new Dutch Masters commercial. Ernie told her to put the call on hold and went into the house, sat at the typewriter for five minutes, and then dictated to the agency a Clio award-winning commercial. "Writing fast is the only way for me," he always said. "If I start tinkering with a thing, it sounds labored."

Whether writing for one of his shows, working on a novel, or composing his "Strangely Believe It" page for *Mad* magazine (a labor of love), Ernie took as his subjects the mundane and commonplace—the people, places, and things around him—but saw them from a different perspective from the rest of us. I came to call his creative process "back of the head" comedy: Whatever would flash across the back of Ernie's head would come out on the television screen, almost a photographic process of inverting an image onto film. "The world's really at an eighteen-degree angle," he said; his cerebral camera saw things upside-down and then turned

them around again. Much like Eugene Ionesco, Samuel Beckett, and other playwrights of the theater of the absurd school, he realized that very few things in life made sense. Unlike them, however, he did not conceive of the absurd as terrifying. He saw laughter as a means of survival, and created a television of the absurd as a video fallout shelter—Ernie would have tripped Godot when he finally did show up.

One of his most memorable "back-of-the-head" creations was the famous Nairobi Trio. During a rehearsal in New York, Peter Hanley, then appearing with us as the traditional "boy singer," brought in a recording of "Solfeggio" and suggested that Ernie listen to it. Within minutes, Ernie had us in place for the premiere performance of The Nairobi Trio. In subsequent engagements of this famed troupe, friends of ours such as Jack Lemmon, Frank Sinatra, and Tony Curtis would be among those who appeared with this madcap threesome.

Never at a loss for ideas, Ernie carried with him, always and everywhere, English notebooks with tissue-thin sheets on which to jot down impressions and ideas as they occurred to him. If we were riding in a cab, he might take a long look at the driver and then write down "nostrils like razor blades." And sooner or later, a character whose distinguishing trait was "nostrils like razor blades" would emerge in a sketch.

It was, though, my mother's house that provided Ernie with a grist for one of his most critically acclaimed creations: Eugene. A Victorian refuge in the modern world, my mother's house was homage to late nineteenth-century artifacts, including a spindly china cabinet full of long-stemmed glassware that sounded eerily like the Bodhi Tree Temple bells as one tried to tiptoe past it. At dinner, everything was served on so many doilies and tinkling trays that one could not say "pass the pickles" unless absolutely certain of steady hands around the table. The inherent squeakiness of my mother's house stayed in the back of Ernie's head, later to appear as Eugene's squeaky shoes, noisy intrusions in a staid men's club.

The origin of *Eugene*, later known as *The Silent Show* for which Ernie was awarded an Emmy, best exemplifies his willingness, even his eagerness, to take risks. NBC needed to fill a half-hour time slot following a sixty-minute Jerry Lewis special. Jerry, who had just split with partner Dean Martin, was then at the height of his popularity and no performer wanted to follow a hit—no one except Ernie. And no one except Ernie would have utilized thirty minutes of network time to showcase a single, silent character. Yet to him, the greatest sin was to play it safe. "It's no fun if you play it safe all the time," he said. "I don't want to get to the point where I'm satisfied to do a 'nice' show, any more than I want to eat boiled meat or look at ugly girls." We never ate boiled meat, Ernie never looked at ugly girls, and he never once played it safe.

That one of his greatest achievements was realized in silence was ironic considering Ernie's almost passionate interest in and use of classical music. When we were first married, his knowledge of it was limited to what might be characterized as "classical music-of-the-month," a simple familiarity with and vague appreciation for the masters. Eventually, however, my Juilliard influence triumphed and Ernie's own record collection ultimately totalled 4,000 albums, and classical music, parcularly that of Tchaikovsky, Haydn and Bartok, became integral to his work.

Whether listening to Tchaikovsky or American composer Deems Taylor, Ernie envisioned pictures of music—"sound insight." "Everytime I hear a little Deems Taylor," he once said, "I'm just naturally reminded of celery stalks breaking, so I make pictures of it." And that, of course,

is exactly what he did: Celery stalks breaking in time to Deems Taylor music, sardines in the can arising in chorus line dance, a cow shaking the bells around its neck as video accompaniment to the church bells in the "1812 Overture"—they all comprised Ernie's own MTV.

One of his more well-known music videos was "Jealousy," which aired on the last of his specials in 1961. An office environment animated through music, "Jealousy" pictured file drawers moving in and out to slide trombones, a switchboard whose connectors were paced to a piccolo, a pencil sharpener that spun to "Sentimental Journey," and a rotary telephone that dialed in tune to percussion. His signature for many of his "sound into sight" pieces was *Kovacs on Music*, with a visual of two feet stomping on a Stradivarious—Kovacs *on* music.

Musical or monologue, all of Ernie's work was testimony to his love of electronic gadgetry, a fascination that extended to our house and his den, his creative nerve center. An electronic control was installed in his desk and from there he would operate a stereo and intercom system that extended to all the rooms in the house, the pool area, and the patio. Over his desk a stuffed rhinoceros was mounted from whose mouth flowed a waterfall. When he was writing, a sign outside the den would flash a warning to all of us— NOT NOW! In 1960, we were the first in Beverly Hills to have an answering machine, a gadget then such a novelty that it didn't even have a name.

Unlike most comedians, Ernie's personal life was not an angst-ridden existence that could be relieved only by the catharsis of performance. Even with his

electronic toys and personal pastimes, Ernie managed to incorporate his sense of play. The answering machine greeted callers with a perfectly modulated English accent; the newness of the wine cellar he overcame by spray-painted cobwebs; we barbecued on a lava rock grill; and Ernie's pet was not a dog or a cat, but a donkey that answered to the name of Piccolo.

In his life and his work, the most important thing to Ernie was to have fun. Of all the things he taught me, I am most grateful to him for that lesson. "It isn't 'how you play the game' that counts," he used to tell me, "it's 'how much fun can we have?'" and we had a hell of a lot of fun!

The 1959 NBC special Kovacs on Music, *probably the best demonstration of Kovacs's aim to transform "sight into sound," included his special version of "Chopsticks," with male dancers jumping on piano keys;* Swan Lake, *with gorillas; "Sweet Mystery of Life," sung by Edie Adams in front of a Wagnerian chorus.*

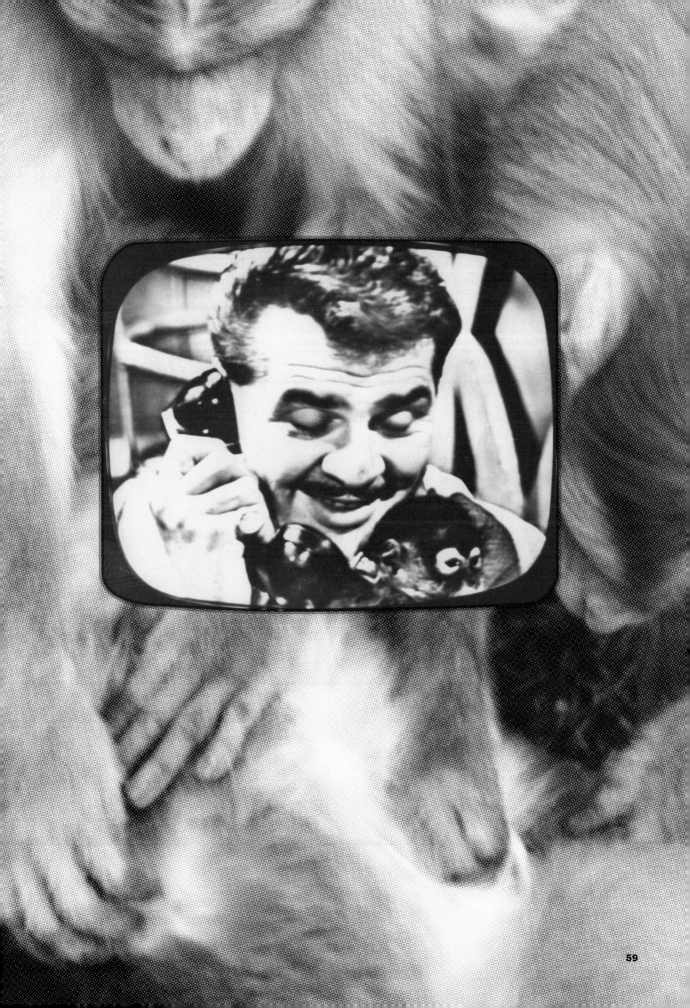

after hours

Vol. 1

No. 2

IN THIS ISSUE

TV'S ERNIE KOVACS
LILY ST. CYR
SPECIAL JAZZ PORTFOLIO

ERNIE KOVACS

by **GEORGE GLAZER**

Our Man-of-the-Month rates high in the

entertainment department for his fresh

and inventive TV approach

"This was my campaign photo while running for president of EEFMS (the Early Eyeball Fraternal Marching Society)."

"**S**TEVEN," the coach used to say, "when in doubt, punt!"

"My name wasn't Steven, (even though the coach thought it was) and I don't know what he mean but somehow, its always inspired me and guided me through life."

So says 33 year old (or 34, or 35—all these ages are included in the biography from NBC) Ernie Kovacs, a frequent baby sitter while his wife, Edie Adams, stars in the Broadway show "Li'l Abner," and one of the funniest guys to shove his mobile mug into a television camera since Ben Franklin started the whole thing by flying a kite.

The tip-off to Kovacs the entertainer is Kovacs, the private citizen.

In his 16-room duplex apartment on Manhattan's West Side the family home contains, in addition to the Kovacs family, a Japanese butler by the name of Ed, a Polish cook, Mrs. Sumati, who's Ed's wife, and Elvere, the Haitian governess who cares for Ernie and Edie's two little girls, and who only speaks "French and maybe a little broken English."

Trenton, N. J. (What Trenton Makes the World Takes, says the

ABC morning show
week, they called me
ked if I cared to bet
eek of my life and
h the show."

"I said I'd be happy to—that
there was no strain, no pain,
no sweat involved."

"The day they put that paint
remover in the martini glass—
Wow! Things like that can
really shake you."

"Actually, it wasn't the money
I liked about that drugstore job
—it's the only place I've ever
been able to get free cigars."

Ernie as "Pierre Ragout, the French storyteller,"
one of the hiliarious characters created for his
night-time TV show.

bridge across the Delaware River at Trenton) also made Ernie. That is, he was born there, and started his carer officially in a Trenton radio station.

But between there and New York, was a stopover at the NBC affiliate in Philadelphia.

Recognizing his obvious talents, station officials had Ernie make his start in TV on a cooking show that ran from 7 a.m. to 9 a.m.

Usually, the show consisted of a visiting cook, who was interviewed, and then made his or her favorite dish before the cameras.

One day, the cook didn't show —and that was the day Ernie Kovacs became an accepted TV comedian.

"It was bad enough having an early morning show anyway," he recalls, "but to have to do a cooking show without a cook was worse yet."

"I remember thinking that maybe I could pull it off by myself, since all the cooks who would possibly be up at 7 a.m. would be cooking for a living, and couldn't get off from work to do the show. So I did the next best thing—I sent some of the crew out to get some vegetables and things, grabbed an old cook book that was in somebody's office and tried to pick out the easiest thing.

"It was horrible—we didn't have all the ingredients, I couldn't cook in the first place, I had no idea what the utensils we had were for, and I kept getting the notes for the recipe I had made mixed up with the notes for the commercials.

"You never saw such a mess in your life. I finally gave up on the thing, and started making jokes, faces, imitations and anything else I could think of, and by the time 9 a.m. rolled around, I was a nervous wreck."

Nervous or not, Kovacs' program underwent a change, and he emerged as a full-time funnyman for early rising Philadelphians.

The network heard about it, and pretty soon Ernie and Edie were on their way to New York. In 1951, he did the first Ernie Kovacs show for NBC, and between then and now has also had shows on ABC and CBS, and for a time worked all three at once.

At ABC, he was in the early morning (6 a.m. - 9 a.m.) slot again and, instead of sleeping like normal people, he kept on the go with his other shows. To keep himself awake and looking human, he sometimes shaved four times a day and in one stretch had five steam baths in additon to several showers every day for a week straight.

"Pretty soon, I got a welt on my leg, and went to a doctor. He examined me and said 'You know, you may think I'm nuts, but do you take many baths? I think you're water-soaked.'"

Besides the fact that he couldn't take enough baths to keep himself awake for the rest of the day after an early morning show, Ernie likes night-time programs best.

"You have to temper yourself in the morning. You can't be too funny with an audience that for the most part hates to get up, and isn't fit to talk to until about two hours after you go off the air. At night, you can let yourself go." (said in the true *After Hours* tradition.)

While most of his now-famous characters were born on his early morning show, they didn't reach maturity until he began reaching people that were really awake.

Miklos Molnar; Pierre Ragout, the French storyteller; Skodny Silksky, ace Hollywood reporter; boozehound Matzo Hepplewhite and Percy the poet are results of people he's known or seen, as is usually the case with comedians who "invent" characters.

But these brainchildren of Ernie's have a way of getting back at him for the ridicule he subjects them too, although they are aided and abetted by the technical crews on his shows.

"Percy the poet is the guy that really hurts me. Percy usually sips a martini during his bit. So one time the martini glass had a goldfish swimming in it, and another time somebody slipped tequila into the glass, instead of the water.

"I didn't know, and swallowed it at one gulp and thought somebody put paint remover into the glass by mistake. I figured it would be the first time TV would have on-the-spot coverage of death by poisoning.

"Old Matzo Hepplewhite got me once too. For that skit, I have to have a tray and a phony bottle of whisky. This one time, I was supposed to drink out of the bottle and drain it at one shot.

"Three quarters of it was gone before I realized this was the real McCoy. The hot lights and the fact that I hadn't had anything to eat made me one sick boy before that show was off the air."

While most people figure Kovacs to be a talented guy, few know how much ability he really has.

For a year after he came to NBC, he wrote the entire

A frequent visitor at Ernie's TV Show, Edie finds that her husband is just as zany as any dogpatch character.

program himself. He still produces his own show, and on that special Saturday night show he did in January of this year, he both wrote and produced the entire thing himself.

"I really stuck my neck out on that one. It was the first television show to be done entirely in pantomime—except for a little opening bit, I didn't say a line during the entire show." As it turned out, it was probably one of the most spectacular one-shots in the history of TV, from the point of ratings (he licked his competition on CBS, Jerry Lewis, unmercifully) and audience acclaim.

"If I hadn't, I would have been finished. There were no writers to blame, no producers to take the rap for me—there was just me."

This pantomime show started out with one of the funniest of the Kovacs bits.

He announced that before the pantomime began, he would like to give the answer to that old question, "If nobody's near a tree when it falls, is there any noise?"

The camera turned to an obviously stuffed squirrel perched on a log. A hand reached out, and stuffed cotton into its ears and then turned it away from the camera.

Next came a shot of a tree falling into the forest.

No sound.

Back goes the camera to the squirrel, the hand reaches in, turns it to face the camera, removes the cotton and a tremendous crash follows immediately.

"One time, we spent a couple of hours working on a bit that took exactly four seconds to perform. The scene is a psychiatrists' office. The door opens, a patient walks in and the doctor escorts him over to the couch. The

The camera catches the
lovely Mrs. Kovacs
backstage as she watches
Ernie in one of his
frantic routines.

ent lies down, and the couch goes flying into the
, patient and all."

he well-known exit used by Jimmy Durante on his
show provided more fodder for Kovacs.

We came on camera with three light spots that re-
bled the three spotlights Jimmy uses when he goes
you know, he puts on his hat and coat and starts
walk away from the camera. At each spotlight, he
s around and waves and its a real socko ending.

We decided to do it in reverse, so at the far end of
stage, this figure appears in one of the spots that
s just like Durante. The audience starts to applaud
ttle, and the applause gets louder as he moves into
second spotlight.

The applause is at its height just before he reaches
third spot, closest to the camera. He walks into this—
disappears—goes straight down. We had taken some
te paper and stretched it over a trap door in the
r. It broke the whole audience up."

He seems really to have enjoyed writing his own shows,
ost as much as actually performing them. At one
e, he was offered the job of head writer on another
w, but it came up at a time when he was to be given
ther show of his own.

As it turned out, I would have made more as a
ter than I did on my own show. The only time writ-
my own show nearly got me into trouble was when
TV writers were supposed to go on strike. I wasn't
l at anybody—and if I was, it had to be at myself,
e I was the performer and the producer too. It's a
d thing there was no strike; I don't know what I
ld have done."

Ernie was asked how he manages to get around the
ffs" that inevitably occur on a show such as the ones
does. "We never try. We just incorporate them into
show. Once and awhile there are some real dillies,
then you want to go hide somewhere."

He told of a few, none of which could be printed.
Kovacs, a good looking and well built (6' 2", 200 lbs.)
n, has had a partner in crime since his Philadelphia
s.

Pretty, blonde Edith Adams for a long time appeared
with Kovacs on his shows until last Fall, when along
came the musical comedy "Li'l Abner." Edie pretty well
fills the bill physically as Daisy Mae, and she's got a fine
voice and sense of comedy to go with it—so what could
be more natural than casting her for the role of Dogpatch's prettiest girl for the Broadway version of Al Capp's
famous comic strip?

The show, of course, was an immediate hit, and Edie
transferred her activities to Dogpatch for the run of the
show.

But while Ernie had his evening show, splitting the
chores with Steve Allen before "Tonight" changed its
format, Edie usually wandered in about midnight and
watched from the wings, frequently getting into the act
unexpectedly.

Incidentally, Ernie himself had a fling at the theater
too.

A high school performance of the "Pirates of Penzance"
netted him scholarship offers to seven dramatic schools.

He spent a season singing with stock companies, formed
his own unit later (where he wrote, directed, designed
scenery and played leads) then got to Broadway for
the annual John Golden auditions.

He made out pretty well, and was offered some good spots.

But then he pulled what can be considered a typical Kovacs stunt—he went to work in a drugstore since he had to support his mother and himself.

That didn't last too long, and it was back to stock work. Pneumonia, complicated by pleurisy, was Ernie's next attraction, and this ran for a dismal year and a half.

A final shot at directing, and Kovacs started the radio career in Trenton that was to eventually land him in New York.

An excellent radio journalist, Kovacs received the H. P. Davis award in 1948 for his newswork.

In between times, he was a gag writer for night club comedians, did some song writing, and voice work for a movie cartoon outfit.

Even at this tender stage of his development, Kovacs was doing some weird stunts for the listeners—like broadcasting from dirigibles, boats, trains, planes and construction cranes.

He got a clear newsbeat on interviews with witnesses to the killing of 11 people in Camden, N. J., when a gunman ran amok.

"I very casually worked the people around to standing under a certain tree—a tree where a microphone was hidden in one of the branches. Worked pretty good."

Ask Ernie if he thinks any of these stunts, or subsequent ones are a little "abnormal" and his reply is that to him, they're quite normal—and they must be to a lot of others too, otherwise why would he still be on the air?

An extremely likeable guy, Kovacs has won the friendship of some of the most critical people in the TV industry—his technical crews.

It was over five years since he had been at CBS the night he put on his pantomime show—but among the pre-show messages he got was one signed by the crew he had worked with at CBS, while another was from his gang at NBC.

In the hardboiled television industry, that's a pretty good vote of confidence for a performer. ▲

Cigar in hand, actor-writer-producer Ernie Kovacs ponde his next assault on the TV scene.

NBC

HUDSON THEATRE
141 WEST 44TH STREET • NEW YORK

NBC TELEVISION NETWORK

TUES.
20
NOV.
1956

tonight

starring

ERNIE KOVACS
11:30 PM TO 1:00 AM

DOORS

CLOSE

11:10 PM

NATIONAL BROADCASTING COMPANY 00685
COMPLIMENTARY TICKET—NOT TO BE SOLD
This card of admission is void unless presented at the Studio within ten minutes preceding hour specified on the face hereof. Children under six years of age not admitted.
Children under sixteen not admitted unless accompanied by parent or guardian. As
this is a complimentary ticket, NBC reserves the right to revoke it at any time.
SMOKING AND USE OF CAMERAS ARE PROHIBITED IN STUDIO. In accepting this
card of admission, the holder consents to being televised directly or by means of
television recording and releases the Broadcaster, the Sponsor of the program and
its Advertising Agents from liability for loss or damage to person or property and
agrees to comply with all rules and regulations of NBC.

GO BEHIND THE SCENES OF RADIO & TELEVISION—ASK ABOUT THE NBC TOUR

PHILCO · V
RADIO & TE

WPTZ
PHILADELPHIA
ERNIE IN
KOVACS LAND
MON. TUES.
& THURS.
ESTINGHOUSE
VISION CENTER

It's Here at Last!

Television's best disc jockey show
with Television's greatest disc jockey

- **LATEST HIT TUNES**

- **ACCURATE TIME YOU CAN SEE AND HEAR**

featuring . . . . **ERNIE KOVACS**

SEE "3" TO GET READY

- **NEWS EVERY HALF HOUR**

- **WEATHER INFORMATION**

EVERY MORNING 7:30-9:00
WPTZ CHANNEL 3

ERNIE KOVACS SHOW

THURSDAY, MARCH 1, 1956

"KAPUSTA KID"

ANNOUNCER:

TIME AGAIN FOR THE ADVENTURES OF THE
KAPUSTA KID IN OUTER SPACE. WELL, THINGS
ARE REALLY HOPPING ON THE SQUARE PLANET.
THAT MYSTERIOUS PLANET WAY OUT SOME PLACE
IN THE SOLAR SYSTEM. WHEN WE LAST LEFT
THE KAPUSTA KID AND HIS FRIENDS, CO-PILOT
OBRIEN AND CO-PILOT ALBUMEN WERE TRAPPED BY
THE PAPER PEOPLE. OBRIEN AND ALBUMEN
LEARNED THAT WHILE THE PAPER PEOPLE ARE
NOT PARTICULARLY AWESOME IN APPEARANCE,
THEY HAVE THE POWER OF CASTING A SPELL
UPON ADVENTURERS WHICH WILL CHANGE THEM
INTO RAG PULP TO BE MADE INTO PAPER FOR
THE PAPER PEOPLE MILL. AS WE LEFT ALBUMEN
AND OBRIEN THE TEENG, THE PRINCE OF THE
PAPER PEOPLE, WAS JUST COMPLETING HIS
SPELL UPON THEM. LET'S JOIN THEM AND SEE
WHAT HAPPENS.

WIDE SHOT OF PLANET
DOLLY IN
CROSS FADE TO SET

AUDIO: THEME
         FADE OUT WHEN WE TAKE SET.

NOTE: WE WILL HAVE FILTER MIKE,
       FOR EDITH.

ALBUMEN:

DO YOU ACTUALLY MEAN TEENG, THAT AS
PRINCE OF THE PAPER PEOPLE, YOU ARE
NOW GOING TO CHANGE US INTO PAPER
PULP?

PAPER PEOPLE: (FILTER MIKE)

PRECISELY.

OBRIEN:

AND DERE ISA NOTHING WHICH WILLA SAVEA
US?

PAPER PEOPLE: (FILTER)

NOTHING. NOTHING WHATSOEVER EXCEPT...
BUT OF COURSE THAT'S IMPOSSIBLE.

ALBUMEN:

A, WHAT IS THAT IMPOSSIBLE? THAT LITTLE

(MORE)

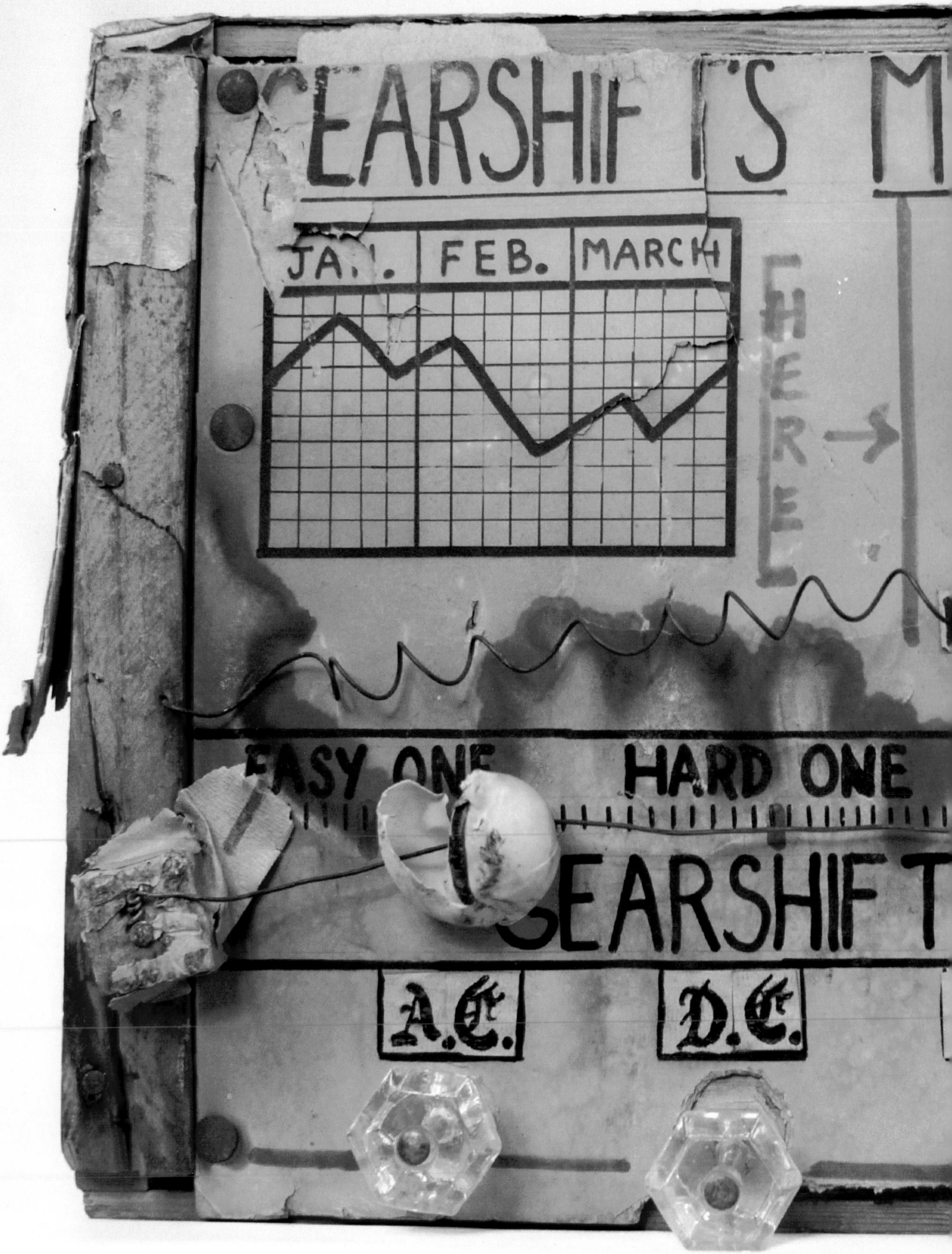

EARSHIFT'S M

JAN.	FEB.	MARCH

HERE →

EASY ONE   HARD ONE

GEARSHIFT

A.C.   D.C.

HANO ALMANAC

FF

KNOB
← →

OFF

INGOING

OOZIE DOUBLE-DOOZIE

GRAPH

HIS HERS

MEMORANDUM ON THE INVENTION OF THE WHEEL

Ernie Kovacs

* * * * * * *

I am not here to necessarily debunk Caesar ("Caesar" only
in expression, actually in this instance, The Wheel), nor to
bury it (to continue), nor to praise it (still Re: to the
Wheel....OR Caesar, if you feel you must read innuendo into
simple statement of fact).

Spectactularly, the art of debunking is most easily come
by for we have become a generation of rather fidgety peoples
("peoples" is not necessarily plural but a distinguishing form
of the word to set it apart from more earthly xxx mundanity).

(italics)   The calculated and quite deft application of "peoples" here
is tinglingly reminiscent of some oral (as opposed to the antonym)
repartee. I once found myself the center of some repartee in a
couturier's retreat not too far from the Barbizon Plaza in an
Eastern city over the utilisation of the phrase QUICK GRASS over
COUCH GRASS....but some other time for that.

Returning to "fidgety peoples"....fidgety peoples who, already
glutted on history which can be ratified,have fled to the flowing
pen of those who dig up scurrilous data on those things which we
were once taught, hypothetically, in school. (This is a condition
which the more stable refer to as the terminal point of the aperture).
There is a plethora of works which function as "refuters". (Not
to be confused with "REFRUITERS" which are horticultural in content
or, in more extreme cases, biological.). These volumes enjoy eager
consumption with such zingers as.. "George Washington was not a

dentist, he was an optometrist who hated dogs"...and/or..."---at the battle of the Alamo, it was not Davy Crockett, but Irving Crocket, a racoon salesman who ---etc.,etc.,".

Therefore, I say again, this is not an article debunking the wheel but, rather, a <u>rounding out</u> of the subject. Furthermore, this <u>petite treatise</u> will not be encumbered with confusing and obscure dates which not only constitute dull reading but are somewhat tedious to look up in books dealing with that period. (These books are not easily come by and when they are found, are somewhat difficult to read because of the condition of the volume having been printed in one million B.C.) - (Before Cguttenberg).

The man, actually as we will discover when reading further, the PRE-HISTORIC man who invented the wheel was named Urg. This was either his first or last name. (If it is <u>both</u> first and last names, it makes a rather unpleasant sound and is best forgotten). For purposes of identification and clarity we will assume this was his <u>last</u> name and,to avoid confusion with others with similar last names who might appear in this work, let us give him the <u>first</u> name of Leonard.

One day (see Puccini), in the time period of our history with which we will now occupy us ourselves, Leonard Urg, his wife (or "<u>mate</u>" as they were then known, and believe me "benefit of clergy" was sneered at worse than you folks driving Volkswagons would ever believe) and kids were out on a kind of picnic.

Leonard said to his mate (or to the kids, perhaps. My notes are mislaid on this.).

(italics)
(italics)

(italics)

(italics)
(italics)

(italics)

<u>Memorandum on the Invention of the Wheel</u>:

"Get the Ornitholestes out of the cart so we can eat lunch."

(italics)   So his wife (or kids if it <u>was</u> they....actually, there was a
kind of vague state of/development of the human form at that time
and the difference wasn't that perceptive, not only between adults
and children but between male and female as well. This, many
times resulted in some zany and somewhat perplexing, for they were
a simple lot, errors...however...) so his wife pulled the ~~Ornitholestes~~
Ornitholestes (which caused some giggling because of the relative
sound of the word...these peoples were not without humour) and
hauled it over to the picnic site, a grassy spot.

"By golly, Leonard" said his mate "this is one of the heaviest
Ornitholestes (again the giggle) I've ever hauled, certainly in
many a moon, or whatever that round thing is up in the sky."

"He surely is a fat fellow" said Leonard, "why don't we use
the new invention of that nut who lives a couple of caves from us
and cook it. You know, that frere...or firkin, or whatever he calls
it."

"You mean 'fire'."

"Yes, that's it. Fire."

"All right, but don't expect me to come up with any fancy
sauces or sometihng. I came for a picnic myself, not to whip
up an Icegivingsday dinner."

(italics)   <u>This era was before Thanksgiving but after the Ice Age</u>.

"Why don't you," she continued, "go play with the kids and
I'll get lunch ready."

"I'd take you out to dinner dear, except that I forgot my
Dinosaurs' Club Card," laughed Leonard for he was a ready wit

ZOOMAR

a novel by Ernie Kovacs

To Edie, my dear wife,

It is difficult to say, in this dedication of a book which, to be so dedicated, should be a collection of fine poems or at least prose of deep tenderness, how much I thank you for your love and the great kindness and happiness you have given me. This is hardly a private place to say very much. So for here, at least, on your reading this as you open the first volume, know that without you, there would have been no book, ever.

1

THE ANT WALKED THE FULL LENGTH OF THE BRASSIERE STRAP … SIX-STEPPED lightly across the foam rubber … forded the short breach … more foam rubber … more strap … across the cold buckle … and up the side of the economy-size Kleenex box.

He traveled the length of the pop-up tissue, which wasn't, at the moment, and down the other side of the box … gingerly over the cuticle scissors …. He shuffled along the surface of the mirror, un-Narcissusly, and came to a halt when Eileen Moore put an eight-ounce jar of Special Night Cream on him.

If there was any chance for survival, it diminished considerably as Mrs. Moore pressed into the cream with two nicely manicured, but average-weight fingers.

Actually the ant had no business walking about on Eileen Moore's dressing table. The Moores were a fairly financially comfortable young couple whose income had crept with progressive regularity into the "town-home, country-home" status. Moreover, had the ant been born into the other residence, the country home, his chance for survival would have been increased by the fact that the occupation period in the country by the Moores was shorter than in the city.

However, this was offset somewhat by the unhappy fact that Eileen used sixteen-ounce jars of Special Night Cream in the country. These were eight ounces heavier, especially for ants. All in all, the percentage of life expectancy for the ant ran about 60 to 40, country house over town house. But the ant was no longer concerned with actuals of longevity. In fairness to his demise in the town house, it must be said that there was a certain distinction to it. How many country ants were laid to rest by Elizabeth Arden?

And now that he had passed on, the secret of the foam rubber in the brassiere was safe again. Perhaps Eileen Moore had unwittingly coined a phrase, "Dead Formicidae tell no tales." But then again, perhaps not.

Eileen opened an eye and peered out through a little volcano of Special Night Cream to look at the round, jeweled clock on the dresser. The clock had been a gift from Tom for their second anniversary.

Tom Moore had just been hired by Cunningham, Thurber and McClean, who had, in turn, just been handed the Belleau Soap account. Tom had been made account executive after his slogan for Belleau Soap had been enthusiastically accepted by the client.

J. Walter Cunningham had issued an office mobilization to summon his regiment of crewcuts in charcoal gray, Madison Avenue's khaki, to him. They presented ball points-at-arms, ready to advance to their wall-to-wall battle stations, there to give birth to a volley of saponaceous, soap-selling axioms with orders to raise the rear sights on their ball points to public range J. Walter began with one of his military sallies.

"None of you has asked for this assignment, but it's a job we've got to do. It can be rough. Someone may get hurt." He actually did not use those words, but the army paraphrase was his connotation. He paused then, and a ten-second pause was shared by the group. It was a moment of reflection, individual confession booths fitted with mirrors. He continued: "Tomorrow at 1300 o'clock--"

"What the hell time is that?" someone's secretary whispered, her pencil hanging inutile at the sudden road block.

"At that time," continued Cunningham, "you will present your Belleau slogans to Mr. Forsythe and to Mr. Cregar or to Messrs. Forsythe and Cregar." Appreciating laugh from Forsythe and Cregar and others. Acknowledgement by J. Walter.

" ... who, upon receiving them, will select the three best and bring them to me. I am meeting with the Belleau executives at 1430 o'clock."

"Christ," murmured the secretary.

"A decision will be forthcoming by 1430 o'clock."

Her pencil snapped.

"Good luck," J. Walter concluded, denoting his being a regular guy. ESP took over as all chairs scraped back in acceptable unison. Thurber and McClean, their secretaries flanking them like distaff attachees, shook hands with Cunningham not without solemnity and the executive heads left the heavily paneled room in geese-to-the-south formation.

"Hep, two, three ... hep, two, three," thought Tom as they left. "Well," he said aloud, "it's 0012 o'clock already, hardly seems more than 0011." Only Miss Loeb, his secretary, laughed and went to put a fresh point on her pencil as she returned to the office with him.

Tom's office was exactly like the other junior-executive offices. The Cunningham, Thurber and McClean decor was antique European. Thurber had made extensive purchases abroad of antique furniture and bric-a-brac, all past the age limit which allowed duty-free entry. The interiors of the advertising company were one of Thurber's clever tax-saving accomplishments. As the furniture aged further, it increased in value, and still received the 10 per cent depreciation allowed by the government as a little bonus. The financial security of the operation was even more ensured by the fact that any piece, contributed to a museum, was deducted by Thurber at the valuation set upon it by the museum appraisers.

They naturally were generous in their appraisal and Cunningham, Thurber and McClean were quick to compound their generosity.

Tom sat in his anthemion-backed chair at his Queen Anne desk and looked at Miss Loeb in her Bergdorf-Goodman. Karen Loeb had a way of sharpening a pencil that was more enjoyable than coffee break. And whoever had installed the pencil sharpener at its low position was half of the conspiracy, for Miss Loeb had to make new pencil points at a forty-five-degree angle. Her right wrist made circles, a kind of chain reaction took place, spreading from the wrist on up the arm and down through the body. It had just reached the it-must-be-jelly-'cause-jam-don't-shake-like-that section, when she stopped. It was entirely possible that centrifugal force would one day bring down the building about them. At this point, from some sequence of events that forever remain unexplained, Tom decided to buy his wife a clock.

2

EILEEN MOORE TISSUED OFF SOME OF THE CREAM AND LOOKED AGAIN AT the clock on her dresser. There were fourteen semiprecious garnets around its edge and a small green stone representing each of the hours. The clock was gold-plated and had one hand. She had never mentioned the fact that one hand was missing because of the second-anniversary glow and the always outside possibility that this was the way it was supposed to be. She had decided that the one hand was the hour hand and now it lay just between the green stone where a five would have been and another green stone where a six could very well have been.

Five-thirty ... "That'll give me an hour and a half," she thought. The clock had been there for almost a year. Tom's slogan for the Belleau Soap Company had lasted quite as long. When J. Walter Cunningham had returned from the Belleau meeting, Miss Loeb passed on his message to Tom that he was requested to come to Cunningham's office at his first opportunity, which meant at that moment. Entering the suite of offices of the Big Three and passing the secretaries was like playing a game. Rounding one corner, he almost expected to see "You have taken a wrong turn. Go back three blocks and spin the arrow again. If you pass 'Go', do not collect two hundred dollars."

A last secretary, just outside J. Walter's door, looked up as Tom came near. She was the solid type. Tom compared her quickly to Miss Loeb and decided that the only thing the two had in common was selection of washrooms. "Mr. Moore," he said.

"Mr. Cunningham's expecting you."

"Thank you."

She opened the door and said, "Mr. Moore." He said "Thank you" again and regretted it. His voice had suddenly changed. He knew he wasn't nervous, but there was that damned dewiness about his palms and a preshaving-age throwback in his voice.

Tom Moore bad met his obstetrician on a warm day in July in Philadelphia thirty-six years ago. His resemblance to the man who had nervously awaited his arrival was a strong one. It was also a fortunate one, as his father was a handsome man. He, too, was more than six feet tall by two inches and had cast the mold for Tom's excellent nose and strong features. If Tom or his father were seated behind Cunningham's desk, the over-all appearance would have been quite acceptable. However Mr. Cunningham was there at the moment and not his father.

"Come in, Moore. You know Mr. Thurber and Mr. McClean of course."

Nodding his agreement supplied the necessary seconds to reset his voice level.

Then the pause. Three executive sets of eyes lay in his direction. All in synchronization ... aperture opening F.8; shutter speed 1/25. Mr. Thurber, Tom discovered with some alarm, was slightly cock-eyed.

'I just lave Belleau," said Mr. Cunningham softly.

"It's a good soap, sir."

"I just lave Belleau," repeated Mr. Cunningham, oblivious to Tom's statement Tom decided to say nothing this time.

"Mr. Moore"-and Cunningham bad risen and was walking around to the front of the desk-"you decimated the competition."

He took Tom's hand and made him doubly conscious of the wet palms he had tried surreptitiously to wipe when he saw the hand-shake coming. Looking straight into Tom's eyes, Cunningham's lips parted and the words drifted slowly toward Tom like cigar smoke over a poker table. "I just lave Belleau ... "

In every man's life there are certain moments of discomfort ... from poorly fitted underclothing to doors opening unexpectedly, but there are some occasions which remain uncategorized. Mr. Cunningham's eyes were approximately five inches from Tom Moore's. His right hand held Tom's right. His left hand was on Tom's right shoulder.

"Genius," softlied Mr. Cunningham, "need not lie in the voluminous tomes of Proust, Rousseau, Puccini, Descartes ... "

"Puccini?" thought Tom. "He's got something bollixed up there."

"Genius"-and here the grip tightened, the pupils descended to F.22 the shutter speed increased to 1/100-"can lie in four words ... four words ... sit down, Tom."

Tom decided that as soon as Mr. Cunningham let go his hand and shoulder he would take immediate advantage of the invitation. Unfortunately, the mood of retrospect still hung in the atmosphere ....

"I just lave Belleau," Cunningham mused.

For some reason, old movie cliches began passing in front of Tom as he stood trying to return the gaze ... the words went past much in the fashion of technicians' credits at the end of a television show ... the words were superimposed in orderly fashion, one line at a time over the unsuspecting Mr. Cunningham's eyes ....

"If I had a son, he would have been about your age ... "

"I've never told you about your mother ... "

"You're my kind of folks ... "

"I wasn't always president of a bank. Once I was arrested for .. , Like an announcer's voice with "station identification," Cunningham's voice broke through the titles. Releasing his grip, he strode back to the desk and said, "I think this calls for a little celebration. We tried a new chain on the old three-wheeler and the sprockets turned them around."

Tom hated the little agency sutras and was usually only half through translating them into basic English when another would be in the air. Staring at a jade bust on the desk, which looked like Bebe Daniels, Tom smiled and desperately tried to figure out just what the hell was going on ....

"We threw a handful of pebbles into the reservoir and four diamonds came out of the faucet, eh, Thurber?" And now the small key was removed and the door to the liquor closet was opened ... "Four diamonds" ... and the crystal decanter was in Cunmingham's hands. He turned ... became motionless .... "We will set those diamonds, Tom, set them to make them shine in the eyes of every woman in America .... Gentleman" -and he poured scotch into the four glasses that Mr. McClean set upon his desk-"gentlemen, we drink to the success of our new association with Belleau Soap." Grateful for the intermission, Tom's drink was half down his throat as he remembered. 'I just lave Belleau" ... it was the third slogan Karen Loeb had added to his list as a gag.

3

THE NEXT YEAR WOULD HAVE BEEN A BIG YEAR AT CUNNINGHAM, THURBER and McClean for Tom Moore had not the Belleau Soap Company gone into bankruptcy. After twenty years of washing the public the Belleau Company's factory stood silent. Its huge empty mixing vats gave out hollow sounds to footsteps on the concrete. The wrapping machines had been dismantled and sold. The building inside and out was gray ... the peculiar gray of failure, and only the pigeons were impressed by the huge 'I just lave Belleau" sign which ran the length of the building.

The Belleau Company had begun a remarkable business when Tom Moore was sixteen. The soap was brown in color and brown in shape. It gave off a profound medicated smell before, during, and after using. The accompanying aroma did everything the ads had promised, substituting "theirs" for "yours." Suddenly a generation of soap buyers, who either had no personal body difficulties or, at least, assumed they had none, refused to smell as prescribed by the Belleau people. The Belleau profits fell off to some extent, but the company still managed to operate at a profit. It was only when they changed color, odor, and slogans ("I just lave Belleau") that they failed completely. Arnold Katz (Mr. Belleau) committed suicide and Tom had felt personally responsible.

He was given the news by Cunningham, who had returned to calling him by his last name and Tom had gone straight to "21," where he spent the greater, or at least the major part of the day drinking. Karen Loeb came in at five with his brief case and hat. She didn't say anything as she stopped by Tom, but her body held a scintillating conversation with all males present as she walked the length of the bar.

After she had finished her first drink they left the bar, sat at a table, and ordered again. "I guess I knew what I was doing when I wouldn't let you give me credit for the Belleau slogan," she said. Someone had been using a phone at the table and the wire lay across Tom's shoulders. Karen reached up and across to unplug it and the contact created an intimacy that changed to embarrassment when the telephone plug stubbornly stuck. Realizing that only full body English would effect it, Karen withdrew her arm and said "it's stuck." Her remark and the action preceding left him a little confused, as he hadn't been aware of the telephone wire and still wasn't. He wondered why he felt warm on the side nearer her. The martinis made it difficult for him to reason ... body temperatures were just about the same, 98.6 ... if hers was 98.6, why should her 98.6 be so much higher in temperature? There were three classifications of girls when it came to shoving their chests up against a male: those who had did it on purpose; those who did it by accident or were unfeeling or were too padded to know where the hell they were pushing; and three, those who simply didn't. Karen was in the final classification.

"I wonder how long it will be before I'm canned," he said.

"Mr. McCormick stopped by after you left and ... I'm sorry, Mr. Moore."

"Oh, already? Guess the sprockets on the old tricycle slipped out of the chain, hm?"

Karen felt this was one of those things which pass without comment.

"Pebbles in the reservoir," he added. "You know what I'd like to do in their damned reservoir?"

"I could go for a cup of coffee ... you?"

The waiter came to the table and took the order. As he was leaving, he reached across Tom and pulled out the telephone plug.

"Oh," Tom said, remembering her actions earlier, 'I guess I should have known better."

"You're not making much sense ... "

"I wished ... wish, that is ... I wish I lived in the country. Then I'd have to catch a 5:35 or something. I feel like a 5:35 tonight. Why don't we just take a train ... a little suburban job ... go for a ride on the island and come back. I'll fold up my newspaper like a commuter ... maybe I'll just fold myself up ... at least if I'm washed up, I did it with a good soap."

"I've got to get home, Mr. Moore. Anything I can do?"

He wanted to suggest something cute and off-color but hiccuped instead.

"No, Karen. Thanks and good night. Good-by, too. So long and in the words of the old maestro, yowza, yowza."

"Goodnight, Mr. Moore."

He watched Karen's shirred ... sheared ... he always mixed up words after drinking ... sheared beaver ... the other one was for eggs ... sheared beaver go. It rounded the comer and with the logic of the very dry gibson, he knew she was in it at the time. He couldn't see her after the turn but pictured her passing the cigar counter ... one of the few in town that carried the dark-leaf Havanas ... now she must be passing the check room ... he wondered if the boys ever took change out of overcoats ... now Carl must be opening the door for her ... those crazy legs would be taking her up the five steps to the sidewalk ... he could see those crazy legs disappearing into a cab ... actually Tom's leg visions were always better than the real thing, he never visualized crooked seams.

Tom Moore had long ago substituted the word visualize for day-dream and had made a rather exact process of it. The general categories were limited to two: sex and the other category. Both were highly inclusive and subdivided into various facets which sometimes, because of the common denominator of the first classification, combined with each other.

The sex category was broken down for visualization into two main groups: one in which he remained faithful to Eileen and the other in which he did not. The alcoholic atmosphere of this afternoon's encounter with Karen had put it into visualization rather than reality. She had ignored his half-serious invitation for a train ride. He had shown disappointment only because he had felt it was the thing to do. Actually he had expected, wanted, and was relieved to have the situation end as it did. There was also the comfort of the absence of finality to its ending. Karen would be in and out of bed with Tom ten times before he saw her again. He would probably picture her with a mole. There was one shortcoming to those daydreams. Tom tried to keep his cast of characters true to their basic natures. He also preferred setting up the scene with his final administering of the amatory coup de grâce as a conciliatory gesture ... this helped his conscience. But Karen, if he were to remain honest to his rules of daydreamed affairs, wouldn't force him into this *coup de grâce* . . . .

Tom Moore sat at the table with the soft photostat of Karen's legs in his mind when Harvey Atkinson, vice-president of the Central Broadcasting Company sat down. Harvey was on the inside roll of a high alcoholic loop.

"Thinking of buying the place?"

"Um? Hi, Harv. What're you drinking?"

"Plenty, but I'll stay with scotch, Teddy."

The waiter, Teddy, walked over, transferred Atkinson's order into a scribble, and added one for Tom.

"What's new at the plant?"

"Just sitting here now, Harv, kicking it around. Been talking with Eileen a lot lately about that setup. She wants me to leave."

"Bad hours?"

"Well, you know the business, Harv, but it's more than that."

Might as well begin looking now ... "She feels I should drop this end and get into another phase ... get involved in production somehow."

"You mean a package outfit?"

"Package ... or network operation ... I dunno. Haven't put that much thought into it ... package would be fine I guess."

"Yeah ... lot of good packaging outfits ... some of those quiz outfits have a lot of shows on the air."

"Yeah ... packaging or network operation."

"We have a couple of good quiz shows on now, one of 'em has a helluva rating."

"Primarily, Eileen was talking about network operations."

"Give me a good package outfit. Going to quit someday and get some good boys together ... maybe you'd like to think about that, Tom."

"Count me in, Harv. Helluva good idea ... you know, it just hit me. I ought to kick around with some network to kind of round out some ideas that I've had and knock out the kinks ... file a few notes ... kind of get ready."

"Would you consider fooling around with Central for that idea? We have a helluva operation. Lotta screwballs running the store, but we get out the shows. Took six out of the top ten. United made it with three, with 'Ricksha' over at Independent taking up the last spot. 'Ricksha's' a helluva show. There's a helluva lot of commercial appeal in that Ming Dynasty crap. Where the hell have you been, Teddy, out making little olives out of big ones?"

"Right you are, Mr. Atkinson."

"You know, Harv, I think you hit it. I could get a damned good rounding-out at Central."

"What about Cunningham, Thurber and Mac?"

"Hell, I can pull out of there tomorrow if I want. They'll probably want a month's notice but I've done them some favors ... I'm pretty sure J. Walter would release me."

"Christ, look at the chest on that one over there in the corner. She makes Marilyn Monroe look like Dean Acheson."

"Va va voom, eh, Harv? Hell, look, I'll just chuck it. Cunningham, I mean. I'll drop over there first, explain it to old J. Walter, and shoot over to your spot at about eleven. I've got a lot of faith in what you and the boys are setting up on that package deal. Here's to it, Atkinson, the Boys and Moore, packagers."

Sipping with eyes down, Tom thought, "I just lave Belleau ... screw Belleau, screw Cunningham, Thurber and McClean and the Atchison, Topeka and Santa Fe, Manny Moe and Jack and the Paterson, New Jersey, quads," whose picture had been on the front of the Daily News that morning, for which they were included in his random auf Wiedersehen ... The last gibson had a kind of settling effect. It was as if Tom had been trying to make up his mind to become drunk and had arrived at a decision ... it had the finishing touch of the little boy's initials in a freshly laid sidewalk ... Harvey Atkinson was past the initials stage. The Lord's Prayer had been fingered into his sidewalk and the Gettysburg Address was well under way .... He beckoned to Teddy, with the subtle gesture of drunks, similar to runaway trucks and falling redwoods.

"You have," said Tom, referring to the gesture with a pleasant thickness and security of the man well employed, "the manner of the French Sûreté."

"The French Sûreté are slobs and fags. Give me John J. Ryan any time. Teddy, a little after-dinner cordial. What was that I had after lunch?"

"Mirabelle, Mr. Atkinson."

"Made from raspberries," confided Harvey to Tom.

"Plums," said Tom.

"I meant plums."

"Crème de menthe, kirschwasser, quetsch, and slivovitz," he added with the grand vagary of an off-stage Hamlet.

"Pardon?"

"Also made from plums."

Right as rain, Harv. Va va voom."

Washed with paddles in ... a wooden tub ... allowed to ferment ... distilled twice to the lot ... pits, too. Oil from the pits important."

"Check-o."

"Check-o."

"Plum pits in slivovitz." "What the hell, I say." "Teddy, bring us one." ⊙

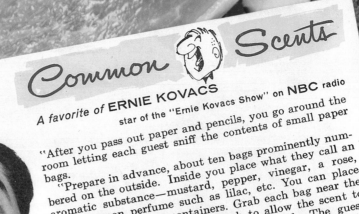

Common Scents

Daisy Dean's Fritos recipes

High

ERNIE KOVACS

·

JACK REYNOLDS

·

JERRY LIEBERMAN

·

FRANK BROOKHOUSER

·

WILLIAM W. BALDWIN

3

e set the stage, but she wasn't following
e script

ONE afternoon, after Tom Moore, producer of the
"Miss Wipe-Ola Beauty Hunt" program, had come
back from one of the Roman orgies which Madison
Avenuites looked upon as business lunches, his secretary,
Karen Loeb, told him there was someone to see him. A
young lady.

"Mary Willoughby," said Karen, not leaving to bring
her in.

"What does she want?"

"She wouldn't say," said Karen. Miss Willoughby however, wasn't fooling another woman.

"All right, but buzz me in ten minutes with an appointment."

Karen left, and when she reopened the door Mary Willoughby, five feet nine with red hair on top, took over the
room.

"I'm Mary Willoughby," she said.

Her voice was the kind a man hears on business trips, so
(Continued on page 71)

much so that it was almost a take-off on intimacy. Somehow
Tom decided to overlook the satirical aspects of it.

"Won't you sit down, Miss Willoughby." Miss Willoughby crossed a pair of what were probably the longest
legs in New York. They looked like the kind of stilts a
sex maniac would turn out on a home lathe. If there was
such a thing as phallic legs, these were it. She had the
ampleness of bosom that children would like to have
romped in, although the age category for romping therein
was not that limited.

"What can I do for you?" he said, and wondered if it
had sounded like what had occurred to him as a likely
project.

"I just wanted some advice, Mr. Moore. I know you're
busy and I won't take much of your time."

She was a little late with this. He had already decided
to kill Karen Loeb if she buzzed him in ten minutes.

"Not at all, not at all," he said. "Cigarette?" Why the
hell didn't he keep the king size in stock? They took
longer.

"Perhaps I shouldn't really come to see you, I'm one of
the contestants in the 'Miss Wipe-Ola Beauty Hunt.' " She
said the name of the show with the awe a tourist bestows
upon the Taj Mahal. "But I haven't been on, yet," she
added hastily.

And unnecessarily, for anyone would have remembered
if she had.

"Oh, I don't think you need worry about that." Need
worry your pretty little head about that, that is. "Would
you like some coffee?"

"Love some. Black, please, no sugar."

"Yes, Mr. Moore?" from Karen at his buzz.

"Karen, would you get us two coffees, both black, no
sugar, please."

"All right. I believe your appointment for this afternoon
has been canceled."

"Oh, thank you. Make it for sometime next week."

Karen was gone and Miss Willoughby, seeing something
in her eyes, had waited for her to leave. "It may sound
silly but . . ."

"No, no, go on." He was hoping wildly she was going
to ask him to go to bed.

"Well, I'm on next week in the contest. Please don't
think I'm here to find out anything about whether or not I
can win or anything like that."

"Of course not." But if worse comes to worst . . .

"It's just that I don't know where to go from here. What
does one do after one leaves a beauty contest. I mean, how
do you go about getting into the business in New York?"

Sweet sufferin' Saint Orthicon! This kid would have
about as much trouble getting that body into the business
as Roy Rogers had with an underweight rustler.

"That is a kind of tough question, Miss Willoughby.
There are an awful lot of beautiful girls like yourself who
wonder the same thing." For about eight minutes.

"I know and I just can't face the thought of knocking
on door after door and having them slammed in my face."

Tom figured she wouldn't go much beyond one door and
if it were slammed, there were other segments of her that
would prevent her face from making contact.

(*Continued on next page*)

"Here's the coffee, Mr. Moore."

That was the fastest delivery of coffee he had had since he began working at the United Broadcasting Company. Karen must have gone out for it herself. He gave her a dirty look.

"Well, you're an attractive girl, do you do anything . . . sing, act or dance?"

"I do dance but I haven't the nerve to audition. I don't think I'm that good," she said, wide-eyed.

"There are a lot of people in the business who aren't Maria Tallchiefs."

He could see by the thoughtful way she was drinking her coffee that she didn't know who the hell Maria Tall-chief was.

"Or Ruby Keelers," he added. "What kind of dancing do you do?"

"Kind of impressionistic."

"Modern?"

"Cum si, cum sera."

A good-looking Sam Goldwyn. "A kind of mixture, hm?"

"Yes, I do what I feel."

A reflective moment of approbation over this one, then: "Perhaps I can arrange an audition for you."

"I know I'll sound ungrateful but I just couldn't—not the first time, anyway—do it in front of strangers."

Oh, dese folks all wants to be yo' friends, honey, dey yo' friends . . .

"Well, there's got to be a first time, Mary." Well, he had managed that switch neatly enough.

"I know but . . . look, this may sound silly—"

Mary had a "silly" complex, but somehow on her it didn't look bad.

"Could I dance for you?"

Tom could see the whole thing now. This huge red-headed broad dancing to something he was humming and Karen walking in with That Look.

"I don't think that would be too much to your advantage here."

"Oh, I didn't mean here." And the wide eyes said that where she *had* meant, surely, was a place something like the Cloisters, where monks sat nearby intoning their day's prayers, if he was thinking now that because she had mentioned "someplace else" she meant anything improper.

"Well, I believe that would be possible. I have a kind of full day today and tomorrow. . . ." He was looking at his desk calendar, knowing darned well she wasn't planning to dance in the cold light of day.

"Perhaps some evening when you wouldn't be too tied up with the show," she said innocently.

Now it had come to win, place, and show. He knew that he had gone through the hazy wall of his daydreams and was connecting wires to something far more palpable. How far could he go with this and still retreat? Tom had never consummated the act of cheating. It had really never occurred to him beyond his daydreaming.

Karen came in with a note. She said that Helen had taken it while she had been out for the coffee. It was from his wife Eileen, who said that she was calling from downtown with her mother who had come into the city to shop, and, with the bad roads, felt she should drive home with her. If it was all right with Tom, Eileen would stay over with her parents and her father would drive her back the next day.

Tom felt that kind of tickling he experienced when he sat in a wooden chair and something heavy vibrated the floor.

He folded the memo twice; he was making a decision. It was half made on the first fold and resolved on the

second. "I could manage it tonight, if that's convenient to you."

"That would be fine." To make it sound less like a proposition, she added, "I'm very grateful to you for taking the time to do this. I know how many people must bother you."

For an awful moment he was afraid that she was legitimately planning an actual audition, but then dismissed it as a face-saving device she was using.

"I'll be up at about eight." He didn't have the nerve to start it with dinner.

"Fine, if it's okay, I'll fix a little snack. You'll probably be starved by then."

Lord, now he'd have to kill time without eating until eight o'clock.

"That's very kind of you. If I finish with the meeting with Mr. Travers any earlier I'll come straight over, if that's all right."

"Fine. It's just a snack, really. I can get it ready in a moment."

He was sure of this from any viewpoint. "All right. Oh, isn't this silly? What's your address?"

"Here, I'll write it down for you."

As she bent over, it seemed his eyes could go down the front of the low-hanging neckline, past the stomach, under and through the legs, up her back and over her clavicle, and back to where they had started. She handed him the slip of paper as Karen opened the door.

"Mr. Travers called and asked if you and Mrs. Moore weren't doing anything tonight; he's stuck in town and would like to take you out to dinner."

"I'll call him back." He still hadn't taken the address from Miss Willoughby's hand. She held it, waiting for him. Karen stood waiting for him to take it, although she was ostensibly there for a further answer to her question. He took the piece of paper with an absent gesture and dropped it on the desk as if Miss Willoughby had just returned a doodling she had admired. "Good-bye, Miss Willoughby, thank you for coming up."

"Thank you so much, Mr. Moore, and I hope I didn't take up too much of your time."

(Continued on next page)

"That was the best excuse for coming home late that I've ever heard—unfortunately, you've in the wrong apartment!"

Because she didn't mention "tonight" in front of Karen, m felt another one of those on-wooden-chair scrapes.

stopped in at the Stork for a drink. Three different tains asked him where Mrs. Moore was tonight. For no e reason he found himself concocting extravagant ex- antations.

He looked at himself in the mirror. He never felt less e doing what he was going to do in his entire life. He ered another drink.

After he was halfway through the one following that didn't feel quite as much "less like doing it."

he walked toward the east Eighties, he saw himself, a few moments, madly frolicking in the nude with Mary e Red. He wondered if the nickname would hold up er she was undressed. He could see himself ricocheting those magnificent breasts . . . "Cringe, Mount McKin- s, you should practically be ashamed of yourselves."

It was the kind of semiintoxicated talk a man makes en he's alone. He knows he's not that drunk and he is ally trying to say things he feels he would say if he were t drunk.

Tom waved a cab to the curb and got in without mment.

"Where to, buddy?" resignedly asked the driver, with e weariness of all cab drivers who had to make a living nsporting drunks.

"Just a minute, please." Tom was fishing through his ckets for Mary's address.

He got off a block from Miss Willoughby's, with the ution of a man throwing off followers, passed the house mistake the first time, and then returned to enter. The sciviousness he had tried to drink into himself had left m completely, and the only feeling he had now was one imminent disaster.

Tom looked at the small brass-rimmed cards, found one beled Mary Willoughby, and pressed the button. He mped a little when he said, "Oh, hi. My, you *are* early." ary Willoughby was standing behind him. She was car- ing a large paper bag from the delicatessen. He decided t to remove his hat and took the bag instead.

"Here, let me."

"Oh, fine. Thank you."

She unlocked the outside door and they walked up three flights of stairs to her door. It had F-8 printed on it. Tom was trying to hide his exertion from the climb as he walked in behind her.

"Where shall I drop these?"

People who found themselves in situations that had been done and redone in pictures or plays reverted to the dialogue that had accompanied those scenes: "Here, let me . . . where shall I drop these?" About the next thing someone always said was, "Quite a climb." He tried to think of something else to say, but "Quite a climb" was all that came to his mind so he said nothing.

"That's quite a climb," said Mary, taking the bag.

"Yes, it certainly is. Great for the figure."

One of them had to say that line, too, sooner or later. He figured it was her vernacular and if he was going to have an affair with her, he might as well establish a relationship as her being "his kind of folks."

"Let me have your coat," she said.

"Thank you. Just throw it on a chair."

"Oh dear no, I'll hang it up—hat?"

"Thank you."

"Nice hat. I like a nice man's hat."

Me Tarzan . . . You Jane . . . Me Boy . . . he thought. Aloud, he said, "Yes."

What the hell do you say to, "I like a nice man's hat?" "I have a nice scarf, too," he said. Seeing her blank expression, he decided this was not the type of humor that brought out her risibilities. And with the thought of bringing out her risibilities, he said:

"How about a drink?"

"How about a drink?"

They had both said it together and they laughed like in the movies.

She had taken off her mouton and was wearing a one-piece knitted dress. It was beige—big and beige. He looked around, making a complete circle. He closed his eyes for a moment. He had heard what happened to Arctic travelers going snow-blind. Was it possible to get beige-blind, too? This was drunk talk, he realized. Something about the beige brought back two dollars' worth of the gin he had had and he turned in time to see her walking toward the kitchenette.

Her legs, which were about twenty feet long, supported a fanny that Lucrezia Borgia would have poisoned out of sheer jealousy. It consisted logically enough, of two separate halves whose rhythm was bum-ba-ba-bum when she took them with her, which, being a saving girl, she always did. They were like twin pendulums, ticking away the hours from this monstrous eight-day timepiece that was Mary Willoughby. When she walked he could almost see an invitatory finger between them, like an animated prehensile tail beckoning him to follow.

She turned around, her breasts following her body a half revolution late. "Scotch or gin?"

"Fine with me," he said with a little giggle. She laughed, too, and all he could think of at the sight was, "What time do the balloons go up?"

She threw together a one-ingredient Martini which would have made a lumberjack cough. They sat on the beige sofa with the beige-blond coffee table in front of them.

"Here's how," she coined.

"I like that," he said, "here's how to you."

"You don't say 'to you,' you just say 'here's how.'"

(Continued on next page)

He digested this bit of incunabula and drank. The drink had all the quality of Brillo pads. "Smooth," he said, double vision hitting him for the moment, producing two Mary Willoughbys, two bosoms, and consequently, four of the component parts comprising the bosoms.

"Shall I dance for you or would you like to eat first?"

He nominated the food and she stood up, using the northern section of his thigh for support to heave her twins upright.

"I'll bring it in here."

Mary had one large white flower floating in water in a brandy snifter on the beige coffee table. He removed the flower, put some of the water in his Martini, and replaced the flower. He looked around the room. Mary was interested in modern art. Tom knew very little about modern art but accepted the cubistic Mona Lisa as all part of this new form.

She returned in a few moments, carrying a little tray of cold cuts and pumpernickel. "That's Danish salami," she said informatively, pointing to some dried objects which bore an unhappy similarity to something else which escaped him for the moment. "Try one."

He demurred and took a piece of boiled ham, rolled it, dipped it into the mustard which she served *au naturel* in the jar, and told her how delicious it was.

She thanked him and a wave of garlic hit him like a wet battering ram. He began eating the Danish salami too, as defense. He spread coleslaw and potato salad on his burning tongue in the manner of carbon dioxide fire-foam.

"Par'm me," she said, switching a large piece of salami to a favored side of her mouth, "shall I make some coffee now or after."

"After" could only mean that there was all doubt removed as to what they were going to do shortly.

"How about that dance," he asked, fighting a feeling of nausea from the garlic.

"All right, but you won't laugh?"

'Laugh,' no, but there were a helluva pile of other verbs he wasn't going to swear abstinence from.

She stood up again, her hand on his thigh leaving five salami lines on his trousers, and began turning off all the lights. She lighted a large candle which had been originally in the image of Santa Claus and had burned down to a point where the wick was in an embarrassing location. She took an album from a wire rack, and stacked three or four L.P. records on the automatic machine.

"What do you dance to?" he asked, breathing deeply to combat his indigestion.

"Oh, this is some music entitled, 'Background Music for The Goya Horrors of War.' See, in the front here are some of the sketches and this fellow, Rim-sky Pro-kor-see-koff, wrote the music for it. See?"

He looked at the sketches of large soldiers raping thin women, slamming ankle-held infants against walls, castrations and close-ups of gangrene infections. He pushed the platter of salami a little farther toward the opposite end of the coffee table.

Mary set the first record and left the room.

The salamied air began to throb with tympany and then a speaking chorus chanted:

"Rape and rob,
Rob and rape,
Cut from him his manhood then
Take his wife and do his mother
Woe to war, woe to war."

A thin flute passage began and Tom had the feeling that he was in another country. The wick in its phallicism o Santa Claus made Tom feel acutely conscious of his ow aims and he shifted his gaze to the cubed Mona Lisa.

Then Mary entered. The little time she had taken to p on her costume convinced Tom that Mary Willoughb did not wear underwear beneath her street clothing. He costume, a two-inch width, three-foot length of wrinkle velveteen, hung from a string circling around her bod below the navel, which, incidentally, stared at him like a accusing gouged Cyclops. She wore nothing else. Her mi givings about auditioning at United were understandabl She danced squarely before him, stopping momentarily t push the coffee table to one side. She was too close for hi to focus on her as a whole. He had to shift his gaze fro area to area. He would liked to have enjoyed an over-a view.

"Rape and rob,
Cut from him
The source of life."

He was glad that this uninhibited female had no pro knife included in her presentation. He crossed his leg anyway, as a reflex action.

War, war, oh woe, oh woe,
Rape the daughter, rape and woe.

Mary did bumps on the verbs and grinds on the noun Conjunctions and adverbs were left unchoreographed. H sat there hopefully waiting for a long sequence of intrans itive verbs from the chorus. She had come uncomfortabl close now. The velveteen was slapping at him on such verbs as "run," "race," "rape," and "render." Keepin her hips swaying in time to an ambitious kettledrum solo she took the end of the velveteen and threw it about th back of his neck. By keeping her grip on the free end an rotating her hips, she injected a South American touch Unfortunately the movement turned his head from left t right and with the motion, the garlic, and the indigestion he was having a difficult time staying with it.

With a sudden gesture accompanied by trombone, sh pulled the velveteen free and dropped the costume on th floor in an untidy little heap. Not knowing quite what wa expected of him, Tom occupied himself with folding th piece of velveteen neatly. Now completely without cos tume, she began sliding to the floor in a dancer's split . . dropping an inch or two with each bar of the music. Whe she had completed the split, she swung the leg that wa behind her to a parallel with the front, did a slow roll ove toward him, which put the twins up, and she again exe cuted a split, contortionist fashion, face and arms on floor legs in mid-air.

Tom wondered nervously if he had stumbled onto a nut How could this beautiful girl be demented? He tried t remember how she acted in his office, but with the gi taking effect, he couldn't even remember what the UB building looked like. By some arrangement with her mus cles she was suddenly on her knees before him, holdin out her arms and rising slowly. When she was upright sh put her hands on his shoulders and, twisting him as sh pushed, laid him flat on the beige sofa.

From his supinery Tom peered up into what looked lik the concentric circles one sees in the throes of high feve That whirligig with the frustration of the red lines in barber pole which seem to begin nowhere and to en equally indefinitely. Mary Willoughby's long red hair ha

(Continued on page 82

PRIVATE SHOWING
(Continued from page 77)

joined in some manner beneath her chin; making her face look somewhat like a gigantic archery target. Her eyes, blue as a Folies-Bergère backdrop, looked down at him like ink defying gravity. Her large red mouth was open so wide he could almost hear echoes and see spelunkers. Her soft palate hung in the rear of her mouth like some great pink stalactite. He visualized Injun Joe chasing Tom Sawyer and Becky in and out of the tonsils. What the hell would A. E. Housman have said. Her mouth loomed close and he felt he could place his entire head within it with the tonsils cradling the sides of his temples like slippery ear muffs. . . .

"Helloooooooo down there," he wanted to shout. The red tongue lay there like a pebbled gangplank for the *Ile de France*, and when it came closer he felt like Mickey Mouse about to be slurped by an overzealous Pluto. Her increasing emotion drew back her teeth like the MGM trademark. Man, this was living! Suddenly she pressed her mouth on his face with the relationship of a kitchen plunger to a stopped-up drain. What the hell was that schoolboy, Lyn Travers, doing at *this* moment? he sneered. The medicine-ball breasts were against him like two bald-headed men. What an act this would make on the "Ed Sullivan Show!"

There was a certain frustration in not being able to kiss her in return. She was, he decided, the aggressor. He felt tiny and defenseless and clear of conscience as far as Eileen was concerned. What could he do about this, short of socking her in the face? He decided to relax and roll with the blows. Briefly he worried that she might be a little mentally short and that this really was her idea of "The Dance," but he put that away with the realization that nobody could be quite that nuts.

Her mouth remained against his face like a soggy inner tube, and he wondered what she had scheduled next. She slipped upward quickly and placed the bald-headed men squarely on his face, and while there was something aphrodisiac to it, he was falling short of fulfilling the enjoyment by an inability to breathe. He finally twisted his head enough to allow a tremendous intake of breath which she mistook for passion and shoved his head back into Othello's pillows.

Cutting down his oxygen intake gave an impetus to the gin the manufacturer would have taken pride in. Tom knew he was not only practically asphyxiated but he was pretty drunk, too.

"Tom . . . Tom," she said, and he wondered how she knew his first name. The grand manner that comes with certain forms of inebriety brought forth a resentment at the familiarity.

"Mr. Moore, if you will," he tried to say, but the only effect was a vibration of his lips against her chest, which seemed to excite her.

"I've never done this sort of thing before," she said.

"You're quite good for a first try," he would have answered.

"Tom . . . Mr. Moore . . . Tom . . ."

This was beginning to sound like a gang job.

With a change of heart he attempted to tell her that she could call him "Tom," but he was lucky enough to sneak in enough air just to remain conscious.

"Oh, Mr. Moore, Mr. Moore."

Dammit, that *really* sounded silly.

"I hope you don't think I'm this kind of girl."

Good heavens, what could possibly, possibly have given him that impression?

"I don't know what you must think of me."

Give me a little air and I'll be glad to tell you. He was a little envious of her up there breathing all that good air, with his own nose assailed by garlic, perspiration, and a small bone that miraculously managed to make itself felt between those two white monsters.

"Take me, Mr. Moore, take me, I want you to."

How the hell could he? He lay pinioned beneath the Moby Dick, unable to move so much as a muscle . . . *any* muscle. One of his legs had become numb and the forces of Denmark salami and the distillery had combined in the stomach she had flattened and were now fighting back.

"My God," he thought, "I'm belching zour.'"

She pressed her upper body upright, her two long arms holding her stiffly above him. "You do like me a little, don't you?"

He was inhaling great gasps of air, not wanting to lose one moment of the advantage. She might be back any time.

"Yes," he gasped finally, "I do, my dear, very much."

"Oh, darling," she oohed, and lay back upon his face. The movement removed the pressure from his leg artery and he could feel the tingling of the blood returning to his foot.

After a few minutes there was suddenly no more movement above him. Had she died? He could visualize rescue parties jacking her off the sofa to find "Tom Moore of the United Broadcasting Company" there. Recalling the great attention the press had given Floyd Collins, he began jostling her a little.

"What is it?" She had fallen asleep and was one of those people who flails about wildly on awakening in strange beds.

"It's me," he said urgently, to enlighten her before she could begin screaming, "me, Mr. Moore."

"Oh, darling," she said, getting up. "You must think I'm pretty dull to fall asleep. Would you like some coffee?"

COFFEE? How the hell long did she think she'd been sleeping? My God, was she under the impression that she had fallen asleep 'AFTER'?

"Excuse me, dear, woman's little work, you know," she said coyly. She went to the bathroom, throwing a conspiratorial wink at him over her shoulder.

He looked at the Mona Lisa and it was beginning to make sense. Miss Willoughby came back with two cups of instant coffee, snapped on all the lights, including an unshaded three-bulb affair on the ctiling, and sat down beside him on the sofa, placing herself so that she was sitting squarely on a cushion and not on the space between.

"Cream?" she asked, with the manner of a naked Eliza Doolittle after a few rounds with Professor Higgins.

"No, black," he said. He was looking at her sideways. She sat there with the aplomb of a woman beside her satiated male. He knew that he could not recommence relationships with this woman who was drinking her Nescafé with this air of finality.

Somehow, he, too, felt that he had had it.

She brought him his hat and coat as if she were wearing clothes.

"Thanks for coming up, Mr. Moore. I hope I'm lucky Saturday night."

Tom walked down the three flights of stairs with the air of a man prepared to be surprised to find that he wasn't on the planet Mars when he stepped outside. ●

by RICHARD GEHMAN

he wacky world of

ERNIE KOVACS

This hasn't been a good year for comedians—except for madcap Ernie Kovacs. He goes right on living like a munitions manufacturer and gambling like Nick the Greek

ROUND the television networks, this has been known as the year the cowboys clobbered the comedians. hile James Arness and other grimy stalwarts reigned in uine splendor, the funny men went thataway. Sid Caesar d Jackie Gleason disappeared from the screen. George bel had to divide his time with Eddie Fisher, and many her comedians for whom shows had been planned, among em Jack E. Leonard and Red Buttons, had to seek em oyment elsewhere.

In view of this situation, the behavior of a six-foot, ack-mustached Hungarian from Trenton, New Jersey, ristened Ernest Kovacs, was strange indeed. Kovacs was fered his own weekly show by NBC. He declined it. Over res then were made to him by representatives of ABC. e again said no. CBS apparently did not feel it was worth uying him the $50 lunch at Twenty-One that is standard rocedure in opening negotiations for talent. The word had ne out that Kovacs was saying no like a stammerer.

"We probably would have tried to get him," said one BS executive, with regret, "if we'd thought there was a

chance. But we knew he just didn't want his own show."

Kovacs was not playing the aloof bit; he simply had other plans. He wrote a novel, *Zoomar*, about the television industry (a zoomar is a lens that quickly brings far-off action in close). He went out to Hollywood and made a movie, *Operation Madball*. He appeared on the Polly Bergen Show, in *Topaze* on Playhouse 90, on the Perry Como show and in various other shows. He became a temporarily permanent panelist on *What's My Line*. It soon became apparent that by turning down his own show he had been displaying his native Hungarian shrewdness; by not appearing regularly, he was enabled to appear irregularly often enough to earn close to $200,000. It was a gamble that paid off, and that was eminently typical of Kovacs. He is a gambler of such intensity that beside him Nick the Greek looks like a two-dollar horseplayer. Unbelievable though it may sound, Kovacs' principal reason in rejecting offers to be the proprietor of a weekly show was his desire to have more time to gamble—principally to play cards.

Kovacs plays cards anytime *(Continued on next page)*

with anybody he can find for a game. If no friends available, he attempts to draw his house man or chauff into a game. He plays poker, gin, cribbage, euchre, casi pinochle, five hundred, hearts, rum, hasenpeffer, beziq canasta, bolivia and the old Hungarian game known va ously as klabiash, klaberjass, kalaber, kalabrias, klob, kla clob, clab and clabber. If no servant can be enticed into game, he plays Flinch or Old Maid with his two little gir If they are bored or up to something else, he plays solitai He sticks strictly to cards, following the adage coined the sportsman Lee Meyers: "Never gamble with noth you can't shuffle." Sometimes, however, he and a frie named Herb Susann will play "Monopoly," using r money instead of the scrip that comes with the set; justifies this by explaining that the "Monopoly" cards ha to be shuffled at the beginning of each game.

So great is Kovacs' passion for cards that he cares no ing for the stakes. "I'm a lousy poker player," he says, " cause I just don't care." He will play for pennies with

KOVACS CLAN builds human totem pole. The kids, Betty (*top*) and Kippy, are by Ernie's first marriage, but present wife Edie is crazy about them.

BIG, FAT CIGARS are Ernie's trademark. He once smoked one while deliveri a cigarette commercial. Edie says clearing out cigar boxes is an all-day cho

BROADWAY gave Edie Adams her first break in "Wonderful Town," and Kovacs soon joined her in N.Y. Later, they were married in Mexico.

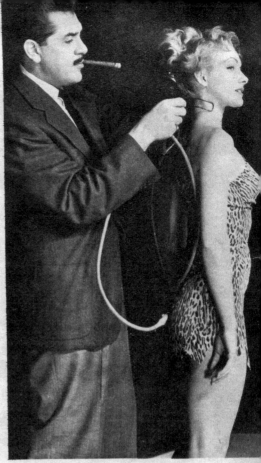

ERNIE and Edie have commuted 3,000 miles to be with each other.

ZANY Kovacs girds victim for TV prank.

arter limit or he will play in games that set no limit at
. He drops $3.76 or $3,000 in an evening with equal
andon. This does not mean that he is not fiercely serious
out the game. As he plays his eyes take on a fierce glitter,
d his heavy mustache seems to droop into the handlebars
the old Mississippi riverboat sharper. He eschews the
all talk and the banter of friendly games. One day last
ll, during the World Series, I suggested we have a game
gin while watching the third game on television.
Great!" Kovacs cried. We settled down to play. Another
iend had told me that the best way to get to know Ernie
uring an interview was to play cards with him; the trou-
e was, I had forgotten the rules of gin. That made no
fference to Kovacs. He explained the rules patiently. The
ct that I was an amateur, and an inept one at that, meant
ss to him than the compelling fact that I was an op-
onent. He played as though I were Hoyle himself. He
ayed with such concentration that he drew me into the
irit of the thing. Two hours later, we happened to glance
the television set. There was a Western on. "My God,"
id Kovacs, "who won the ball game?" After totting up
e score, it developed that I owed him something like $82.
e refused my check.

This was a characteristic gesture. Kovacs is a genuinely
iendly, easy-going fellow, and when he says the money
eans nothing to him, he means it. For a time, he and
ackie Gleason played gin in the afternoons, day in and
ay out. He beat Gleason consistently. Gleason presently
ook up golf and kept urging Kovacs to go out on the

course with him, believing he could recoup some of his
losses. Kovacs is no golfer, but he bought himself a set of
clubs just to give Gleason the opportunity to win back
some of his money. They went down to Fred Waring's golf
club at Shawnee-on-the-Delaware, in the Pennsylvania
Poconos. There, it developed, Kovacs couldn't lose at golf,
either.

Gleason is possessed of a Falstaffian amiability, but he
is a keen competitor and hates to be bested. Kovacs needled
him unmercifully throughout the weekend. On the way
back to New York, each was riding in his own limousine.
Kovacs has a telephone in his. As the two long black auto-
mobiles pulled up beside each other at a stop light in New
Jersey, Kovacs' telephone began to ring. He answered it
and rolled down the window, extending the telephone toward Gleason's car. "It's for you, Jackie," he said. "I think
it's your golf pro."

The automobile telephone is symptomatic of the boyish
delight Kovacs takes in living like a munitions manufacturer. Ever since he began to make big money in television, he has been slightly, but not offensively, ostenta-
tious. He hired a chauffeur even before he could afford a
limousine. One day a couple of years ago, when he and his
wife, Edie Adams, had a morning television program on
NBC, I saw them come out of Toots Shor's at lunch time.
She was wearing a long mink coat with a hood collar;
Kovacs was wearing a cream-colored leather trench coat
and a homburg and smoking his usual long, expensive cigar.
At the curb was parked a modest- *(Continued on page 74)*

WACKY WORLD OF ERNIE KOVACS continued from page 37

PUFFING like chimney, Ernie goes over busy day's itinerary at breakfast with Edie.

priced convertible with the top down and a liveried chauffeur in the front seat. The Kovacs' got in the rear seat like a couple of Whitneys and the car drove off.

The incongruity of the sight amused me. It amused Kovacs, too. It was his own way of kidding his own taste for the showy way of life. There is a certain ambiguity in his attitude. He says he hires his chauffeur because the man's salary is much less than the amount he and his wife would spend on cabs in a single week. "Also," he points out, "by having a chauffeur you also have your own car whenever you want it—you don't have to wait for cabs." These practical sentiments still do not conceal Kovacs' pleasure in being able to afford a chauffeur.

The Kovacs' have a 17-room apartment (with eight baths) overlooking Central Park. Actually, it is not as expensive as it sounds; it is on the West Side of Manhattan, where the rents are comparatively low. Kovacs gets it for about $500 a month; a comparable shelter on the East Side would cost three times that much and possibly more. But no East Side apartment is more elegantly furnished. Stepping into the Kovacs' home is like stepping into Biltmore, the fabulous pleasure dome decreed by George Vanderbilt in Asheville, North Carolina, around the turn of the century. Ernie's guest must dodge jutting spears held by suits of armor; there is enough armor in the place to outfit one of Richard III's platoons. The crystal chandeliers could be used for a whole series of Franz Lehar operettas. The dining table is about as long as the one in the great hall at William Randolph Hearst's San Simeon. The ivory concert grand piano in the living room seems lost

in one corner. Kovacs and his wife sleep in a tremendous bed; at the foot are two portable television sets, his and hers, so that there is never any dispute about what show will be viewed.

Near Kovacs' dressing room is a special room in which his cigars are kept. Kovacs imports these cigars from Cuba. They are huge dark brown *immensa meduras,* all but unobtainable except by special order. "Nobody wants to buy this color of leaf," Kovacs explains. He believes he inherited his fondness for cigars from his father. Kovacs sticks a cigar in his face the instant he awakens in the morning, and he is never without one for the rest of the day, except while he is eating. He smokes about 20 per day. He even smoked a cigar, once, while he was delivering a cigarette commercial on TV; the cigar is so much a part of his personality that not even the advertising agency men noticed it. His stationery trademark is a black mustache and a burning cigar; at the top, incidentally, it says, *From the desk of Willie "Dutch" Sutton* or *Mary Margaret Gabor* or somebody like that . . . Whenever Kovacs' cigar supply runs low, he and his wife and two daughters get on a plane and go to Cuba for a weekend; he long ago learned that each individual may import 200 cigars duty-free, for his own use. Curiously enough, the customs men have never questioned the Kovacs' children's liking for *immensa meduras.*

Kovacs takes great pride in his home, so much, in fact, that he rarely uses the country place he recently bought in Rockland County, New York. At home in the apartment he spends most of his time in his study, a paneled niche in which his gun collection adorns the walls. Kovacs

buys guns the way he buys old suits of armor. His prize is a German blunderbuss of the late 19th century, its wooden stock inlaid with ivory hunting scenes—dogs and hunters chasing stags and boars, etc. He also owns an Austrian wheel-lock. "The guns are all in firing order," he says, "but I really ought to spend more time on them. In fact, that's another reason I turned down the weekly TV show—so I could put in more time on the guns." The den is pleasantly cluttered with papers and various bits of equipment that reflect Kovacs' interests—a tape recorder, an electric typewriter, an Italian *espresso* machine, a portable phonograph and piles and stacks and shelves full of books and records. There is a well-stocked bar; Kovacs is an enthusiastic, but moderate, drinker. He prefers 12-year-old Scotch. In addition to the guns, the walls are covered with pictures, mainly of Edie and their two daughters. There are also the plaques showing the various awards he has won; in 1956, he knocked off three of the Emmys given by the Academy of Television Arts and Sciences—best new show, best comedy writing and best continuing show.

It was in this room that Kovacs wrote his novel, *Zoomar*, He wrote the novel in, he swears, 13 days, which is a feat comparable to running the mile in one second flat (come to think of it, if challenged to run the mile in one second flat, he probably would figure a way to do it). The novel reads as though it had been written in 13 days. Despite the occasional insertion of words like "saponaceous" (meaning soapy), the whole work is veined with bad grammar, careless metaphor and uninspired imagery. It is full of toilet jokes.

JACK O'BRIEN, the television critic for the New York *Journal-American,* said flatly, "It is a cheap book." Kovacs responded to this criticism by tearing off the price from the dust-jacket ($3.95) and sending it to O'Brien in a plain envelope. He himself had seen nothing remarkable about writing a 348-page novel in 13 days (it took twice that long to collect the material for and write this piece, by the way). "Hell," he said, "some days I wrote thirteen, fourteen hours a day. Some nights I wrote forty pages. I mean, I just started to write and kept on until I was finished, sending hunks of it to the publisher. They read the manuscript, suggested three changes which I made in about a day, and put it into type. My editor said he'd never seen anything like it." Kovacs' particular editor used to be a Y.M.C.A. Boys' Work Secretary. It is a platinum-plated cinch he never saw anything like Kovacs' book in those days. The characters are in and out of bed like customers in a Honolulu whorehouse. Frequently they do not even bother to use beds.

Kovacs always works with lightning speed when he is creating. He wrote a night club act for himself and his wife

74

night while they were sitting with ...e friends in Billy Reed's Little Club. ... wrote it on a napkin and tucked it into ... pocket. This act, which they later ex-...ted to patrons of a Las Vegas club ...ed Tropicana, earned them $100,000 ... a month last November. "We did it ...nly to give Edie something to do after ... left *Li'l Abner*," Kovacs said. Miss ...ms was the star of that Broadway ...w, although her name was not billed ...ve the producers', which was a matter ... irritation to Kovacs; he is a hard, ...ewd bargainer, and is as tough about ...dits as he is about money.

...ow much money Kovacs carted home ... after earning the $100,000 in Las ...gas may be open to question. It is a ...tainty that he dropped some at the ...d tables, and his living expenses cer-...ly were not inconsiderable. Wherever ... goes, he spends money in a style that ...als Mike Todd's. While making *Opera-...n Madball* at Columbia studios in Hol-...wood last summer, he lived at the Bev-...y Hills Hotel, one of the most expen-...e hostelries on the North American ...ntinent. His bill there was something ...e $1,500 per week. He earned only ...5,000 for his work in the picture; he ...d taken the job against the advice of ... agent solely because he wanted to get ... feet wet in films. Considering the tax ...acket his $200,000-per-year income puts ...m in, he could not have taken home ...ch pay for the work. He did not care. ...*Madball* was a ball," he says. "I enjoyed ...ery minute of it."

Also, he picked up some valuable ex-...rience. It is Kovacs' firm intention to ... a movie director-writer some day; ac-...ally, he now considers himself more ...iter than comedian. This is a source of ...itation to directors assigned to work ...th him. "I never could get close to the ...y, I never could get him to do what I ...nted him to do," says one man, a vet-...an television comedy director. "When-...er I had a suggestion, he always wanted ... do it *his* way." There are other direc-...rs who respect Kovacs' views and his ...sistence upon his own way, however.

"I began working with Ernie early in ...6," says Perry Cross, currently produc-... of the Jack Paar show on NBC. "We ...d a morning show on NBC five times a ...eek. From that we went on directly as ...mmer replacement for Sid Caesar on ...s Monday night hour-long spot. Ernie ...rote the bulk of that show, although ...ere were three writers on the staff. As a ...sult of that one summer the show won ...ur Sylvania awards and five Emmy ...minations.

"Ernie is a warm, unfunny guy—by ...at I mean he's a regular human being ...hen he isn't performing. He doesn't sit ...round trying to crack jokes like many ...medians do. I would say his type of ...omedy is just a slight exaggeration of his ...fe philosophy. He always finds some-...ing funny in commonplace situations.

When he's onstage he's making a social commentary or an observation on human nature. Take his Coty Girl bit, for exam-ple. I'm sure he watched the straight ver-sion on TV dozens of times and probably in his subconscious he got sore. You know the bit—first you see the hat, then the girl raises her head and says, 'Hi, I'm the Coty Girl.' With Ernie, the feeling of rage ultimately emerges as a highly comic se-quence. He put on an almost identical Coty girl, but as soon as she got her head up a custard pie hit her in the face."

The Coty people, incidentally, were de-lighted with this bit, which perhaps got them more attention than the original. To show their appreciation, they made a spe-cial film for Kovacs, showing their own girl with a huge mustache and a cigar. Kovacs howled when he saw it. Later, when he was a guest on the Polly Bergen show, he conceived the notion of coming on and saying himself, "Hi, I'm Polly Bergen." Unfortunately, Polly's sponsors did not think this was funny, and it never was used.

There are those who believe that so much of Kovacs' humor is based on in-side jokes that he thus far has not been as appreciated by the general public as he should be. Certainly many of his stunts do depend upon the viewers' familiarity with other TV phenomena. Once he con-ceived a great notion for closing a show. During the season, Jimmy Durante had been winding up his show by walking off into the distance, pausing in pools of light from overhead spots as he went, raising his hat in sad farewell. It was a touching way to go out. On Kovacs' show, an actor walked away at the end, pausing in the spotlights, imitating Durante to perfec-tion—except that the third spotlight was a trapdoor, and the man fell through the

floor, disappearing completely from sight.

"This was a great success," says Perry Cross. "That actor, by the way, was a stunt man, and Ernie worked out dozens of situations where it was logical for him to fall through the floor. He did another wonderful bit that involved all kinds of planning and machinery—just for a five-second blackout. The guy walked into a psychiatrist's office and laid down on a couch. The doctor leaned forward to speak to him, and as he did the couch sprung up and catapulted the guy through a wall. That was all there was to it, but it was wildly funny and demanded tre-mendous preparation.

"Ernie is meticulous and a perfection-ist, that's true," Cross adds. "He never goes into tirades or anything of that kind, but he demands that everything be well-rehearsed. If something goes wrong, he goes to whoever is responsible and tells them that he was displeased, but never in rage, never in anger. He's very popular with the stagehands. He used to work in the Hudson Theater on 44th Street for that morning show, and now that I'm on the Paar show the guys always ask me about him, if I ever see him, how he is, when he is coming back to work. That's very unusual in this business."

The stagehands liked Kovacs despite the fact that he could never remember any of their names. This is his foremost failing. One of his principal triumphs in recent years has been to recall unfailingly that his wife's name is Edie Adams. His favorite director in television is a man named Barry Shear, who this season is doing the Eddie Fisher show; Kovacs, who has been working with Shear for years, still occasionally calls him "Barry What's-his-name." Once Dr. Frank Stan-ton, president (*Continued on next page*)

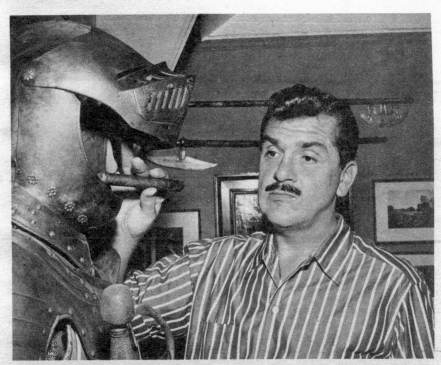

COMEDIAN and friend: the butts of Ernie's pranks often need armor instead of skin.

of CBS, approached him and congratulated him on a show he had done. "Thank you, uh . . . ." said Kovacs, and stopped, panic-stricken. "Now, Ernie," said Stanton, gently, "I'm going to tell you my name once again." In Hollywood, after he did *Topaze,* he gave a party for some friends in his hotel suite. "I timed it so that when the guests arrived, I would still be in the bathroom," he later said. "This gave them the chance to introduce themselves to each other, and saved me the bother of having to remember their names."

Kovacs does not know why he cannot remember names. A psychiatrist might interpret this quirk as a kind of overt act of hostility against the world, bolstering this contention by pointing out that much of Kovacs' humor is cruel and sadistic. But it is doubtful if Kovacs will ever land on a couch for this or any other reason. He is dubious of the value of psychiatry for a person like himself. "I think a person ought to help himself," he sometimes says. "I haven't even been to a doctor for years. If I have to take a pill for dieting, I feel that I'm slipping. It could be sheer Hungarian stubbornness, but I feel that a man must rely on himself." In these days when people are hurling themselves upon psychiatrist's couches like so many lemmings throwing themselves into the sea, this is a most refreshing, not to say heartening, attitude.

G OD knows that Kovacs might well have good reason to consult a psychiatrist about his inner tremors and anxieties. He came from a home where the mother and father were both of volatile disposition. They quarrelled constantly. "He called her 'Dad' and she called him 'Mom.'" Kovacs once said to me when I asked him their names. This was a wittily oblique method of expressing the contention between the two. The father, Andrew, had come to the New World from Hungary at 13 and had worked at odd jobs until he was old enough to land a post on the Trenton, New Jersey, police force. It paid around $10 per week, which forced him to keep his family in a poor, run-down neighborhood. Ernie was born in 1916. His brother, Tom, nine years older, left home as soon as possible (Tom is now working at an air base in New Jersey), which left Ernie for the mother to shower with all her pent-up affection. Ernie wolfed down her cooking voraciously; he was a fat little boy, and the butt of his schoolmates' jokes. To make matters worse, his mother was fond of dressing him in little velvet suits.

The fact that Kovacs was an exceptionally quick and bright child did not help matters. Most kids are prone to pick on the brightest in the class, out of envy or just plain resentment of authority. Ernie skipped two grades. His teacher suggested

to his mother that he might be happier—and would progress even faster—in a private school. The mother was in despair—the family could never afford that.

But, curiously enough, the Kovacs were able to afford it within a relatively short time. One reporter, Jhan Robbins, has written that Kovacs' father went into "the beverage business." He wrote that in a family magazine. In this one, where men are men, we can call spades spades. The old man went out and began selling booze. In no time at all the family was living on a large estate complete with dogs and horses, and Ernie was going to Miss Bowen's, an exclusive private school. Thus Kovacs cultivated the taste for luxuries that he has never been able to lose. But almost as soon as his father made his money he lost it and Kovacs went back into the public schools.

U P TO this time Kovacs had had no special notion of what he would do when he graduated. Then, in high school, a teacher named Harold Van Kirk recognized his natural ability as a mimic and encouraged him to think about going on the stage. With Van Kirk's assistance he got a scholarship at a summer theater, and in the fall he enrolled at a dramatic school in New York City. He was miserable there for many reasons, not the least of which was the fact that he had no money. He was also homesick, and he did not have money enough to go back to Trenton for a visit. One day he awoke with a terrible pain in his chest. A kindly neighbor found him and sent him to the hospital for public charges on Welfare Island. There his condition was diagnosed as pneumonia.

The year was 1939. None of the doctors expected him to live. Kovacs himself had just about given up hope. About the only man who seemed optimistic was a clerk from the draft board who came to register him. Kovacs will never forget the man. "I was lying there scarcely able to lift my head," he recalls, "and this joker came in and began asking me the usual questions and filling out the forms. Finally he got around to 'Complexion?' He peered at me. Then he wrote down 'Sallow.'"

New York and New Jersey then had a kind of reciprocal trade agreement for penniless hospital patients. Ernie was shipped to a Jersey state hospital, where he languished for several months. Gradually his health returned, and one day, over and above the protests of the sawbones, he stole his clothes from an attendant and departed. He has not been to see a doctor since.

Back in Trenton, he went to live with his mother, who was divorced from his father. He took a job as a director of a small-time theatrical organization; it lasted until one of the directors disappeared

with the advance receipts. Then he wer to work as a disc jockey for radio statio WTTM. He soon developed such a fo lowing that it was no problem at all t talk the editor of the local newspaper, th *Trentonian,* into permitting him to do column. He began to smoke cigars; h was a big man around town, in his ow way. Unfortunately, up to this point h had not yet developed much perspicacit in human relations. A dancer came t town with a traveling show and he ma ried her before he quite knew what h was doing.

The marriage lasted about five yea and produced two children. When his wi moved out Kovacs was left with the chi dren, which was all right with him, for h adored them. Betty was then three yea old and Kippy, one. His mother move in to take care of them while he wa working, and he began slaving in order t make enough money to give the babi every possible advantage. For a time h had radio shows not only in Trenton, b also in Philadelphia, 40 miles away, ar in addition he worked nights as a mast of ceremonies at dinners and partie Presently he developed a small reputa tion around the Philadelphia area, whic ultimately led to his being offered a jc in New York.

Before that occurred, he met the lad who was to change his life. Her name wa Edith Adams; she came from a sma town in upstate Pennsylvania. She ha studied for an operatic career, but late decided the musical comedy stage wa more to her liking. Kovacs was struck b her the instant he saw her, but his fir marriage had left him with such a bitt taste he was not inclined to try it agai Then came the New York offer. NB wanted him for $1,500 a week, which wa more money than he ever had imagine At around the same time, Miss Adan landed the second lead in *Wonderf Town,* the musical comedy starring Ros lind Russell. Kovacs moved his moth and children to the metropolitan area, n only because of his job, but also becau he wanted to be near his girl.

N EVERTHELESS, it was some time befo the two were married. Kovacs' fir wife made an attempt to get the childre The divorce and settlement were conduc ed in that atmosphere of anger and r crimination that characterizes all break ups, no matter how "civilized" both pa ties declare that they are going to b about the whole thing. Meanwhile, Edi left New York to go on the road with th musical. Kovacs endured the separatio as long as he could, then flew to Texa and took her to Mexico to be married.

That this is a love match is instantl apparent to anyone who ever sees the tw together. When Edith was out of towr during the tryouts of *Li'l Abner,* Kovac followed her to Boston and Washingto and Philadelphia whenever he could spar a day away from (*Continued on page 78)*

New York. When he was in Hollywood making *Operation Madball,* she literally commuted to the west coast from New York on weekends; she would get on an airplane at 11:30 P.M. on Saturday night, arrive in Hollywood Sunday morning, and leave for New York on Monday morning for her 8:40 P.M. curtain.

THE new Mrs. Kovacs is also crazy about his children, and they, as evidence of their feeling for her, began calling her "Mother" virtually the instant she moved into the home. On afternoons, when Edith and the children go out on shopping expeditions in the limousine, they keep in constant touch with Ernie by telephone. The girls went along to Europe when Kovacs and Edith finally had a honeymoon the year before last. "They always had a room of their own, next to ours," Kovacs said recently, "and they were hell on that room service. One day they made thirty-five calls to room service." Kovacs, Edie and the children dine together every night; guests are seldom invited to this meal. Kovacs maintains a strict, old-country formality about dinner. He lounges around the house in hideously-colored sports shirts and old pants all day long, but for dinner he puts on a collar and tie and coat. Yet he is not stuffy about it.

John O'Hara, the novelist, once wrote in his *Collier's* column about a day when he observed the Kovacs family on a train going between Philadelphia and Wilmington, Delaware. He was impressed by the affectionate congeniality and warmth that existed between the four individuals, and said it was a pleasure to watch them. Kovacs was deeply touched by this observation. Indeed, such is Kovacs' nature that all compliments seem to please him inordinately. Shortly after *Topaze,* I remarked to him that I thought it was the best thing I had seen on the idiotic little screen for months. "Did you really?" he said, with an air of wonderment. "Gosh, I'm glad to hear that. It meant so much to me, that part. I worked so *damned* hard on it. And when some of the reviewers didn't like it, I was crushed. It's wonderful for me to hear from somebody who likes something I've given my best to."

Kovacs invariably gives his best—as far as he can (some of his critics say he gives too much of himself; that he never knows when to stop). Even when he was preparing to go on *What's My Line,* he used to think up a few jokes beforehand. He was regarded as the successor to Fred Allen on that show. Actually, this was no special distinction, since the other panelists—Dorothy Kilgallen, Arlene Francis and Bennett Cerf—are not primarily comedians.

But Kovacs brought new life to the format. Once, when Henry J. Kaiser was the mystery guest, the panel determined that an automobile was named after him.

"Are you, by chance, Abraham Lincoln?" Kovacs asked, innocently.

There was a general roar of laughter, during which Kovacs could be heard saying, "Pardon, I didn't catch the answer."

What's My Line is not Kovacs' idea of his best work, since he does not think of himself as a stand-up, one-line funnyman. He believes the characters he has created —Percy Dovetonsils, Charlie Clod, Wolfgang Sauerbraten and others—and the special effects he uses, are more in line with what he believes he can do better than anything else. He takes an unusually objective view of his own abilities and limitations. In *Zoomar,* a critic obviously modeled after John Crosby discusses Ernie Kovacs as follows:

"Too erratic . . . His comedy is too extreme and too frequently he gets its punch line from the grisly side of life . . . man being torn apart by horses . . . trick golf expert missing the golf ball and bashing in his assistant's head." The question now arises: if Kovacs recognizes such qualities in himself, why doesn't he do something to make himself less erratic?

KOVACS can't answer that question. Nor does he appear much concerned by a need to find an answer. Actually, his use of a fictitious critic to hold forth on the subject of Ernie Kovacs in the book is nothing more than another Kovacs joke on Kovacs' critic. It is prompted by a sense of well-being second to that of nobody else in the business. Kovacs turned down the weekly show offers because he wanted to be his own boss, wanted to do his own jobs, wanted more time with his family— and above all, wanted to play cards. Most of all, he wanted to hang around his own house and enjoy what he has worked for during his 38 years. "You know," he said to me one afternoon, "I'm so lucky—I have a terrific sense of security here." He smiled, half-apologetically, and I thought: it couldn't happen to a nicer guy. **END**

THE DAY

Villa was r
rived on Ma
to the tow
and lodged
Hotel but
conspicuou
of March
Camp, an
erator, wh
El Paso b
that somet

Others
Lamar Co
Paso, tele
"Villa lef
March 1,
Mexico.
Grandes
he intend
and hop
Military
zona, re
ward th
miles south of the New Mexico boundary.
The El Paso *Times* published this fact. A
great many persons knew Villa was coming.

...d to
that
...nre-

...finite
e of
...vmen
...l and
llistas
Boca
...s fled,
...inney,
...rode
...oners.
...o met
...rd re-
...nd for
...Vith a
...rup of
...self up
...g him

...party,
...io and
...0 miles
...in the
...er, told
...colonel
placed extra patrols along the border that

liable" information had been received that
Villa intended to give himself up to the

Real

FIRST CLASS MALICE

A quickie course in the art of writing complaint letters from the double edged pen of the late comedian, published now for the first time — by ERNIE KOVACS

The most widely-used form of letter-writing is The Letter of Complaint. To write such a letter is not simply a matter of blatantly stating one's distress, discomfiture or chagrin. That is the mark of the *scribe gauche*. Here is such a letter taken from the files of a leather-products manufacturer:

Brute-Strength Luggage Corporation
Stanford, Virginia
Dear Sirs:

Last Tuesday, I bought one of your brief cases. The handle fell off this morning. What do you intend doing about this matter?

Yours,
(name withheld)

While it is possible that this letter might result in the replacement of the malfunctioning article, it does little to enhance the writer to the Brute-Strength organization. Consider this form, instead:

Brute-Strength Luggage Corporation
Stanford, Virginia
Hello, there!

I have many times admired your attractive factory, while passing through on my way to visiting friends in nearby Charlesville. The well kept lawns, the happy, open countenances of your employees as they drive home in their expensive convertibles have been a constant joy to me.

Something (as I am writing this) has just come to mind which you may find amusing, as you all seem to be a rather jolly group. Last week I was fortunate enough to purchase one of your few remaining simulated double-fold, Magi-lock brief cases (a brown one). As I am employed by the Pentagon (administrative head of Security and advisor to the CIA), I am frequently obligated to carry top secret documents from one end of the country to the other. After purchasing your handsome brief case, I put the plans for a new nuclear submarine into it, handcuffed the case to my wrist and boarded a government jet.

Imagine my chuckling reaction when, as I was about to fasten my safety belt, I noticed all that remained was the handle and the handcuffs! (We had quite a laugh about this back at the Pentagon, as you can imagine!)

As we were not successful in locating the missing section, I wondered if you might not see fit (perhaps at a discount) to more or less furnish me with the large section that fastens on to the handle.

Warmest regards,
(name withheld)
P.S. My mother's maiden name was Brute-Strength and she was a darling.
(N.W.)

A good example of latter 15th Century letters of complaint is shown in the following. This was at the time of the Medici-Borgia fuss and the Borgias were trying to dispose of as many Medicis as time and convenience allowed. Just when the Borgias thought they had completed their project, another Medici would pop up and it was always Lucrezia Borgia's job to retire him. Mostly, her efforts were successful but there were times when everything wasn't quite like clockwork, as this letter (found in a Florentine snuffbox in one of Savonarola's old cassocks) would seem to indicate:

Torregini Galli
23, Via Morte del Sera
Florence, Italy
Mio Caro Torregini

Lasta night, I'm poota onna my finga, you new poisona ring. (By the way, itsa no fitta so good . . . I'ma scratcha my knuck.) Guilio Medici isa comma to sup.

First, we have a littlea antipasta . . . denna, some nice minestrone . . . den, some *crazy* chicken cacciatore! (Mio madre, whatta sauce!) I'ma say to Guilio, "Hey, Guilio, looka hup. How you like our new chandeliera, atsa wassa comea from Venezia."

Guilio isa looka hup. Hesa say, "Lucreetch, you gotta da glass!" (Atsa kinda jokes isanuff to poisona him even if heesa name was Jones.) While hesa looka hup, I'ma poosha da ring and da stuff you wassa poot inaside isa fall in his cacciatore.

After hesa feenish his cacciatore, we eata some rumma cake, drink some chianti, a littlea expresso, somma Fernet. Den, hesa belch. (I'm say to myself, "Hottadog, Lucreetch, hesa deada duck!)

"Hekascooze, please," hesa say, "I'm musta go to the johna. Par'm me, to the johna. Gettit Lucreetch? *Parmagiana!*" (Boy, I'ma tolla you, Torregini, atsa Guilio isa cornaball.)

Well, hesa go to the johna and justa when I'm tolla da busaboy to cleana-hup hisa place because hesa feenish,

FIRST CLASS MALICE from the forthcoming book *Please Excusa da Pencil* by Ernie Kovacs © 1962 by Doubleday & Company, Inc., trustee of the estate of Ernie Kovacs.

hesa come back! Hesa laugha like hesa halfa nuts. Hesa say, "Hey, Lucreetch. Guessa what? I'ma joosta pee *blue!*"

So, Torregini, facet-brut, what kinda junk you poota inna da ring? If I'ma wanna play jokes, I'ma go to the drugastore and buy "funny" pills.

Senda me a fresha batch of poison and donna tink I'm gonna pay unlessa Guilio isa fall onna his ass!
Revederci,
Lucrezia Borgia

This same approach is seen in a letter written by Benjamin Franklin. It was found recently one Sunday on Broad Street in Philadelphia.
June 3, 1752
Tite-Locke Lock Co.
8th and Lexington
New York, New York
Gentlemen:

I am the same man who wrote to you some days ago complaining about the lock I ordered for my filing cabinet in which I keep notes for my new book, tentatively titled, "Poor Albert's Almanac." (I am not happy with the title, but, on the other hand, I am not happy with your lock.)

As I wrote you before (and I will risk boring you with repetition in the event that you have mislaid my previous letter), I found that the key which was sent with the lock failed to turn properly. When I tried forcing the key, it bent. In your last correspondence, you informed me that your representative was staying here at the Bellemont Hotel. As I was in the hotel one afternoon having lunch, I inquired as to his room number and went up to speak with him. A rather petulant and vulgarly-proportioned young lady was with him, and when I tried to show him how badly the key was bent from my patient endeavors, he shouted, "Go fly a kite."

So, yesterday, I tried this. Unfortunately, there was a thunderstorm at the time and I damned near got electrocuted. I fail to see how, even in clear weather, this could have helped.

I have reached the limit of my patience and either you will send me a new key (serial #2342) by return mail or I shall consult with my barrs baristt attorneys.

Sincerely yours,
Benjamin Franklin
221 19th Street
Philadelphia, Pa.

Note that both Miss Borgia and Mr. Franklin resort to the personal approach, thus introducing a sort of camaraderie. A letter of complaint, couched in careful thought with only a delicate hint of remonstrance, will alleviate possible sticky situations. The replies so elicited will always reflect the congeniality of the relationship. Look, for instance, at the reply of Torregini Galli to Miss Borgia's letter:

September 6, 1491
Lucrezia Borgia
Palazzo de Medici
Florence, Italy
Mia Cara Lucrezia:

You unadated letter wassa receive and filea. What you flappa you big bocca atta me for? Itsa you own fault, stupido! Whenna you was come to my shoppa, you gotta da mout full a pizza. You talka so fast, you garlica breath almost knocka me out. Next time, takea da pizza outta you mout' whenna you talk. I'ma no know you wassa say *poison*. I'm tink you say *paisan*. Please takea you biz and you breatha someplace else.
Prenda la gasso!
(¹)
Signor Galli

It may be obvious to the student of letter-writing that the examples of these complaints are examples of what the author calls Letters of Complaint Regarding Specific Articles of Merchandise. On the whole, they are fairly lengthy. This must not, however, give the impression that a well-written complaint need be of duration. Brevity often is effective because of its succinctness.

This short note was found stuck on a desk spindle at the Weymouth Wig Corporation in Coventry, England. It is dated either 1060 A.D. or 1066 A.D. (The last digit has the spindle hole in it and is difficult to make out.)
Weymouth Wig Corp.
Coventry, England
Gentlemen:

When I asked you for a *"hair-fall,"* I did not mean to be taken literally.
Yours,
Lady Godiva

When the author showed this letter to his publisher, the latter snapped his finger (a somewhat difficult performance in his case as he has an arthritic thumb and the finger must snap by itself). He said that he remembered having seen a letter lying on the comb and vaseline shelf in the men's room. Rushing from the room, he returned a bit later (it must be admitted, in no small dishabille), triumphantly waving the letter above his head, much in the manner of Tom Swift. The letter proved, indeed, to be from the same person and read as follows:
Buckingham Riding Academy
Coventry, England
Gentlemen:

My husband would like to know who was responsible for sending me those two smart-alecks in the horse costume when I asked for a proper mount this morning.
Yours,
Lady Godiva

Returning to the longer type of letter, here is one dated July 4, 1807.
Pre-Fab Bomb Company
Louisville, Ky.
Gentlemen:

Several days ago, I remitted my check for one of your Super Pre-Fab Bomb kits. This was sent me disassembled with as complex a set of instructions for re-assembly as I've ever seen.

First off, please let me point out that whoever it is with your organization that writes these instructions is a nut. It is completely impossible to "assemble this device with any small coin used as a screwdriver." Some of the crossbeams in the kit weigh over three hundred pounds.

However, this is not my major complaint. I worked on your Super-Bomb kit for three days in order to be ready for the Fourth of July. Following the somewhat bewildering instructions, I constructed the Super-Bomb, as the instructions suggested, on the river (I live *(continued on page 64)*

(¹)—Some of Galli's clients unfortunately lacked a sense of fun and took his remarks at their face value. Galli's business gradually fell off and he spent his remaining years eking out a living by tainting fish for peasants conducting cheap poison vendettas.

FIRST CLASS MALICE

(*continued from page* 56)

near the Hudson and am not complaining about the distance). I promised my friends that I would set it off at noon and quite a few of them gathered to watch along the river bank.

Gentlemen, I cannot possibly put on paper the embarrassment I suffered when, after igniting the fire, instead of *exploding,* two large wheels on the sides began to turn and the entire Super-Bomb paddled down the water like some damned boat, whistling 'til it was out of sight.

I have disassembled it and it is in the mail to you. When it arrives, will you be good enough to refund my money.

Yours,
Robert Fulton

There are too many instances of a letter of complaint being simply an out-and-out nonconstructive gripe. Last month, a Mau Mau, picked up by the South Nairobi police for blowing berry seeds through a sheet of paper rolled into a tube at whoever was in power at the time, was given six months in jail. In going through his personal effects (one loin cloth, heavily laundry-marked, and a jar of blue ointment), the magistrate unrolled the paper tube and saw that it was a letter from General Hannibal, dated 218 B.C. Inasmuch as the Mau Mau still has five months to serve and will not be able to blow berry seeds until then, the magistrate was kind enough to lend me the letter for this article.

Somewhere in the Alps
September 23, 218 BC
You-Guide-It-Elephant Rental
Chief Nagutu II
Grass Hut A
No. 6 Tsetse Street
Nairobi, S. Africa
Dear Chief Nagutu, The II:

As you can see from my address, I am somewhere in the middle of the Alps and I am pretty mad.

When I rented this herd of elephants from you at the "fleet price" you guaranteed me that I wasn't getting any used elephants. Let me tell you, chief, all you have to do is kick a few of the legs and you can tell that some of these boys have put in a lot of kilometers. I got one soldier who does nothing all day but shove back the loose tusks and we're gettin' about six kilometers to a bushel of peanuts. Half of the big slobs are so old they have no getaway power at the crevasses. I'll be lucky to get forty-year old camels on the trade-in. And as for those "roomy trunks," about the only thing you can carry in them are French horns. The trunks are always curled up.

I know the price was for "stripped" jobs, but I think you went a little too far. What the hell you gonna do with all them ears, anyway? Speaking of ears, my private elephant . . . the souped-up Pachyderm 8 with the lance-proof legs (these legs, by the way, were supposed to be white and there was supposed to be a gauntlet-compartment for maps and facial tissues) . . . anyway, those ears of his are lousy as no-draft vents. He keeps 'em folded up alongside his head and I get no more wind protection than the other guys get on the stripped jobs. And as for those ears keeping flies off me, that's a helluva extra! You ever see any flies in the Alps in January?

And about this thing you taught them of walking single file with the elephant in back curling his trunk around the tail of the elephant in front. . . . You ever been around when one of the elephants in the rear trips and nobody lets go? It takes you two days to pick up all them ass holes.

In disgust,
General Hannibal
Carthage
P.S. How the hell do I get 'em to stop trumpeting? It's not so bad out here, but when we get to Rome and they start blowing off in front of a church or library. . . . Also, who's the wise guy who taught my elephant to blow the first four notes of *The Call to The Gladiators*? I'll leave these wrecks at the River Ticino. Have somebody pick 'em up.

Not all letters of complaint deal with a product. There are complaints registered which deal with less tangible things, such as character, action or misrepresentation. The following is an example of too much diffidence on the part of the complaining party. This is the type who shies so from complaining that he sometimes fails to get his point across at all. This letter was written by a timorous dean of women at a fashionable girls' school in Alaska to the parents of one of the students, who had all the signs of being a somewhat zealous lesbian. At school only one week, she had reduced the major portion of the student body to quivering wrecks and was making progress on the faculty.
Mr. and Mrs. (name withheld)
(street address withheld)
Boston, Mass.
Dear Mr. and Mrs.—:

Fall again in Massachusetts! How I envy you! The russet leaf upon the darkened bough . . . the leaping pickerel . . . bobbing for apples. What joy! Although Alaska, too, is quite nice and not at all like you people from the states picture it. (Gracious! I'd almost forgotten. Alaska is *in* the states now, isn't it? I must have been thinking of Hawaii.)

Well, the excitement of entering the first semester is upon us and, goodness knows, time will fly and the girls will be looking forward to going home for Thanksgiving. (Although, they will miss each other dreadfully . . . sometimes, when they're only parting to retire for the night, some of them kiss each other quite desperately for hours. They're most affectionate. Your little Lesbo (what a darling name! How did you ever think of it?) seems to love everybody. Really, *everybody*. Sometimes even *I* have to virtually wrench her arms from about my neck. (I *do* have to get *some* sleep. Ha-Ha.)

But now for a surprise! This year, we decided to do something quite unique. We held a popularity contest at the *beginning* of the school term. The faculty voted to see who was the most popular student and guess who won! ! ! (I'll bet you already have!) Lesbo! The prize is most exciting. The whole year to spend at home with her parents!

I must stop writing now as the plane is leaving in an hour and we are all going to the airport to see Lesbo off.

Hurriedly,
(name withheld)

Complaining to parents about their offspring is always a touch and go proposition. While some adopt the diffident approach of the previous letter, others strike out a bit more boldly.

A letter dated 220 B.C. and authenticated by the curator of a museum in Hyannesport, North Dakota, and addressed to Zeus, the god of thunder and lightning, goes:

Tuesday-March 8, 220 B.C.
1321 Augeias Drive

The Honorable God Zeus
Gracie Mansion
Mount Olympus, The Firmament
Dear G.Z.:

You don't know me. I'm just one of the little guys down here on earth. I'm a monk at a local monastery. My job probably sounds a little dull to you, what with Apollo and Eros and that bunch you have up there. I do a nine-to-five brown cassock bit, punchin' the old sun dial five days a week. Saturdays and Sundays I like to spend at home. We got a little place just outside Athens.

I don't know if you know it or not, but I did you a favor some years back. Down at the monastery, the big profit item is brandy. The boys knock out a few barrels a week and we use the profits for buying new bell ropes. I been putting out the monastery newspaper, *The House Organ,* as the boys call it. It's not a bad little sheet. No advertising, you understand, strictly nonprofit . . . few local items and some war stuff.

Well, anyways, I do a little gossip column, too. You know, the usual stuff. (Like, "What King of Hades has been looking for a recently deceased mortal who's been fooling around with one of the Furies sisters?") Well, Z., when your son Hercules was born a lot of the boys down here at the monastery knew damned well it wasn't your wife Hera's kid. It so happens that one of the boys was delivering a fifth of B & B to a local chariot-stop and he saw you registering with the little Theban princess, Alcmene. He checked the register and saw that you had signed in as Mr. and Mrs. Sam Poseidon. What I'm gettin' at is this, Z., I never printed one damned word in my column about it!

Well, I been kind of following these "labors" that your son Herky has been signed up for by King Eurystheus. All the boys know that your old lady egged Eurystheus into tagging the kid with these lousy jobs and I wanna tell you, Z., I seen some nutsy-Fagin deals, but this takes the apple turnover. I think your kid's got a screw loose some place for getting mixed up in it in the first place. Worse than that, *he ain't makin' any friends, either!* When he did that first labor (You remember, he was supposed to knock off the Nemean lion?), well, we were all for it. Ask the neighbors, nothing smells worse than a wet lion after rain.

Then he dumps that broad with the eight snake heads, Hydra. We were all for that, too, as that damned eight-way hissing all the time wasn't gonna win her no popularity contest by a long shot. But he louses up again by dipping his arrows in the blood which is as poisonous as leaving mayonnaise out of the icebox in July and everybody gets off the cross-town chariot whenever he gets on. (He killed two conductors last week, just by handing them chariot tokens.)

Next, he goes after the Ceryneian hind (that white moose, or whatever-thehell it is, with them brass hooves and golden horns). Well, he chased that miserable thing around for the better part of a year . . . runnin' across everybody's front yard, heavin' rocks and arrows at it day and night, the damned thing blowin' those damned golden horns, WOO-GAH!! WOO-GAH!! until everybody was half nuts. Finally he catches it and we're all hopin' his next booking takes him on the road, maybe.

Nosiree! Monday morning, bright and early, he's racing up and down after that friggin' Erymanthian boar! Finally, he hauls that the hell out of here and we figure, what with the fact that there ain't no more kooky animals left that, at long last, the old neighborhood is going to go back to quiet evenings of barbeques and quoits. Then who shows up on Tuesday, carrying a shovel the size of an elephant's rear end, but your kid.

"What're you gonna kill for the special this week, Nutty?" I ask him. He tells me, "Nothin' ", and explains that he's gonna clean out King Augeias' stables next door. Well, the wife is as happy as Bacchus with a bag full of grapes. You can't blame her for gettin' a little excited. King Augeias has about five thousand head of cattle next door in those stables and nobody, I mean *nobody,* so much as goes through the place with a whisk broom. The flies are *murder!*

So, even I get a little misty-eyed and wish the kid rots of ruck. But can he go in there like a normal human being and shovel the stuff into a wheel barrow? Not *this* goof-ball. *He* has to chop a hole in the wall and let the river flow through and wash it out. But where's it end up? And who lives next door? Right! *Me!*

So, tell me, *who's gonna get this stuff offa my lawn?!*

Yours,
Brother Lapidus

The Zeus letter of complaint is also illustrative of the Letter of Frustrated Complaint . . . the protest against the irrevocable *fait accompli.* The Greeks, being a fairly even people, are wont to rhetoric, but other nationalities are somewhat prone to stronger censure. In the author's interest in the varying degrees of vehemence, he wrote to a cousin who has established residence in Corsica for the purposes of securing a Corsican divorce. In his letter, he asked, if any letters written by Corsicans might be found lying about would his cousin be so kind as to send him one. In the return mail, he received one written by a General Napoleon Bonaparte to an innkeeper in Toulon. The letter is dated 1793, September 3.

L'Hotel Sanitaire
16, Rue Pediculous
Toulon, France
Monsieur:

Last week, while conducting my siege of your city, I spent the night at your hotel. At that time, you will remember, I questioned the price of the lodgings (50 francs incl. continental brkfst) and you told me the reason you charge a bit extra was because of the additional costs in maintaining strict dietary and sanitation rules.

When I pointed out that the "men's room" was in a somewhat dingy state for that price, you assured me it was simply the poor illumination of the cheap candle I was carrying.

I would like to point out that for the last three days I have been driven almost insane because of a fierce itching in the groin area. I strongly suspect I have picked up a case of "crabs." I scratch secretly all day long and have almost been caught at it by photographers. Only by sliding my hand quickly up to my chest did I avoid embarrassing pictures.

I shall return!
Napoleon Bonaparte

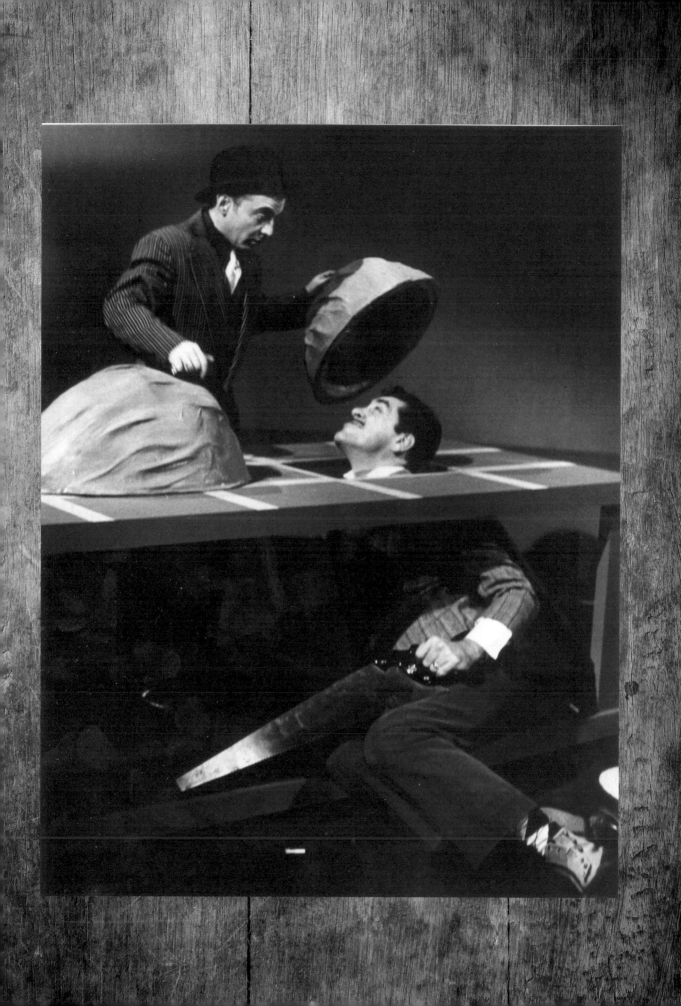

Ith watching the string that holds me tiedxin Cyril's greasy fingers
He's eating a sausage pizza and his grip no longer lingers.
The string is itxx slipping siwftly now, I'd be grateful, quite a lot
If he'd stop eating the pizza long enough to tie a little knot.

Oops, it's out, I'm rising now, it's awfully hard to stop
Well, there is something I never knew, Cyril's bald on top.
Up into the skies I go, makingxxxaparxixakxx I'm making vapor tracks.
Oh, look down there. I see the Giants. They;re carrying valet-packs.

I'm filled with helium you know- and while I hate to be crass,
I wished they'd used just plain old air- I suffer so from gas.
I'm floating up by RCA- I believe I've floated far "nough.
Someone's shooting pins at me- I think it's Robert Sarnoff.

Oh there's another room I see- it's filled with pretty maids.
Well! Goodness me, aren't we prim! (Those hussies, they've pulled down the
                                                              shades)
Here comes a flying jet- you'd better order flowees--
The pilot has an accent- it isn't one of ours.

                    An Orange
Thoughts of /ixRed Balloon Released From a Four Year Old Child"s Hand,
                    Named Cyril, As It Goes Up.

118

Number
56

COWBOY SONGS

25c

C.D.C.

FAVORITE FOLKTUNES

PERCY DOVETONSILS
ODE TO A DUDE RANCH

FRIDAY LAST, I SAID GOODBYE, TO DEAR OLD UNCLE HARRIET,
PACKED SOME SOCKS AND UNDERWEAR AND OF COURSE, I PACKED MY LARIAT.
I BOARDED A TRAIN, MY INTENTIONS WERE PLAIN, I WAS HEADING BOY FOR THE
WEST.
I CARRIED A WESTERN NOVEL TO READ, T'WAS WRITTEN BY EDGAR GUEST.

BEFORE I HEADED FOR THE RANCH, I WENT INTO A STORE
BOUGHT A MAUVE SOMBRERO AND CATTLE, THREE OR FOUR.
WHEN I FINALLY MEANDERED OUT ON THE RANGE (IT WAS JUST BEYOND
EL PASO)
I LOOKED LOVELY WITH MY CAPEZZIO BOOTS AND MY NEW CHATRUESE SILK LASSO

THE GUEST RODE ON THE BRIDAL PATH, BUT I DIDN'T CARE TO MINGLE.
I EXPLAINED THE BRIDAL PATH WAS NOT RIGHT FOR ME, AS I WAS UNMARRIED
AND SINGLE.
EACH GUEST RECIEVED A NICKNAME LIKE SPIKE, SOME WERE "SHORTY" OR "HAM".
I'M RATHER PROUD OF THE ONE THEY GAVE ME...I WAS KNOWN AS '"SEERSUCKER
SAM"

MY SEERSUCKER SLACKS FLAPPED IN THE BREEZE, MY HORSE DID FAIRLY FLY.
I WAS AFRAID TO FALL ON THE CACTUSES...OR PARDON, IS THE PLURAL CACTI
THE HORSE THEY BROUGHT FOR ME TO RIDE WAS A TERRIBLE MONSTER NAMED "MILLER,"
I CHANGED HIM FOR ANOTHER ONE THAT THE BOYS CALLED DOROTHY MILEER.

DOROTHY WAS A PINTO...SHE'D JUST TROT A LITTLE
SHE DIDN' LOPE, SHE DIDN'T DASH, SHE'D GONE TO POT IN THE MIDDLE.
THE SADDLE I RODE I BROUGHT FROM NEW YORK...T'WAS CONSIDERED MORE THAN
PETITE.
I HAD THE HORN ADORNED WITH LACE...SPONGE RUBBER WAS SEWED IN THE SEAT.

BUT IT DIDN'T HELP THERE MUCH AT ALL, I BOUNCED UP AND DOWN
IN THE SADDLE.
I WENT UP AND DOWN SO DARN MANY TIMES, MY SPIT CURLS WERE STARTING
TO RATTLE.
WHEN CHRISTMAS ROLLS AROUND NEXT YEAR, I ONLY HOPE THAT SANT'LL.
AVOID THE FIREPLACE AND COME THROUGH THE DOOR, CAUSE I8LL BE EATING OFF
OF THE MANTLE.

"Television is a medium."

"So called because it is neither rare nor well done."

ON THE RECORD WITH

Percy Dovetonsils

Ernie recorded an album for Warner Bros. in 1960 entitled *Percy Dovetonsils....Thpeakth* that was never released, due to creative interference from the label and Ernie's staunch resistance to that interference. Rights for the project went to Vanguard, and then to Cedars-Sinai, and eventually years later back to Edie. Tracks from this were included on *The Ernie Kovacs Record Album* released by Columbia in 1975 including one that ends with Percy saying, "Ready for side two...?" This prompted Kovacs archivist Ben Model's search for the elements for the album, and a eureka moment when going through the holdings of Ediad Productions.

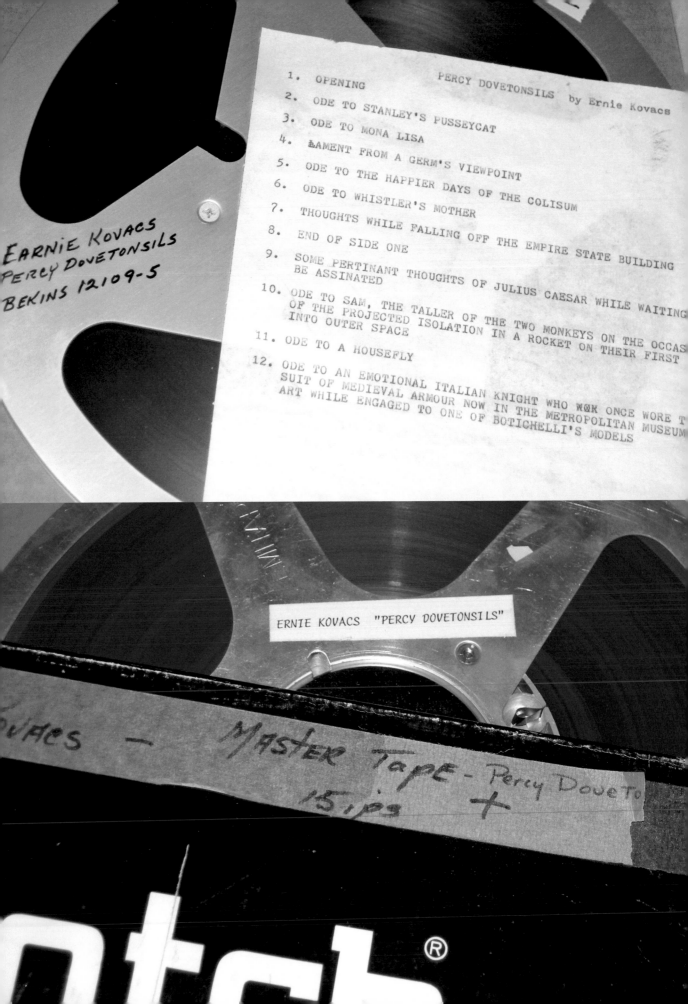

PERCY DOVETONSILS   by Ernie Kovacs

1. OPENING
2. ODE TO STANLEY'S PUSSEYCAT
3. ODE TO MONA LISA
4. LAMENT FROM A GERM'S VIEWPOINT
5. ODE TO THE HAPPIER DAYS OF THE COLISUM
6. ODE TO WHISTLER'S MOTHER
7. THOUGHTS WHILE FALLING OFF THE EMPIRE STATE BUILDING
8. END OF SIDE ONE
9. SOME PERTINANT THOUGHTS OF JULIUS CAESAR WHILE WAITING
   BE ASSINATED
10. ODE TO SAM, THE TALLER OF THE TWO MONKEYS ON THE OCCAS
    OF THE PROJECTED ISOLATION IN A ROCKET ON THEIR FIRST
    INTO OUTER SPACE
11. ODE TO A HOUSEFLY
12. ODE TO AN EMOTIONAL ITALIAN KNIGHT WHO WQK ONCE WORE T
    SUIT OF MEDIEVAL ARMOUR NOW IN THE METROPOLITAN MUSEUM
    ART WHILE ENGAGED TO ONE OF BOTICHELLI'S MODELS

Earnie Kovacs
Percy Dovetonsils
Bekins 12109-5

ERNIE KOVACS "PERCY DOVETONSILS"

...ovacs — Master Tape - Percy DoveTo
15 ips +

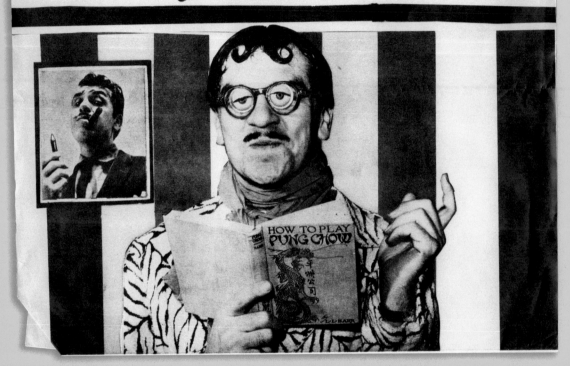

The unreleased Percy Dovetonsils record is mentioned by Ernie in an interview he did for the CBC in 1961 on their show *The Lively Arts*, which is on the *Ernie Kovacs Collection* DVD box set. The surviving tape is unedited and unmixed and seems to have been done in a few uninterrupted takes, as Kovacs is heard going in and out of character in a couple of spots. At the very end of the recording, Ernie yells to the engineer, "Now, with 88 bars of music between each line, it'll come out even!"

The album was released in 2012 by Omnivore Recordings, and in going through boxes of stuff Edie Adams saved, Edie's son Josh found this artwork that had been designed for the record way back when. Omnivore used this for the cover art for the CD and for the vinyl LP.

THIS IS PERCY DOVETONSILS WITH A PERSONAL MESSAGE FOR THOSE
OF YOU LISTENING TO MY NEW ALBUM - HI ! - OR SHOULD I SAY
HI FI !

I'M SITTING HERE BESIDE MY ITALIAN HARPSICHORD WITH IT'S
GENUINE QUILL PLUCKS. BEHIND ME IS A MARBLE BUST - WELL,
PERHAPS NOT A BUST BUT THEN, IT WASN'T A COMPLETE SUCCESS,
EITHER.

SO - NOW - GREETINGS ACROSS YOUR TURNTABLES AND WITH A
LITTLE SIP OF MY MARTINI ( ) - (A FRACTION TOO MUCH
VERMOUTH) - SHALL WE BEGIN --- ?

intro: SIDE II - PERCY DOVETONSILS ALBUM:

WELL, HERE WE ARE, ALL FINISHED WITH SIDE I - THAT WASN'T
SO BAD, NOW, WAS IT ?

READY FOR A GO AT SIDE II ? ONE LITTLE SIP AND (   ) -
BRUCE, THERE'S STILL TOO MUCH VERMOUTH - YOU MUST
PRACTISE MODICUM, ~~THAT~~ ~~DEAR BOY~~, ~~AS AS~~ PERCY ALWAYS SAYS,
EVERYTHING IN MODICUM -- (HONESTLY, SOMETIMES THAT BOY ---)

ODE TO A BOOKWORM

Oh hail to thee thou streamlined fellow
You go through books like a dog through jello.
You bore your way from book to book
Eating things raw because you can't cook.

I saw you first, so trim and so spruce
As you gummed a few pages of my Mother Goose.
You were so happy - in your eye was a twinkle
As you chewed through the index of old Rip
                          Van Winkle.

 The next time I saw you, I was slightly miffed
For that day you ate the climax of Young Tom Swift
And you made little bites, so round and so tidy
All over the back of my copy of Heidi.
As
As I grew older, I still heard you munch
And you were big enough to eat Ivanhoe for lunch
I knew you liked travelling, I first got the notion
When you chewed through my Atlas and fell in the ocean.

And then you reached manhood , I recall with some pain
When you first bit your way, into Mickey Spillane.
When you reached Chapter two, I saw you were gushing
Then on Chapter thirteen, I noticed you were blushing.

Oh, we have had many years of joy,
When yo u first nibbled the books I bought as a boy.
A banquet for your anniversary, bookworm, my friend,
I give you a gift that should last to the end.

You will get this gift and nibble for long..
And the night will be filled with your nibbling song.
Your bookworm friends will envy you once
I enroll hou in the book of the month.

by Percy Dovetonsils

TAKE CARD:
    "BLACK DAY AT WHITE ROCK"

AUDIO: MUSIC:
Heavy, dramatic
with interjections
of "Old West"

Hold 8 bars..
fade b.g. for
voice off

CROSS DISSOLVE TO TIGHT SHOT
OF 3 OR 4 SMALL TOY HOUSES GROUPED
TOGETHER ON SAND (WE ARE SHOOTING
FROM ABOVE)

VOICE OFF: THIS IS "WAYOUT". NOBODY

                        KNOWS HOW THIS TOWN GOT ITS

                        NAME.

CAMERA ZOOMS UP ... WE SEE VAST
STRETCH OF SAND IN ALL DIRECTIONS
AROUND TOY HOUSES... MODEL R.R.
TRACK RUNS STRAIGHT THROUGH PICTURE,
ENTERING FRAME AT BOTTOM, LEAVING
AT TOP INTO ENDLESSNESS. OCCASIONAL
MINIATURE TELEPHONE POLES SPREAD
THROUGH "TOWN"...

VOICE OFF: TOWNS HAVE A FUNNY WAY OF GETTING

                        NAMES. NOBODY KNOWS HOW THEY GET

                        THEM, OR WHY, BUT THE NAME ALWAYS

                        STICKS AFTERWARDS. EXCEPT IN THE

                        CASE OF "WAYOUT" WHICH WAS CHANGED

                        TO "WHITE ROCK".   THERE DIDN'T SEEM

                        TO BE ANY REASON FOR THAT NAME EITHER.

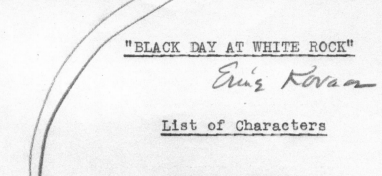

"BLACK DAY AT WHITE ROCK"

Ernie Kovacs

List of Characters

Stranger... Sid Caesar

Bessie Lou... Nanette Fabray

"Crunch" ... Howie Morris

"Sneer" ... Carl Reiner

and others

SNEER

Take title card:
"Black Day at White Rock"

OPEN ON SHOT FROM ABOVE. *TIGHT ON* 3 or 4 SMALL TOY HOUSES GROUPED TOGETHER ON SAND... OCCASIONAL MINIATURE TELEPHONE POLES STRETCHING PARALLEL TO HOUSES	(AUDIO)	*MUSIC:* Opening music.. Heavy, dramatic with interjections of "old West" Hold 8 bars.. fade b.g. for Announcer *VOICE OFF*

VOICE OFF:
ANNOUNCER: (on camera)

          THIS IS "WAYOUT". NOBODY KNOWS

          HOW THIS TOWN GOT ITS NAME.

CAMERA ZOOMS UP .. SHOWING
VAST STRETCH OF SAND IN
ALL DIRECTIONS AROUND
MINIATURE...

AFTER SHOT IS ESTABLISHED..HOLD
AS ANNOUNCER CONTINUES

ADD: (A strip of R.R. tracks
runs in a straight line
completely across set. this
strip is parallel to the
town .. tracks enter frame
and leave frame into endlessness

VOICE OFF:
ANNOUNCER:

TOWNS HAVE A FUNNY WAY OF GETTING

NAMES. NOBODY KNOWS HOW THEY GET

THEM, OR WHY, BUT THE NAME ALWAYS

STICKS AFTERWARDS.. EXCEPT IN THE CASE OF

"WAYOUT" WHICH WAS CHANGED TO

"WHITE ROCK". THERE DIDN'T SEEM TO

BE ANY REASON FOR THAT NAME, EITHER.

THIS WAS GOING TO BE AN UNUSUAL DAY

AT "WHITE ROCK" AND WOULD HAVE SOMETHING

TO DO WITH THE 12:03 WHICH WAS DUE TO

PASS AT ITS USUAL TIME, 1:17.

THE CITIZENS OF "WHITE ROCK" DIDN'T
          AT 11:59,
KNOW THAT THE 12:05 WOULD AFFECTxTHEM

ATxI CHANGE THEIR LIVES AT 1:17...

THAT A STRANGER,WHO ALWAYS KEPT ONE HAND

IN HIS POCKET, WOULD GET OFF THE TRAIN

THIS DAY....

                              AUDIO: BRING MUSICUU

132

(1) "Black Day at White Rock

Cross-Dissolve to

(2) ~~Fade in~~ ^Tight shot
of 3 or 4 small Toy
houses grouped together
on sand — (we are shooting
from above)
~~Cross. (infode~~

(3) Camera zooms up... we
see vast stretch of sand
in all directions around
toy houses... model R.R.
track runs straight
through picture, entering
frame at bottom, leaving at
top into endlessness. Occasional
miniature Telephone poles
spaced through "town"...

(4) Pan down and Tighter
shot to read seal.
"approved by Roy Hines

DREAMS OF AN OPUS EATER

Ernie Kovacs

~~En route to New York from Las Vegas this past May, I entered the world~~

It was about 3:27 a.m., either Daylight Central, Daylight Saving or

the other one peculiar to trains, just passing a Yucca tree, which if

it was/~~light~~ like most of the other Yucca trees, was about five feet tall,

that I entered the ~~world of~~ permanent nebulous world of all night radio,

disassembling cafe express makers, chornological sheep and snore balls.

in our drawing room coming East,   inner smaller size of
At 3:18,/my wife ~~telxxxx~~ left The Annex, that/~~small~~ room the/~~xllxxxxf~~ the

5% wedge in ~~in~~ those graphic financial pies that General Motors uses to

illustrates ~~when~~ where 1/20 of General Motors ~~pri~~ profit goes, and told

me that the john was jammed/ and wouldn't stop the Niagara Falls bit.

I put down my three constant travelling companions, ~~Conversation~~

Cortina's "Conversational Japanese", (Pan (w)o ippon kudasai, which is

the Japanese answer to Ma tante est un crayon and translated means, Please

pass me two loaves of bread, a sentence obviously fabricated before the

~~x~~ international set became calorie-conscious), a pinch bottle of Haig
                    au astigmatic
and Haig and/~~a~~ small boy who always follows me from the dining room and

with the superiority of my gender(our last stand against Dagwoodism),

went in to stop what plumbers technically call The Flow. (A term con_coted

by a gentile named Sweet Afton, I believe. Who ~~xix~~ could never have

been a pumber so ~~F~~ first-named) ~~x~~

After hitting it ~~with~~ sparately with my three travelling companions, one

of which let out a rather peasant like yell in Japanese (it oould have been

any one of the three), I said the hell with it and went back to bed/ and

to/ sleep.

At 3:26:30, the porter woke me (I remembered having rung for him at

3:24:45) and looked at the john. He told me it could fixed when we got

to Utah which, I assume, is where the experts live.

At 3:27, (see opening line), I found I wasn't sleepy. It ~~is now three week~~

...en instant coffee must have looked good on paper...about as tall as a migrant Wambesi...teeth made Ernie Bognine look like a pepsodebt ad....

It is now 4:45 a.m., five weeks later, and I am still not sleepy. Since then, I have won 8,004 dollars at poker, lost 425 dollars at Gin, spent$1.20 for two sleeping pills which didn't work, and am still wide awake.

Perhaps it was finalized that first morning at 7 a.m. when the porter told me that our running john had exhausted the water in every bedroom, drawing room and compartment in our car. My pepsonal responsibility over this became clear when the unshaven and unwashed of that car passed me on the way out. The One room (Bedroom C, as I recall) was miraculously three inches deep in water, kxxxxxxxxxxx the porter was badly tipped by all, kxxxxxxxxxxx Cortina's Conversation Japanese was soaked in the idioms and the little boy caught xxxxxxx cold trying to find a drink for his Easter Bunny who wouldn"t/accept the Haig and Haig, being aware no doubt, of his being purchased on a relgous holiday. When the/little red-eyed girl came out of Bedroom C with her bag of potato chips all soggy, x I'd have given ten dollars for a TWA ticket or a knockdown to Cluny Brown.

OPENING *ALL CAPS*

The picture opens without titles. A 35mm shot of an
orchestraxsymphony orchestra taken, presumably, from the first
balcony. The orchestra is playing Tychaivsky's 1812 Overture. A
medium boom in until we have a slight diagonal line of the conductor
in the right side of the frame and Egun Eugene prominent in the upper
diagonal of the left. Eguen

Eugene's clothing iuxx is formal and similar to the
others but there is an undifinable in the lack of proper fit. He is
standing in the manner of the cymbalist, cymbals poxiud poised, reading
the score and ixg looking up at the conductor. His cue comes, he spreads
the cymbals, crashes them together and the entire floor beneath him,
an area of four feet diamter, gives way in a rending, splintering
crackup and he disappears from view...

As the orchestra continues playing, we boom up and
from the kuix black hole, serpentine and increasing in size, we read
the star's name and the title of the picture as it comes to rest
horizontally.

The ruxt other credits are done in what will be one
of the most interesting of credits ever shown: Ferxexample

> E.G. A single of the trombonist, live, becaomes
> an animated, but exact likeness, of him and his
> trombone loses shape and forms a name...then
> resumes shape and we return to actual performer.
> The bow on the cello, the flute, the strings of
> th the harp, etc....Until t e fonal mass of credits
> are needed, at which time, the keys of the piano

137

climb into a vertical column, names appear on them, they fall back on

30 keyboard in accompnaying piano gliss, the keyboard becomes practial

we go to a shot of the two large tymapny. On the one which is being

played, the name of the producer comes up, we pan to the left, the name

of the director. As the name of the director is read, the tympanist

hits this surface which is not a drum head but a smooth, soupy subatance.

As the sticks disappear into the substance, with tympanists hxndxx arms

anf the startled look, the name of the director becomes equally soupy

and pours into the/mass of the tymapny.
                    liquid

                    DISSOLVE into opening scene of picture. Upper New York State
                         Electric piano background of Euegen's Rhapsody (blues)...
possibly Route 9 W...Eugnne is just walking across a field and kneels down to

dross under barbed wire fence. He is carrying an old suitcase and his

cymbals. One attached to his hand. the ohher under the arm carrying the
                                     Suit case is pushed out on to highway, he to follow.
suitaase. He is face down./The back of his coat gets caught on the

barbed wire. Short attempt to free himself...As his hand struggles, he

sees it is twelve noon...Opens suitcase from prone position, takes out

lunch box. Pullsxiunchbxxxtxxhimsdxx Closes suitcase, pulls lunchbox to self.

One beat after lunchbox is withdrawn, huge trailer truck goes over suit

case immediately in front of him. One wide shot to show truck leavingx

continuing on way...Qpenxxsuiteaseyxand Suticase is flat to highway...He

opens...We see that syitcase has not been flattened but has been sunk,

undamaged, straight into concrete. He takes out small portable radio turns

it on. Voice:"Goodmorning andxweignmex and time for the 11 a.m. news roundup."

Hexlookxxatxwatxh He was just about to parixarx bite into snadiwhc. Stops

midbite. Looks at watch. Realzses he is hour fast. Puts lunch away into

suitcase, frees himself from barbed wire, takes suitcase out of concrete

which leaves shape of suitcase in highway and begins walking along highway.

Walking along the highway, Euegene attempts to hitchike
but is compeltely unsuccesful until he rezlies that his extended thumb
has been hid behind the cymbal attached to the same hand...In this
scene; the cymbal will mirrør the sun into a driver's eyes causing him
to run into a tree...Euegen will lift pant leg to lure motorist who
laughs.-We closeup to see large ankle tatboed on leg...small delivery truck
hits extended cymbal, spins Eugene around who hits back of truck with cymbal...
fly buzzing...he kills fly by bringing cymbals together...stampedes
a small herd of cattle...Qther incdients here until he is picked up by
small foreign car that opens from front. He is slightly puzzled by lack
of door, finally sees owner open from front, sits down facing sideways.
During ride into town, puts hand with symbol on it out and car spins around.

Seeing nothing here, walks down the block a bit to next agency...Scans
list:

SPEED*O AGENCY
JOB OPENINGS
FARMER
FARMER

PEARL DIVER

HINDU

POLO PLAYER
OPERA STAR(Tenor)
BRAIN SURGEON

JEWEL THIEF

HOCKEY GOALEE

RACING DRIVER

cymbalist ←(Penny--small letters here for cymbalt)
Eugene is happy that a cymbalist is needed...In groping for door with
hand still on cymbal, door is opened from inside and coming out of
door in positive costuming, each holding a slip of paper with an
a job address on it, the following group, all happy at having found job:
The farmer, pearl diver, Hindu, polo player, opera star (singing scales),

I (F)

THOUGHTS WHILE FALLING OFF THE EMPIRE STATE BUILDING

by PERCY DOVETONSILS:

WELL, LOOK AT ME, I'M RIGHT AT THE TOP - I'M CERTAINLY GETTING MY KICKS

MY THIS BUILDING IS AWFULLY TALL, ~~THEY MUST HAVE USED~~ *THERE MUST BE* DOZENS OF BRICKS.

THESE GUIDED TOURS ARE AWFULLY DULL, I'LL ~~ALSO~~ SLIP AWAY FROM THE REST,

THERE NOW, I'M ALL ALONE, THIS SOLO STUFF IS THE BEST.

I'LL JUST CLIMB UP UPON THIS LEDGE - GEE WHIZ, MY TROUSERS ARE RIPPED.

PERHAPS I SHOULD GET OFF BEFORE...OH DARN NOW I'VE DONE IT - I'VE SLIPPED.

OFF I GO INTO OUTER SPACE, ONE HUNDRED THREE FLOORS TO FALL TO

LET ME SEE AM I CORRECT, OR IS IT ONE HUNDRED TWO TO FALL TO.

NEVER MIND, IT'S OF SMALL CONCERN, I'M FALLING ANY WAY

I HOPE I CLEAR THE EIGHTY-SIXTH IT SEEMS TO BE IN THE WAY.

THERE, I'VE MISSED THE EIGHTY-SIXTH, NOT ALL DO THAT WHO FALL.

I THINK FOR MY FIRST GO AT THIS, I'VE NOT DONE BADLY AT ALL.

I'M GLAD THE HUNTING SEASON'S OUT, I LOOK A BIT LIKE A DUCK.

SAY, THAT TYPIST ON SEVENTY IS WINKING AT ME, NOW THAT'S A BIT OF LUCK.

THERE'S THAT CHINESE TEA IMPORTER, HOLLERING "CLAZY 'MELICAN!"

THIS MUST BE THE SIXTY-THIRD - I WISH I WERE A PELICAN.

THAT WINDOW WASHER ON FIFTY-FOUR IS CERTAINLY AWFULLY BOLD.

OH DEAR, IT'S RAINING ~~HARD~~ *NOW* OUT HERE, I'LL CATCH MY DEATH OF COLD.

I WOULDN'T CARE TO DO THIS THING TOO OFTEN OVER TOWN,

I'M SO UNCOMFY WAY OUT HERE, THERE ISN'T A PLACE TO SIT DOWN

OH, THERE GOES THIRTY-SEVEN, I HAVE MY OFFICE THERE,

I SHOULD HAVE TURNED THE DESK LAMP OUT, MY LIGHT BILL IS A BEAR.

IT'S RATHER COOL OUT HERE TODAY, WHY GOODNESS SAKES ALIVE

THERE'S ~~GEORGE DIXON~~ *ALBERT JONES*, AWFULLY NICE CHAP, WHAT'S HE DOING ON FIVE.

NOW I'M AT THREE I'LL LOOSEN MY LACES THOSE FOLKS SEEM SURPRISED

JUST LOOK AT THEIR FACES

NOW I'M AT TWO, MY SEE HOW THEY SCATTER

GUESS THE RUMOUR'S AROUND THAT I'M LIKELY TO SPLATTER

9 B

Royalty Writes

by Ernie Kovacs

The enduring legacy
of laughter left
by the late E.K.
never soared higher
than in his
"Letters of Complaint,"
published
posthumously.
Here is his spoof
on the letter-writing
foibles of
the bluebloods.

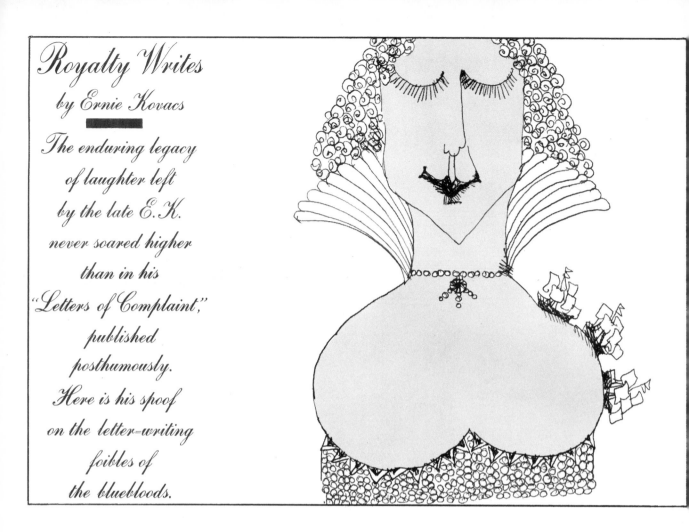

Although members of royalty have been known to correspond with other members of royalty, rarely do they take quill in hand to write Letters of Complaint. Usually, they are more direct and rather prone to dispatching couriers who behead the offending parties.

Now and then, however, exceptions are made to this custom, either because of the physical inaccessibility of the offender or simply because the Royal One has a natural inclination for putting words on paper.

Here is one such letter found in the hip pocket of the pants of a flamenco dancer who passed away last week in a cheap bordello in Spain. Unable to pay for his *arroz con pollo,* he was thrown out of his hotel, leaving his pants behind him. A chambermaid (who has requested we withhold her name as her parents think she is really a bullfighter) found the letter and gave it to the author in a burst of generosity. The letter is from a queen of Spain to a sailor named

"Chris," and it is dated October 14, 1492. . . .

Chris, *mi querido,*

I don't know if this letter will ever reach you. I am going to put it in an empty Port wine bottle and hope it hits your Gulf Stream, or whatever you call it.

As you know, it's been over two months since you left town. (Did you put my garter on the mast of the *Santa Maria* like you promised? Naughty boy!) I hope you're doing O.K. Frankly, Chris, I think you been going a little strong with the Madéira or something because that bit about the world being "round" is too much! I don't want to get on your back, Sweetie, but have you ever noticed, for instance, when a ship is coming over the horizon? You see a little bit at a time. Right? Why? Because it's coming straight up from the other side which is pure perpendicular. Also, if the world was *round,* people would be falling off all the time. That just isn't good thinking, Chris. But I

promised to butt out and I will.

Not much doing around the old palace. (Also, how come, if it's round, I have a square globe on my desk?) We took Granada last week from the Moors. Ferdinand (you remember him) has been chasing the Moors out like crazy. Gets a big kick out of chasing them down the street, hitting them on the head with his sceptre. Ferd says we should get rid of them all. He says they're all Commies. I couldn't care less.

What I'm writing about is this. You know all those jewels I gave you to hock so you could buy the three ships? Well, the other night Ferd and I went to a little off-beat spot for some espresso and Danish, and he asks me where is the charm bracelet he gave me for Mother's Day? I like to died! I gave him some wind about leaving it in the powder room at the Doge's Palace, but I don't think he bought the idea.

I was wondering—could you stick the charm bracelet (if you haven't hocked it, too) in a bottle and send it to me?

Love,
Izz

P.S. Also, if it is *round,* how come the streets don't have big hills on them?

The next letter was found in a box of fresh shirts returned from the author's laundry this morning. It was written, according to the date of the postmark, in 1777. The handwriting is rather elaborate and difficult to read, what with royal seals stamped all over it, but, on examining it closely, it appears to be signed by one Marie Antoinette, Queen of France.

Semi-Fini Cake Mix Co.
Cannes, France
Gentlemen:

I have before me the letter containing your generous offer to endorse your ready-mixed Semi-Fini Devil's Food Cake.

First, let me sincerely express my thanks for your offer. A thousand gold francs and a dozen boxes of the cake mix is a most tempting offer.

However, when I spoke to my husband, Louis, about it this morning, he felt that we should see what the copy is that would go with the endorsement. From your letter, I see that you would want to do an oil painting of me holding the box of the Devil's Food Cake Mix while pointing at it with my forefinger, upon which you want one of the royal rings.

Louis also would like to know: Would this be done with or without the Royal Crown? If it is done *with* the crown, Louis feels that this is worth an extra hundred francs. Also, if any of my attendants are to appear in the painting, would there be some fee designated for them? The last time we posed was purely for promotional purposes, an oil painting billboard with myself and two ladies-in-waiting saying, "See France This Summer." The two young ladies raised quite a stink when they found out it was a freebee. Also, are you thinking of my pouring the milk into the mix? If so, I have a lovely bowl you could use that I brought from Australia with me. It's terra cotta.

But would terra cotta be sufficient background contrast for Devil's Food?

Now, a word about the copy. Louis feels it shouldn't be *too* commercial. He has written some ideas which I will copy down here for you. He feels that he would want either these (or others as dignified) in keeping with our position.

"You Can't Beat SEMI-FINI for Kitchen Funnee."

"When Dad Has a Hard Day in the Fields from Morning to Night, a Cake Made from SEMI-FINI Will Make Things All Right." That one seems to be a bit wordy. But the following one isn't bad.

"What's for Dinner, Marie? Just Wait a Moment and You'll See!"

As for myself, I like them all. (Although I still feel the second one is a bit wordy.)

We're all quite excited about your offer, down here at the Palace. Goodness, I had no idea my little "Let 'em eat cake" would create such a fuss.

Royally (and for "SEMI-FINI," you can bet!),
Marie Antoinette

Sometimes, Royal Letters of Complaint lead to further correspondence and, in one known case, romance. A tourist poking about in an old castle, formerly occupied by a Prince Charming and Princess Cinderella, found this letter written on parchment.

Royal Palace
Castle Road

Cinderella Smith
Frugal Street

Dear Miss Smith:

You may have heard by now that I have been searching all over town for the owner of a glass slipper with a broken heel that was left at my Father's Royal Ball last Saturday night. Reliable sources have informed me that you were the young lady wearing the glass slipper.

I would like to point out a couple of things to you, Miss Smith, that have prompted this search. When you left the ball at midnight last Saturday, one of the pages pointed out that you must have been dancing for free all evening as the back of your hand was not stamped as a paid admission nor were you carrying a press pass.

I think you should know that the one ducat admission charged by Dad for his annual ball is hardly enough to pay for the orange punch and the candles, let alone the cost of the orchestra. (Do you have any idea what Hot Lips Haydn and his Crazy Violas run to for an evening? And the fellow on the vibes is extra.) In all the years Dad has run these affairs, *he has never once increased the price one farthing.* Where else are you going to get for that one ducat charge:

General admission

Barbeque'd Quail

Corn-on-Cob with Whipped Creamery Butter

Dancing to three-piece orchestra (guarantee of six minuets and Paul Jones windup)

Moonlight Moat Ride

Party Favors.

You go into town and you're lucky if a wandering minstrel lets you stand within six feet of him for that kind of money. Only a *deadbeat* would try to beat Father out of the ducat.

Then, there is the matter of those glass shoes. In the first place, glass shoes went out with wedgies. You couldn't be more *declassé* if you showed up in khaki pantaloons. On top of that, your glass heel busted just before Pops went into his specialty *trepak* which he dances in the traditional manner, barefoot! It's a lucky thing you left. He sure would've chewed you out.

So, I run down the steps after you with a couple of guards in tow. But when we get to the driveway, what? We slip and fall on our cans from those slippery pumpkin seeds and all that mice dung. What the hell kind of car you driving, anyway?

I will be up to your place personally to collect the ducat. You be in.

Royally,
Prince Charming

The Missing Letters of Cleopatra

BY ERNIE KOVACS

An entire section from an unfinished masterpiece by the late great E. K. —one of the most gifted, inventive, and truly funny comics of our time

Anybody who has a whole closet full of cigars in his house is my kind of guy. Anybody who has a turntable outside his house so his guests don't have to turn their own cars around is my kind of guy. Anybody who has a wit that fast, that keen, that perceptive is my kind of guy. Ernie Kovacs had all of those, and Ernie Kovacs was my kind of guy. □ We were down at Shawnee-on-Delaware playing golf one time and started home in our limmos. He had a telephone in his. We pulled up to a stop light, side by side, and as we did his telephone started to ring. He rolled down the window and handed the instrument out to me. "It's for you, Jack," he said. □ That was Ernie's gentle way of putting me on. He always found a way to make the ridiculous plausible and vice versa; he was one of the great inventive comedians of our time. People didn't appreciate him nearly enough. He never really knew how much we loved him. It's sad that he's gone, but it's good to know that he left permanent things behind—some hilarious performances in movies, television shows, and now some writings in this book. I miss him. He was my kind of guy.—Jackie Gleason.

April 19, 48 B.C.

Dear Calnivia,

Please excuse the carpet hairs all over the scroll, but wait till I tell you how they got there!

Yesterday, I finally did it. Yessir, I met him! "Mr. Big," himself! Little ole Ceaser in person. As I wrote you, for the last two weeks I've been trying everything at the palace. I put out a real wad on costume and make-up. . . . "Need a new cleaning woman, Boss?" "Wash your chariot, one denarius, make it look like new, Boss?" "Free brushes to everybody over 21 in the house, and a whisk broom for the parakeet". . . . Nothing! Absolutely nothing! Struck out every time.

I'm about to call the whole thing off, and I'm walking down near the Piazza Maggiore, when some beat-up looking guy with a pile of rugs gives me a whistle. "Go chew bay leaves," I tell him, and I'm about to move on when, wham! It hits me like I stood too close to a low-slung belly dancer. I head back to the little guy, with my hips going like it's "Goodbye Sockets," and I run a forefinger around the inside of his bellyband. I can see by the way his curled-up slippers straighten out that he's getting the message.

He tells me his name is Maximus Bigelonius. (Everybody in this town seems to be named Maximus somebody.) He hands me a little piece of scroll, which he says is "his card," and it's got a slogan on it: "A Name over The Arch Rates a Bigelonius on The Porch." It doesn't rhyme, but what the hell . . . if it sells rugs, it sells rugs.

So I give him the pitch. He's to roll me up in one of his rugs and take me in to see Ceaser. (I never can get that damned name right . . . can't remember if it's CAE—or CEA. Anyway, you know who I mean.)

Well, he thinks it over and then suggests somebody roll us *both* in the rug and his assistant will carry us in. "Double your pleasure, double your fun," he snickers, with a corny wink and his tongue flopping outside like a dachshund running up hill. I tell him it's okay with me, but I start scratching. I just stand there scratching. He swallows a little and says he just remembered his assistant is off, because it's Shrove Tuesday or something. So, he rolls me up in an itchy Persian hall-runner and off we go to Caser's. That doesn't look right, either.)

Well, it's a long hike and it's getting pretty hot inside the hall-runner. The sweat is starting to run down my legs like I got busted pores. (Also, he's copping a little feel through the carpet.) Then I hear him grunting and I can tell by the angle of my head we're heading up the steps. He gives me one more quick grab and then pushes the bell.

As soon as the door opens I hear him say, "I'm a traveler from Levant. I have something nice in a rug." (As he says this, he must be pointing at the rug for emphasis, and I got to hand it to the old bugger, he's hitting the bull's-eye every time.) In we go, and he walks for about a half mile and then he stops. I hear a lot of "Hail Ceesering," so I figure we are now at the head roost.

All of a sudden I'm being unrolled, and bingo! it's daylight again and there I am, laying on my back with my dress way up over my head. Quick as a flash, I slap my purse down on what I guess everybody is taking a

pretty good look at. With the other hand, I wave what the early Egyptians used to call a disapproving finger. I hear Ceasser cough a little self-consciously, and I know right away I guessed right. I sit up, not moving the purse until I pull down my dress, and I give him a "Hail Ceaser" with a lot of breath behind it. Well, I can see "Tilt!" light up all over him, and that two denariuses worth of cloves I'm chewing don't hurt none, either.

"Who are you, madam?" he asks. (He's got a lisp, by the way.) I don't know if he's making a crack with that "madam" bit or not, but anyway, I tell him I'm Cleopatra.

"Wasn't your father—"

"Right as rain, Ceser, he was King Auletes, the flute player."

"Didn't he write, 'Ta-ta-te-tum-tum?' "

"Uh-huh. He wrote it as a dirge, after he killed my sister, Berenice."

"Crazy sauce!"

He's a little mixed up, but he's friendly. He asks me if I'd like a Martini. So I come right back with the old bit, "Martini? If I wanted *two,* I'd have asked for it. Just one Martinus, please."

They sure as hell are behind the times in Rome. He laughed at this old gag till his garland fell off. (Back down, Calnivia, a garland is a thing they wear around their heads, here.)

I tell him I'd like to pop into the powder room first as it's been a long trip in a short rug. He comes a little closer to me, swishing his toga, sexy-like, and puts a fatherly hand on my can. Just then a gnat lands on his nose. He slaps his other hand on it and four servants come racing out at the sound. "Did you call, Boss?," they yell. He pretends he's straightening the bell-pull on his toga, and says, "Yes, the lady and I will be dining in here. Bring some food and book some entertainment."

So, I duck into the ladies' room and not a minute too soon. (What with that jerk bouncing me up and down inside the rug all the way from the Piazza. *You* know those lousy kidneys of mine. . . .) Anyway, I comb my hair, put a little distilled Nile Water behind each ear and kind of ooze out of the room and go toward him, like a snake travelling over a pile of ball bearings. He gets so excited, he sticks a fig in his eye. This gives me a good excuse to get close to him. As I'm picking out the fig seeds I can see his other eye running over me like a Ping-pong ball on a hot stove. (I loosened my Made-in-the-Forum bra while I was in the powder room and every time I take a breath, he doesn't.)

Then he claps his hands for entertainment and some broads come out and dance. When they're through, he has them trampled by elephants.

"How'd you like it?," he asks.

"Cute routine," I tell him, "But a little short."

So he brings back the elephants and has them trample on the broads for about ten minutes more as a kind of encore. Then they bring out the food. It's the usual stuff—Hummingbird *Cog au Vin,* Shark's Snout *avec chives,* Stork *au berre* and a pot of Expresso.

"What would you like to do tonight, Cleopatra?" he asks me. "How'd you like to go over to the Coliseum? Great acrobat team that's eaten by hungry lions, and a giant gorilla ripping apart some old ladies. Plus selected short subjects."

I tell him I think I would just like to go to bed and I drop one of my shoulder straps like one of those characters in the Tennisius Willimus southern Greek tragedies.

"All right, Cleo-honey," he says, "I'll have somebody go up and turn down your sheets."

Well, Calnivia, here's what follows. I go to the guest room, squirt some more Nile Water on me and lie there like I'm tied to an anthill. Well, I lie there till I'm getting a cramp in my back. The sand is going through the hour-glass, like a crooked contractor mixing cement, and still no Ceser.

I must have fallen asleep, and when I open my eyes, the sun is shining! I always heard Caesar (that look right to you? That's the way it's spelled on the hand towels) . . . I always heard Caesar was a real swinger. "Omnium Mulierum Vir," they call him. ("Everybody's husband."). . . . You know what I think? "Omnium Mulierum *Fruitus.*"

Yours,
Cleopatra

June 15, 46 B.C.
Dear Calnivia,
My, doesn't tempus fugit? A lot

has happened in these years since I wrote you last.

Remember how I told you Caesar (the hand towel had it right) never laid a hand on me that first night? Well, the next morning he shows up, a glass of papaya juice in his hand.

"XXIII Skidoo!" I tell him. "Beat it, Buster." Then I roll over. *That* is a mistake . . . and I spend the next ten minutes in the john washing papaya juice off my rear end. He thinks he's funny as hell. He's got a kind of "Keystonius Centurians" type of humor.

"I'll bet you're a howl with a couple of custard tartlets," I tell him.

"Sorry I couldn't get back last night," he says, "but Calpurnia's mother came over and we sat around and talked."

"Calpurnia *who?,*" I ask.

"Calpurnia Caesar, my wife."

"Oh, her."

"*She.*"

Well, after that, we started going around together. I asked him if he wouldn't mind knocking off my brother, Ptolemy, as he was getting kind of sassy and talking back. So, he does it. Well, one thing led to another and I took him to my barge for a couple of wild sessions. He suggested that I supply the food and he'll bring the entertainment . . . but I told him the help hated cleaning up after those elephants and to forget it.

A year after that, we had a kid. (Just to give you a small idea of the rough time I had in labor, the kid's name is Caesarion!)

Then some of the Romans started making snotty remarks about all the time he was on the barge and not paying any attention to his work, and stuff like that. So he went out and captured Pontus. He came back so crocked from the party they threw for him, he could hardly talk. ("Veni . . . vidi . . . vici," he kept mumbling to himself like some damned parrot. Half the time, when he gets loaded, I never know what the hell he's saying.)

Sid (that's my pet name for him) says we're going to get married, what with the kid and all. Then I'll be queen. (Get me, hey, Calnivia?! It seems like only yesterday when I was getting grabbed through the carpet.) Sid set up a temple with his image

on one side and mine on the other. It's not a very good likeness of me . . . looks like a passport sculpture. But everybody's supposed to go there and worship. Ain't that the living *end!?*

This Cicero is getting to be a kind of pain-in-the-can, though. He's always knocking me in publius places. Sid don't pay any attention to him. In fact, Sid set me up in my own little spot, right across the Tiber. I hired a faggie interior decorator to do it up in purple and gold. Looks real nice. I had a batch of slaves dipped in wax. They make crazy candles. You gotta come see the place sometime.

Love,
Cleopatra

March 14, 44 B.C.
Dear Calnivia,
Just a short note. Have to get my hair done. Today's the big day! Sid's going to be officially crowned emperor and this makes little Cleo the Queen. Ain't that the nuts?!

In haste,
Cleo

March 16, 44 B.C.
Dear Calnivia,
Well, he blew it!

Always bragging about his big buddies . . . big chums! Big BULL! When that stupid ass stood up to make his acceptance speech, everybody who didn't have bursitis stuck a dagger in him.

In the first place, he'd been up all night rehearsing the speech and he didn't look so good to begin with. But when they finished stabbing him, he looked a helluva lot worse, believe me. (Brutus . . . remember I told you about him . . . his old "Chummie-Boo?" The big "fishing buddy"? Well, "Chummie-Boo" was right in there with the rest of 'em, with a switch-blade going back and forth like he's trying to develop his chest muscles or something. Talk about your fair-weather friends.)

Anyways, afterwards, when they mopped up most of the stuff, folks stood around and talked and it was too hot to go home so I kind of hung around. It's a little warm for March. Usually it's a little nippy this time of year. There were some speeches that weren't too bad. This Marc Anthony gave a pretty good talk.

(Continued on page 40)

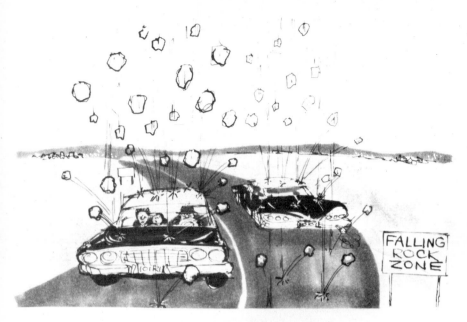

CLEOPATRA'S MISSING LETTERS

(continued from page 14)

And, when he said, "I come to bury Caesar, not to praise him . . .", he was looking right at me. Kind of gave me goose bumps all over. He's got brown eyes.

Afterwards, Marc came over to me and asked me if I'd like a pizza. (There were a lot of vendors around soon as word got out they'd slipped Sid the shiv.) While we were eating the pizzas, he's making jokes. Some of them a little raw, but I can't help laughing. Then, he makes like he's wiping his fingers on my tunic from the pizzas, but I know what he's doing and I figure, what the hell, we ain't kids and it's spring so I give him a little grab right back, while I'm pretending to admire his sword. (He wasn't wearing one, but I've always been lousy at ad-libbing.) So, whether he's mixed up or what from the grab, I don't know, but he tips the pizza vendor a whole estate! Get that, *a whole estate*! (Sid was strictly a fifteen per cent of the tab guy.)

So, we start walking toward the barge like a couple of kids. He's goosing the knife vendors (who don't give a damn—they had such a big day). This little old lady comes up and croaks at him, "Beware the Ides of March . . . beware the Ides of March." He tells her she blew her cue, and where the hell was she all morning, and he's going to report her to Lucullus Equity.

We got to the barge at about IV in the afternoon and I want to tell you, that boy may kid around in the market place, but when he's in the hay, he's not doing Floogel Via!

Thanks for your postcard from the pyramids. It should be nice there in a couple of weeks, before the tourists start. Please write.

Love,
Cleo

July 18, 37 B.C.

Dear Calnivia,

Well, the old B.C.'s are sure rolling by. I'll be glad when we get to the A.D.'s. It just don't make sense the way it is . . . everytime a year goes by, you *subtract* instead of *add*. Next year will be 36 B.C., this year is *37* . . . So what number did they start with and how do they know it's going to come out even in time for A.D., 1? Well, ta hell with it, the whole town's a little ridiculous. It was named after one of those kids that was nursed by a wolf or a chipmunk or something. (Nobody seems to have the story straight on just *what* they were nursing on. Anyway, it certainly doesn't say much for their Child Welfare Society. It's full of some old broads who sit around on their ass playing chess all day while kids are crawling around getting their lunch from kangaroos.) Anyway, these two kids (the ones the town is named after) were twins. One was named Romulus and the other was Remus. Romulus killed Remus so they named the town after him. (Nice people, huh? I guess if you kill your mother here, they build you a shrine, or something.) If it had been the other way around, with Remus killing Romulus, they would've named the town after him,

instead. Can you just hear Marc Anthony saying, "Friends, *Remans*, Countrymen . . . "?

Tomorrow's my birthday and Marc is having two thousand Trojans massacred as a present. It was supposed to be a surprise, but some bigmouth blabbed. I'm not going to tell Marc I know about it, but it's going to be hard acting surprised. Cicero is going to get it, too. (Remember, I told you he was the one that was all the time picking on me?) Actually, massacring Cicero is as much a present for Marc as it is for me. He's with that crowd that's been going around disagreeing with Marc's political platform. They're saying that Marc's promise of "two chariots in every garage and an oriole in every pot" is just a lot of wind.

Anyway, I still don't know how Marc's going to massacre them. At least I have that much of the surprise left. You know, Calnivia, I think Marc is as big a meatball as Sid was. Honestly, he gets taken in by everybody. Right now, he's got some kind of three-way deal going with Octavian and Lepidus. Frankly, I think he's going to get screwed.

A little worried,
Cleo

Sept. 3, 31 B.C.

Dear Calnivia,

I threw a little wing-ding for Marc the other day on the barge. (That reminds me, I'd better get the damned thing painted pretty soon. The friggin' thing is covered with barnacles. It looks like something from "Annius Christius.") Marc asked me what I'd laid out for the party. I told him it cost me a hundred denariuses or drachmas or talents, or whatever the hell they call money here. (Cripes, am I ever fouled up on the exchange system here. Give me Egypt, where two pharaohs equal one dollar.) When he was leaving, I gave him the whole shootin' match as a gift . . . gold goblets, plates, silver, left-over cold cuts . . . the whole bit.

He carried the whole thing into the rowboat that takes him ashore. Boy, for a guy who gives away estates to pizza vendors, you'd think those cold cuts were the end of the world. He was waving goodbye with a piece of Lebanon baloney, and, so help me, I thought he was going to dive over after it when it slipped out of his hands.

He's really a cornball, though I hate to admit it. I've had it up to my garnet-studded navel with some of those corny routines . . . Little wind-up buzzers that go off when you shake hands . . . rubber snakes . . . fake doggie "doo-doo" he leaves around on the rugs. Last week, he hired a diver to hook one fish after another on his line to show me what a big fisherman he was. I cooled him, though. I sent an Assyrian over on the side and he tied a can of sardines to Marc's hook. What a horse's ass he is. I made him a bet that I could toss a dinner party for the two of us that would cost a cool million (of whatever the denomination here is).

So he comes in for dinner that night, trips over the incense burner (damn near setting fire to the barge), and says, "Let's put on the feed bag, baby." Brother! Sometimes I'm almost sorry they did the dagger bit with Sid. So, I start the dinner with antipasta: Some pickled rind of pomegranates with caraway seeds . . . green olives stuffed with black olives . . . Seaweed Vichysoisse, some Hungarian poppyseed cakes, lady fingers shaped a little phallic, Crawfish Corinthian, Hare du Jour, Marinated Monkey avec sour cream, whole Squid (priced according to size), some little cakes with dirty pictures in icing on the top, snails stuffed with barnswallow (or is it the other way around?), quince and chitlin's. Well, this oaf takes a look and says, "I don't see where this cost you a million ducats," . . . (or florins or francs or whateverthehell they are).

"Keep your breastplates on, Shorty," I tell him, "wait'll you see what this vinegar is for."

"Bib lettuce?" he asks.

"No, Stupido. Watch," I tell him and then take off one of my pearl earrings and drop it in the vinegar. It dissolves like lemon sherbet in the seat of a ballerina's leotard during the fast part of Swan Lake.

I say, "That pearl was worth one half million shillings (or kopecks)." Then I drink it. Calnivia, I thought he got caught in his folding chair! You never saw a guy turn so white!

"You must be flippin', Cleo baby . . . (I'm beginning to really loathe that expression!) . . . I can get you all the quince-juice you can drink for a dime," (or a guinea or a German mark. I forget what it was).

"You mean that's something?" I ask. "Watch this, Brown Eyes." And I take the other pearl earring and drop it into another glass of vinegar. He grabs my hand as I am about to drink it and says that vinegar is bad for the stomach. What a square. (These weren't my real pearls, by the way. I had these copies made out of oleomargarine, but Dopey don't know the diff.)

Now comes a messenger swimming to the barge, dodging crocodiles and floating tin cans, with a scroll in his mouth. They haul him aboard and he races in to Dopey with the message. Dopey unrolls it and stares at it intently for about ten minutes, frowning all the time. I ask him what it says and he says he can't read it . . . the ink ran in the water.

So, he throws the messenger over again and tells him to go back for the carbon. The messenger finally returns with the scroll wrapped in gnu skin and tied to the top of his head so it won't get wet. Just as he reaches the boat, a croc grabs him underwater somewhere and all of a sudden he's a tenor. Luckily, Marc managed to get the scroll off his head before the croc gets a good grip and hauls him under. Marc reads that Octavian is kind of pee'd off because Marc's wife (who is Octavian's sister) is getting miffed because Marc and I are having a few laughs.

Marc says the hell with her and says we should go put some more earrings in vinegar and I tell him he knows what he can put in the vinegar and not to go spending my dough so freely. (Those liras or quarters.)

Then, I take a look at my sun dial and realize I am three months overdue. I tell Marc he can expect to hear the patter of tiny sandals on the barge in about six months so we'd better get married.

So, he sends off a divorce to his wife by carrier pigeon and the captain marries us on the barge. We have a helluva party. All kinds of eats and we book Sid's elephant act. The next day, the pigeon comes back looking pretty bushed. He's got a message from Octavian saying that he's coming to attack with a fleet of ships. So Dopey gets a fleet together. I do, too. I figure, what the hell, it's community property Octavian is shooting up and I better protect my half.

Well, all three fleets meet yesterday at Actium (that always makes me think of a skin condition) and I can see in a minute that Dopey is going to get the crap knocked out of him, so I pull out of there fast as they can beat the guys in the slave galley to row. I passed pretty close to Octavian's ship. (This Octavian has the lousiest complexion, but there's something about his blue eyes that kind of makes you forget the pimples.) I sort of flung a piece of paper over to Octavian with the address of my barge on it.

As soon as anything develops, I'll let you know. Well, Calnivia, don't stand downwind of the Sphinx, as they say.

Love,
Cleo

September 30 B.C.
Dear Calnivia,

I guess I just can't get lucky. I got the old double X from that pimple-faced son-of-a-bitch, Octavian. "Come to Rome, Sweetie," he says, like it's "back in the saddle again time." . . . "Come to Rome and I'll fix you up." So, like some hick from Carthage, I go. All bright-eyed and bushy-tailed. Wham! He locks me in and tells me I'm going to be his slave. . . . Not me, Calnivia, Not me. No man's going to tie me down in a kitchen while he's out having fun and orgies and everything. So I decide to give him a little scare. I send a kid out to buy one of them rubber asps that Dopey was always scaring people with. When Pimples comes back, I grab the rubber snake and shove it against my boobs. "Last chance, Pimple-Pete, last chance! You either let me go and give me lots of rubles or farthings, or the snake gets the blue-plate special." He sneers at me with those crummy teeth. "O.K., Charlie," I tell him, "there's some jewelry in my purse. . . . You can hock it and have some caps made for those lousy incisors, but as for me . . . give me liberty or give me death!" and I stick the asp into home plate.

All I can say is, if I ever get my hands on that kid I sent to the novelty shop for that rubber snake! The little bastard slipped me a real one to save dough. And bingo! It bites right through the foam rubber into old Bessie, on the left.

I'm sorry I ever came here.

Au 'voir,
Cleo-The Unlucky

Letters o

The second
in a series
of unpublished excerpts
from the final
comic masterpiece
of the
late great E. K.

A Beginner's Manual

Of all the different types of letters, each requiring its own brand of cautious writing, no letter must be written with more care than The Letter of Apology. Badly-written Letters of Apology virtually constitute a repetition of the offense. While the demeanor of the writer should be somewhat gay, a wild abandonment of the emotions is not recommended. It should also be held in mind that since the recipient of the apology has already been offended, he or she is possibly a person of now increased sensitivity and should so be approached. A nicely-written example follows:

Lady and Sir Chyteworth
King's Road
Kensington, England
Dear Lady C:

Well, I certainly screwed up the week end, didn't I? I was most embarrassed when the hotel manager told me how pissed I was when Sir C. brought me home from your lovely place. I really am prostrate. (That word always makes me think of a finger for some reason.) Really, it just isn't like me to crap up a formal party like that.

I do hope I haven't affected Sir C.'s opportunity to enter The House of Lords. I'm *certain* Lord B. knew I was jollying him when I said, "At least I'd rather have a seat in the House of Lords than back into a meat grinder." Lord B. apparently has one of those quiet senses of humor, typical of that Grosvenor Square group.

In retrospect, I gather that my story on "the high price of clothing" didn't quite come off. Actually, it's quite funny. You see, the idea is . . . First you tell the price of your cravat, flipping it out, as you talk. . . Then the price of your braces, hooking a thumb under them to illustrate. . . And finally, the price of your shirt, as you unzip your trousers. What I was *supposed* to do was to flip my *shirt-tail* out. But, "the best laid plans . . .," as they say.

Anyway, I don't know about you, but I had a *barrel* of fun and only hope my throwing up all over the Louis XV chaise longue didn't cause you too much distress. (I honestly do recommend plastic slip covers.

Apology

by Ernie Kovacs

They're quite inexpensive and great for parties.)

Until next time,
Oliver Finley

Perhaps the reader has already discovered the shortcomings of the preceding note. It is this: While the writer is obviously remorseful over his conduct, he does wrong in *enumerating his indiscretions* of that week end. In all likelihood, his hostess had forgotten all about it and were he to remain a trifle ambiguous in his account, what with the various guests and various week ends, the busy hostess is apt to forget just *who* did *what* to *whom, when.*

The following is a *superb* example of a note written because of almost similar circumstances. In this in-instance, the writer had stayed overnight with his host and attractive hostess. He then breakfasted and was driven into town forcibly by the host, as he had spent the night *with* the hostess in one of the twin beds in the room. The other bed was occupied by her husband, the distance between the two beds being insufficient to avoid discovery during the night's indiscretions.

Dear Sally and Bob,

Many thanks for putting me up last night. It isn't often we see examples of that "Old World" hospitality anymore. Breakfast was swell, too. Where did you ever learn to prepare kippers like that! You're a lucky guy, Bob.

Love (To you *both,* of course!)
Lester

Letters of Apology have been written for many, many years. The next letter was written by Michelangelo (the last name is a bit blurry but it looks like Buonarroti). The author borrowed the letter from a bus boy at Bickford's Restaurant. He has quite a collection of these letters of which he is quite fond.

July, 1536

His Holiness
Pope Julius II
The Vatican
Roma
Your Holinessa:

Lasta mont', when I'ma wassa

looka you hup, you wassa aska me if I'ma painta da ceiling of your uncle's Sistene Chapel. You rememb' what I'ma wassa say? I'ma say, "Shooz, who not? Somea week end whenna I'ma passa troo, I'ma slap a littlea designa huppa dere and gooda luck." You remem'? Well, disa morning, I'ma wassa take my first look atta you Sistene Chapel.

Mama Mia! You know how mucha *room* you gotta hup dere? *Sixa tousand square foots!* Atsa ain'ta spaghetti with clamma sauce—atsa work! Itsa take me forty years to feenisha. You ain'ta got enough ducats inna da treasury to buy the *brushes!* If I'ma was to painta day anna night looka straight hup, I'ma look like a hunchaback inna reverse.

Noncha getta me wrong, You Holiness, I'm notta knocka da Catolics. I'ma on *you* side, but you aska a littlea too much.

Ifa you want I'm paint da ceiling *one-a color,* likea *blue,* atsa hokay. But iffa you want me to getta fancy, forgetta it.

Please excusa da pencil.
　　　Yoursa,
　　　Michelangelo Buonarroti

The ability to make light of little incidents that tend to mar otherwise happy relationships is a strong aid in constructing a Letter of Apology. An example of this is dated Dec. 6, 1941.

Mr. Author Flavin
1132 N.W. 17th
Washington, D. C.
Mr. Fravin,

Yestelday, I reave you house most lighteously indignerent! Missy Fravin, she comprain in roud voice legarding lose bushes I prant rast week.

Who the heck Missy Fravin think she are? Some bigtime whoreticultulist? I are have prenty customels I are garldenel foah. (Foah erven yeals, some of them.) I not need you lotten business. Prease considel this retter as my lesignation as you garldenel.
　　　Good bye,
　　　Toki Yashimiro

A second letter, illustrating our point, was written by the same person two days later.

　　　December 8, 1941
Harro Mr. Fravin, Sir and Fliend!
I are just sitting here raffing with my wife about good times I are having when I tlim you hedge and mow you flont lawn in you attlactive glounds. She and I are raff, too, at way you Flench Poodrle are bite me on reg when I plune you chelly tlee (which incidentarry, are gift flom Japan and *flom heart,* too). Then Aunt Yishi telr us joke he are pulr on you and we raff some moah. Aunt Yishi say day befoah yestelday (Saturday, Dec. 6) she are light you joke-retter and sign *my name* and say I *are lesign!* We raff so much, tear are fahring down cheeck!

As today are Monday and I do nothing on Monday (do nothing Sunday, Dec. 7, yeslelday, *nothing whatsoevah!*), I have time to light you and leminisce how happy I are with my many yearls (and continued so, I hope) I are have with you and you nice famiry.

Say, incidentarry, I are just grance at rast night papah. There are something about some rittle fuss in Honoruru. I do not know if you are lead about this yet. (Incidentarry, Japanese who do this fuss are *norlthen* Japanese, I are *southerln* Japanese. Pelhaps, you are noticed my accent befoah.) My family, Yashimiri family, not even go to Noath Side of Japan, exept to take boat to Eulope now and then.

Anyways, it is good to have raff with you, boss. See you tomollow. Am pranting some nice lhodedenlhlons for Missy Fravin. By the way, she absourutey light about those lose bushes that she comprain about. I dig them up firlst thing in moaning.
　　　Rove and big kisses,
　　　You boy,
　　　Tokileh

Good? Yes. Why? Because the writer pictures his happy home life and brings in chatty current events to make his letter live.

A friend in the motion picture industry, who at present is shooting a picture in Florence, Italy (a film about the ad agencies of Madison Avenue), sent me this letter that a proprietor of an *osteria* gave to him when he complimented the chef on the quality of his ravioli. (And, it's length.) The letter was written by a painter. A Leonardo da Vinci, quite famous (abroad) in his day, he tells me. His letter will serve as an example of the Artistic Apology:

Luglio 10, 1506
12, Via Paletto
Florence, Italy
Monna Lisa del Gioconda
34, Via Sorriso
Florence, Italy
Cara Signora del Gioconda,
(As a convenience to the reader, the author has had the letter translated into English)

You have been most patient with me. To sit so patiently for four years while I painted your portrait! That's a helluva long time, huh? But you know me, Monna, bambino, I just can't put my head on one thing at a time. I get bored and invent airplanes, suction pumps, bobby pins, and all kinds of junk, just to kill a half hour.

I must reiterate my appreciation of your patience. To set for four long years! That's a long time to set in one spot when you have to go to the can. *Somanagunna!* ("Son-of-a-gun")

I almost forgot! Something has been bugging me for these four years. And last night the mystery was solved! My old buddy, Michelangelo, dropped in to look at your painting. (I dropped one of the "n's" of your first name in the caption . . . looks better somewho.) As one artist to another, I told him what had been bothering me. (That constant smile on your face. . . No offense, baby.) Well, Mike takes one look at me and busts out laughing. "Leonardo," he says, "Look at your pants. Your fly is open."

Well, no wonder you were always chuckling. I used to think you were "squirrelly." (Even so, that's a long time to laugh at the same old gag.)

Well, that's about all I wanted to tell you. If you get a little time on your hands, drop in. Maybe we can try a different expression.
　　　Suo amico,
　　　Leonardo da Vinci
　　　(Lennie)

Another difficult task in writing Letters of Apology is in The Refusal of A Loan. The letter is dated six months prior to the opening of a Broadway Musical. (The date and name of the musical are being withheld.)

Dear Moss,
I haven't answered your letter before because I've been a little unsure
　　　　　　　(continued)

LETTERS OF APOLOGY

(continued)

as to how to tell you my answer without hurting your feelings. But I think we've known each other long enough for me to be honest with you.

Regarding your kind offer for me to invest in your forthcoming musical. Moss, baby, you're a big boy. You been around. You know the business —but dammit, Sweetie, sometimes you get a little carried away.

To put it bluntly, I think you're out of your *mind* to toss away all that time and *effort,* Chickie, into putting on that old turkey, *Pygmalion,* as a musical. In the first place, Buddy, Shaw has had it. *Finito, Moss-baby, finito!* Secondly, every high school

and jerkwater stock company has done the damned thing to shreds. Everybody knows the story backwards and forwards.

And in the *third* place . . . (I hope this doesn't hurt too much, Sweetie) . . . in the third place, *Rex Harrison* and *Julie Andrews?* You must be kidding, Chickie. (*He's* going to *sing!?*)

Maybe I'm silly writing. Probably by now you've given up the whole idea. Hey, you weren't putting me on, were you, you old sonofagun?

Give me a buzz next week and we'll have lunch at Sardi's.

Best,
David

The author has just been handed another example of the Artistic

Apology. It is signed by Thomas Gainsborough, an English painter. The date is a little smeared as the letter has been in a medicine chest of one of the author's children and has some cough syrup spilled on it. The writing was done, it appears, some time in the Eighteenth Century.

Mrs. Timothy Slee
12 Knightsbridge Rd.
Chelsea, England
Dear Mrs. Slee,

Thank you for your letter telling me that your son has double pneumonia and pleurisy. I know that, as a mother, this probably upsets you although I do *not* think it gives you license to address me in the sharp manner which you used in your letter.

When we agreed that young Slee would pose for my painting, "The Blue Boy," at a shilling per day, it was with the understanding that there would be certain conditions involved.

As you know, madame, I have a reputation as a perfectionist. When I paint fruit, I use only the best grade of apples, oranges, and grapes that money can buy. I have cancelled out a complete stalk of bananas, simply because I did not like the size of the fruit-flies hovering about it. And when I paint a picture to be called, "The Blue Boy," I want a *blue boy* and not a pink-cheeked brat with a bellyful of beef and kidney pie!

Also, let us not overlook the fact that when I turned the heat off in my studio, to help get a little of that ultramarine in his lips, I was working in the same room with him. So let's not be so damned pickie! (The little bastard is lying, by the way, about the whole thing. In the first place, I do not *own* a mouton smock with a fur collar. *Nobody* does.)

And another thing, if you think it's so damned easy trying to paint in a fur coat, why don't you try it yourself some time!

Yours,
Tom Gainsborough

While William Wyler, the Hollywood director, was in Rome shooting *Ben Hur*, he just missed finding a letter written by the real life Messala to Ben Hur after the big chariot race. The author happened to glance down and saw it lying in the gutter. It was quite dirty, as it is over 1,900 years old, but after washing it off, it was quite legible.

Roma Clinic
Roma, Italy

Ben Hur
XII Via Maxime
Roma, Italy
Dear Bennie,

Right off the bat, whatta you say . . . let bygones be bygones? It sure was one helluva race, huh, Bennie? Gollee!

Hey, by the way, you ain't mad at me, are you? I was just lying here in traction, saying to myself, "Messie, I wonder how your old buddy, Ben Hur, is?" . . . and then I said . . . "Why not drop him a short scroll. I'll bet he got a heckuva kick out of

some of those gags you pulled on him during the chariot race. He always had a great sense of humor."

That's exactly what I was saying, Bennie, lying here in traction. (They tell me they're going to crack off the casts in a month or two. I'll sure as hell be glad when they do. Nothing is worse than these so-called friends who come visit you. They all chisel some corny saying in the casts before they leave. Sometimes the pain is unbearable, when they get long-winded. Everybody's a comic these days, huh, Bennie? Whatever happened to the straight men?)

Getting back to some of those cute gags I pulled on you during the race . . . I knew you'd get a kick out of that sign, SCHOOL—GO SLOW, that I put up on the big curve. I saw you do a heckuva "take," Bennie, a *heckuva* "take." I told my night nurse (I think she's a nympho, but I can't tell with all these casts on) about that take. When it comes to broad comedy, nobody can touch you, Ben-boy, *nobody*. As for sprinkling those oats in front of your horses, I really

figured they'd eat before the race. *Not for one minute* did I expect them to stop dead in the middle of all that action just for a handful of oats. Believe me (and I hope you know me well enough to know that I don't lie), if I thought for one second that your horses would take the gag seriously, I never would've done it.

I got a kick out of your expression, by the way, when you thought I was trying to squeeze you up against the rail. You *did*, get a little white, Bennie, I could hardly tell where your toga ended and your neck started. Then I could see, by the way you looked, that you knew I was just kiddin' around. Say, I wonder if you could do me a favor? I'm trying to find out the name of the dirty rat who put those big iron spikes on my wheels. Why, if those things ever got into your wooden spokes, you could've got hurt, or something.

Sometimes I lay here laughing like heck. Everybody wants to know what's so funny. You know what I'm laughing about? Huh, Bennie? The way you took me seriously when I made a couple of kidding remarks about your being Jewish. *Me* knock you for being Jewish! ! Sometimes, when you look mad like that, I think you're putting me on. Some of my best friends are Jewish. *Christmas,* I'd be the last one to knock my friends, believe me, Beneleh.

Listen, if you get around to these parts, drop in. (I'll give you a knockdown to the nympho if she's on that night.)

For auld lang syne,
Messala

P.S. Did you get my Yom Kippur cards? (M)

P.P.S. Incidentally, I wouldn't worry about that crack I made about your old lady and your sister. It's probably just some kind of summer rash. (M)

P.P.P.S. Did you hear the boffo about the Jewish camp for Indian kids? (M)

Parents, particularly with children, are frequently called upon to get off Apology Notes to neighbors, teachers, and probation officers. A prominent philanthropist and head of the Etruscan Department at a museum in a large city in the Midwest was notified by the teacher that his son was being reprimanded for using profanity at school. He interrupted his research immediately, as a good parent, to reassure her that steps would be taken to clarify to his son the inadvisability of continuing the practice.

Dear Miss Van Breel:

While I was deeply shocked at first on receiving your note about Llewellyn, I am, nevertheless, quite grateful to you for your so advising me. Llewellyn is still a youngster and corrective advice now will be invaluable in shaping his future.

I spoke with him this morning, and you have my complete assurance, Miss Van Breel, that the little son-of-a-bitch knows which way the wind blows now.

Gratefully,
Llewellyn McClintock, Sr.

The following is an Advanced Form of Apology. In this masterpiece of illustration, the offending incident is buried within the chit-chat and potpourri of ambiguity.

The Hotel Peyton
Lorenzo, N. J.
Mrs. Clinton-Haydley Duff Gordon, East Hampton, Long Island
Dear Mrs. C-H Duff Gordon:

(Or may I call you "Thirty" for short? Ha-Ha, that's what I get for reading so many newspapers. "Thirty," you know, is newspaper talk. When they finish a column, they say "That's Thirty." Sometimes they say it at the end of a newcast on radio or TV.) Isn't that the *longest* salutation *ever!*

It's Tuesday already and so the week goes past. Wednesday, Thursday, Friday and it's the end of the week.[1]

Saturday and Sunday (he still has not said *week end,* a grim reminder possibly) with its weather and sea are an exhilaration to be set aside for the Gods.[2] What a glory-combination of sight and mind. To breathe, perchance to dream, as Shakespeare said in his magnificent *Hamlet,* (I would like to send you a copy, may I?).

A thought has just occurred to me.[3] While I am sure that one of your sophistication (I use the word in the *best* sense, of course, to indicate a

level of intelligentsia as to your pursuits and companions) . . . while one of your sophistication can look upon it as a sensitive individual's overt self-expression (although it was admittedly somewhat graphic in its depiction) of today's tensions, I feel that (in the event that I am wrong in this assumption), I should pass upon it.[4] Each of us has,[5] in his day, struck at his particular yoke of oppressing forces in his own way. There are some who are fortunate enough to bear the sword and slashing at tyranny, assuage the torment within. Others pick up the pen and with determined stroke decapitate (as surely as does the cold steel) the malignancy and foul heads of despotism.

I, unadorned with physical prowess of the mental wherewithal of the apt phrase, poor soul I, must employ (as did our ancestors of the cave) other means[6] to delineate one small voice's outcry.

This, then, was my function when I ran (inhibitions severed by an overindulgence of the juice of the grape) into the living room, innocently naked and modestly holding erect the extant symbol of Greek phallicism, shouting, "Screw the Long Island Railroad!"

Please extend my best to Mr. C-H DG, and again my felicitations to you both on your already-celebrated wedding anniversary.

Sincerely,
Leyton Henning

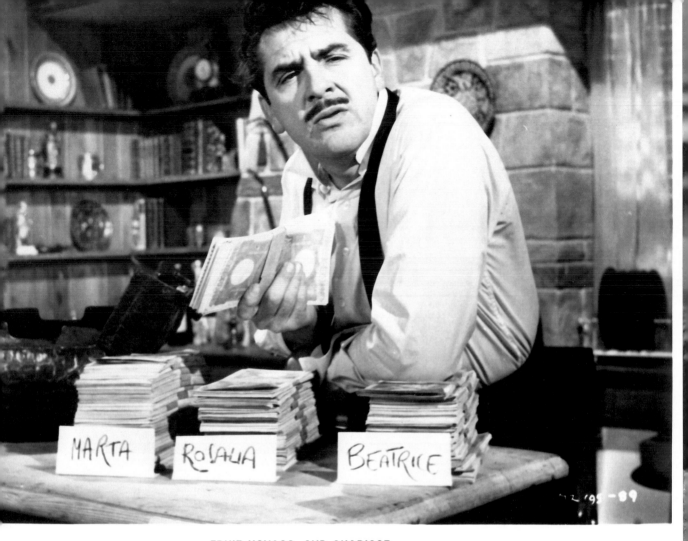

COLUMBIA PICTURES presents A MARIO ZAMPI Production. **ERNIE KOVACS, CYD CHARISSE**
and **GEORGE SANDERS** in **FIVE GOLDEN HOURS**, co-starring KAY HAMMOND, DENNIS PRICE

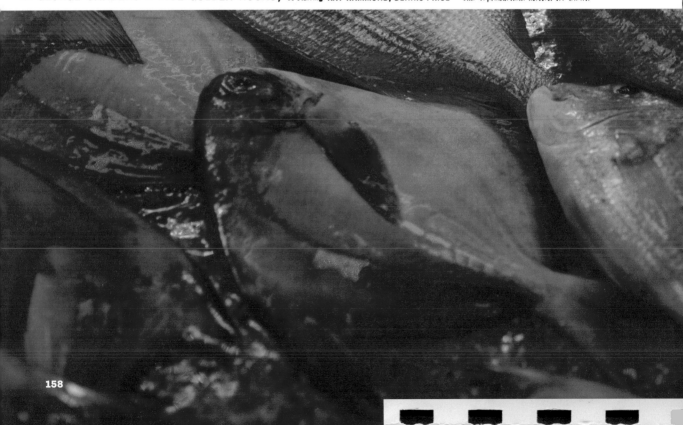

KOVACS
<u>HATES TV</u>

■ When a madman stands 6 ft. 2 in his stocking feet, and when he weighs in at 200 lbs., and when some fearless engineers give him a closetful of crazy electronics gadgets to fool with—the result can only be TV's mayhem-master, Ernie Kovacs.

While early a.m. viewers take pot-luck with Ernie (8:30-9:30 morning show is unrehearsed), on Tuesday Kovacs cuts up at night (8:00-9:00) in a carefully planned insane asylum. The hour is loaded with props (a recent show called for 65—including an axe, a

starring

ERNIE

KOVACS

THE
FUNNIEST
PICTURE
SINCE FUN WAS BORN!

Mervyn Leroy

tops his
"NO TIME FOR SERGEANTS"
and "MISTER ROBERTS"
with

Wake
Me
When
It's
Over

starring
ERNIE
KOVACS · MARGO MOORE · JACK WARDEN · NOBU McCARTHY · and introducing DICK SHAWN

THE FUNNIEST PEOPLE
IN THE WORLD ARE STILL
LAUGHING OVER IT! . . . .

BOB HOPE says:
"For anyone
who needs some
good laughs!"

JACK BENNY says:
"A new tranquilizer!
A real laugh pill!"

DINAH SHORE says:
"The liveliest
one yet!"

BING CROSBY says:
"Like sailing on a
laugh rocket!"

DANNY THOMAS says:
"A dream of a comedy!"

DEAN MARTIN says:
"A laugh riot!"

MERVYN LEROY's
PRODUCTION OF

Wake Me When It's Over

CINEMASCOPE
COLOR by DE LUXE

starring
ERNIE   MARGO   JACK   NOBU   and introducing
KOVACS   MOORE   WARDEN McCARTHY DICK SHAWN
SCREENPLAY BY
RICHARD BREEN

THE MOST RIOTOUS
GET-RICH-QUICK RASCALS ON RECORD!

ERNIE KOVACS · CYD CHARISSE · GEORGE SANDERS

"5 GOLDEN HOURS"

co-starring KAY HAMMOND · DENNIS PRICE

Original Story and Screenplay by HANS WILHELM
Produced and Directed by MARIO ZAMPI
Associate Producer, GIULIO ZAMPI

A MARIO ZAMPI PRODUCTION · A COLUMBIA PICTURES RELEASE

COLUMBIA PICTURES presents
JAMES STEWART
KIM NOVAK
BELL, BOOK, AND CANDLE

COLUMBIA PICTURES presents
JAMES STEWART
KIM NOVAK
BELL, BOOK, AND CANDLE
co-starring
JACK LEMMON
ERNIE KOVACS
HERMIONE GINGOLD · ELSA LANCHESTER · JANICE RULE
TECHNICOLOR   A PHOENIX PRODUCTION

JACK LEMMON

KOVACS

HERMIONE G

ELSA LANCHESTER

AVALON

KOVACS
E CAPTAIN

n

SHOW Tonight-Kovacs AIR DATE Jan 7-8   Date Pre-Show Estimate 1-3-5)
Date Post Show Estimate 1-10-5)

SHOW COST PD. January

Below the Line	Pre-Est.	Post Est.	By	Actual	Above the Line	Pre-Est.	Post Est.	By	Actual
300 Construction	22	—		—	302 Outside Rehearsal Hall	Ping Pong Exib. —			100.
300 Scenery	151	170		168	311 Talent	Toni ARDEN	pau. mc Water	L, Holmes	265.15 / 241.50 / 600.—
300 Painting	48	225		212	312 Temp. Staff	Barb. Pete Mayr.			772.94
300 Properties	747	1100.		1176	313 Writers		→		1225.
300 Draperies	9	50		37	314 Rights	→			—
300 Trucking	296	350		366	315 Prod/Direc.	→			1775.
300 Set Designing	400	380		375	316 Announcer	→			400.—
300 Costumes	448	680		629	317 Talent Pkg.	—	—		—
300 Costume Design.		125		110	318 Commission	—	—		
300 Graphic Arts	63	180		178	321 House Orch.	1500	1500		1460.—
300 Makeup	250	325		336	322 Outside Music/Musc.	—	—		—
Others (Specify)					325 Film Rentals	100	120		100.
Additions					368 Film Print Cost	—	—		
Deletions					326 Film Library	—	—		—
					320 323 D.B. Film Edit. Seasoning	—			13.
					399 Lines	—			
TOTAL Stg. Services	2434	3555		3581	349 WOR-Dbbing Cueing Devices Telepse	—			46.— / 120.
300 Wardrobe	90	180		180	346 Travel Entertainment	—			300.
300 Stagehands	1030	1980		1978	359 Miscellaneous Mimeo Projector	—			50. / 30.
300 Light. Equip.	45	125		100	609 Kine Record	—	—		
300 Spec. Effects	35	28		28	Deferred Writeoff	—	—		
300 Studio	1068	2125		2125	601 Recovery	—	—		—
300 Film Studio	170	170		170					
300 Piano AW Studio Tuning	24 / 5	24 / 5		24 / 5					
300 H.V. Wipes Reh. Hall (NBC) Monitors	85 / 51	85 / 51		85 / 51	TOTAL ABOVE THE LINE				7479.00
300 Basic Crew	1360	1360		1350	TOTAL BELOW THE LINE				10,795.00
300 Prior/Post	440	440		440	SHOW COST				18,795.00
300 FLR Wash Labs Calls Storage	10 / 51	10 / 51		10 / 51	SHOW BUDGET				17,935.—
300 Eng. Per. Outside Reh.	—	—		—	OVERAGE				539.00
300 Equipment	—	—		—	Vito Matta				
300 Sound Effects	190	190		180	Unit Manager				
300 Mobile Unit	—	—		—	NOTE: Please explain any sizeable variances between Estimate and Actual.				
300 AD/FM	450	450		440					
TOTAL PROD. FACILITIES	7533.	10,826		10,795					
SET AMORTIZATION									

BILLING ABSTRACT
DESIGN, ART & SCENIC PRODUCTION

| | ROUGH GUIDE | 1 | | 2 | | 3 | | 4 | | FIRM QUOTE | 1 | | 2 | | 3 | |

DESIGNER ☐ FREE LANCE ☐ STAFF	PHONE	PROGRAM TITLE
BROWN		TONIGHT ** KOVACS
UNIT MANAGER	PHONE	AIR TIME	AIR DATE
MATTI		FROM ___ TO ___	10/29-30
☐ COLOR ☐ B & W ☒ PROGRAM ☐ COMMCL		STUDIO LOCATION Hudson	

		SECTION	Mon 10/29 BUDGET	Tues 10/30 ROUGHGUIDE	TOTAL ACTUAL CHARGES	4 GREEN SLIP ADJUSTMENTS	5 TOTAL SERVICES	6 NET CHARGES
1	402	SET DESIGN GREEN SLIP NO.						
2	405	GRAPHIC ARTS GREEN SLIP NO.	28	✕	90			
3	403	COSTUME DESIGN GREEN SLIP NO.		81	944			
4	404	MAKE-UP GREEN SLIP NO.			120			
5	352	CONSTRUCTION GREEN SLIP NO.	42	63	105			
6	393	SCENIC ART GREEN SLIP NO.	221	151	572			
7		NBC STOCK SCENERY GREEN SLIP NO.	52	106	158			
8	394	PROPERTIES GREEN SLIP NO.	423	331	754			
9	395	DRAPERIES GREEN SLIP NO.						
10	396	TRUCKING GREEN SLIP NO.	✕	✕	✕			
11								
12		TOTALS	1433	1348	2781			

FIRM QUOTE	400
ROUGH GUIDE	2381

GRAND TOTAL

NOTES: COLUMN 2 ABOVE CAN BE: (A) USED AS A ROUGH GUIDE (B) A FIRM QUOTE (C) A COMBINATION OF BOTH FOR EACH SECTION. IF USED AS ROUGH GUIDE OR FIRM QUOTE APPLICABLE BOX TO BE CHECKED, INDICATING THE SHOW OR COMMERCIAL UNIT'S REQUEST. A ROUGH GUIDE WILL BE GIVEN AT ANY TIME UPON INFORMATION AVAILABLE. TO OBTAIN A FIRM QUOTE, ALL INFORMATION MUST BE AVAILABLE AT TIME OF MEETING SO THAT UPON COMPLETION OF MEETING ALL INFORMATION MAY BE FORWARDED BY ESTIMATING SECTION TO PROPER SUPERVISORS FOR EXECUTION. IF ALL INFORMATION NOT AVAILABLE TO SATISFACTION OF ESTIMATORS, ROUGH AND FIRM QUOTE (COL. 2) WILL BE MARKED OUT AND WE WILL FIRM QUOTE ONLY PORTION COMPLETED AND SUBMIT ROUGH FIGURE FOR UNCOMPLETED PORTION. IN THIS EVENT (F.Q.) WILL REPRESENT FIRM QUOTE AND (R) WILL REPRESENT ROUGH FIGURE AS A GUIDE. THESE TWO SYMBOLS (F.Q. OR R) WILL BE SHOWN DIRECTLY AFTER SECTION TITLES TO INDICATE THE CLASSIFICATION FOR DOLLAR AMOUNTS GIVEN.

THE TOTAL FIRM QUOTED FIGURE AT BOTTOM OF COLUMN 2 IS ACCEPTED BY _____

THE TOTAL ROUGH GUIDE FIGURE AT BOTTOM OF COLUMN 2 IS TO BE CONSIDERED ONLY A ROUGH GUIDE AND MAY VARY.

UNIT MANAGER	PHONE	ABOVE CLEARLY UNDERSTOOD AND ACCEPTED BY

OPER-329 7/56

AGENCY

38

Thursday - June 1st

Mr. Kovacs:

If you have the time, please sign those forms I left for you in your
mail folder yesterday. I think they should be returned to Mr. Gadbois
as soon as possible.

Also, I would appreciate it very much if you would sign that check tonight
for the Art Studio Picture Framing. When I went to pick xxxxx your picture
up this morning I was very embarrased to discover that I didn't have enough
cash with me...but the man there was nice enough to let me take the picture
anyway so I'd like to put his check in the mail tomorrow.

Also, to impose on you again, please sign the check payable to you from
the Security Nat'l Bank, in the amount of $5,687.30. This is the money
that is being transfered xxxxx from the Security Bank to the Union Bank.
Mr. Gadbois is closing your account with Security and they could use this
money in your Union account.

Because they are closing your Security bank account I xxx am sending those 3
checks that they made payable to the Beverly Wilshire Hotel (barber shop)
for $15.00 each - back to Gadbois-and in turn he will send you three new
checks from the Union account made payable to the same people for the same
amounts.

pls write to recording company for any others

The only Vardi _of_ string sextet album I could get for you is entitled
"Sutton Place South," which Leonard is picking up tomorrow from the Record
store.

The card game Sunday is at the Beverly Hills Hotel -- 6:00 p.m. --
Bungalow 8. Mr. Blauner said he would be there; Mr. Mikolas said he
will let me know tomorrow.

— _Tell Joe Mikolas_

The editing of the show is set at 10:00 a.m. this Sunday at the Studio.

The deposition has been changed to 9:30 a.m., July 1st.

Dick Rush called -- OL 6-0357. He xx said he's a director and wants to
talk to you regarding a property.

Freddie called from LaRue's and said they have your favorite dish tonight.

Billy Belasco's office number is CR 1-8101; his home number is CR 5-8891.
But if you ever want to reach him at night and he's not at home, you can
call his office, as they have a 24-hour answering service, and they will
usually know where to reach him. (He'll be at the Coconut Grove tonight).

Would it be alright if I got Betty's class picture framed?

Don't forget to call your father back.

Dear Mr. Stein...

Thank you for sending me the proposed profile for Redbook.

While I think Mr. Robbins has done an excellent literary-wise job, I do feel it in the best mutual interests of your publication and myself that some changes in chronology and fact be made. I some instances, the inaccuracy I would correct is one that actually would be known to the general public.

Page two: Item one (see encircled): This statement has been attributed to this poor doctor in two or three press releases. It has never been made in the serious light in which it seems to be at this moment. Your readers, I am sure, would feel this was not quite honest and I think the article's veracity would suffer by it.

Page three: Item 1: While it is true that one of the promoters of the show disappeared with the funds, I think it is safer on the part of your magazine to allege this. This boy may be down and out some place and looking for suit. I also suggest you do not designate the method of transporation used and the city. The sum is innacurate. The sum was a few thousand dollars (approximately four or five). My salaray was to be a hundred or a hundred and a quarter. I went ahead and finished the play as the tickets had been sold and there was nothing to do. The fact that the sum goes into the thousand mark makes it even more necessary for you to take precautions as (although I do not know law) we seem to be going from misdemeanor to felony.

Page three: Item 2! The retail billing for my cigars is approximately $13,000 a year.

Page Four: This implies something which is quite the extreme of what is really true/ That is/ to say, this , according to the two of us, is not quite right. There is one strong difference. While I am inclined to do things impulsively (leave for Havana with Edie and the kids on a five minute notice--or write a book on impulse, etc), Edie is (or was) more inclined to plan things. Otherwise, we have the same tastes in food, music, friends, morals, ideals, furniture, art, etc. It is so close an alliance, we have a strong ESP between us that works day and night.

Page four: Items 2,3,4 and 5...The neighborhood had an occasional violence but was not depressed nor was it ugly. It would be unfair to the neighbors whom I knew and the people who live there now to say that it was ugly and depressed. I had quite a lot of fun there as a matter of fact. Dad was not"nagged"by my mother who is also still living. Their relationship had the storm which accompanies most marriages of two volatile personalities who have the happy supplement of another language to add to their discussions for"color"/ My parents had their stormy times but many, many happy times. As a child I remember many happy parties in our home. My brother didn"t fade out of the argumentative scene.

Page five:Item 1: I once wore a Lord Fauntleroy and had natural curly
hair at the time. I feel the line makes my mother look somewhat like
an idiot. I never said I "stayed inside and read--and ate"...I read
a great deal. ⬛⬛⬛⬛⬛⬛⬛⬛⬛⬛⬛⬛⬛⬛⬛⬛⬛⬛⬛⬛⬛⬛⬛⬛⬛⬛⬛⬛⬛⬛⬛⬛⬛⬛
⬛⬛⬛⬛⬛⬛⬛ But I read after the day was over-- a normal one of baseball,
football and blackjack.(this in refernce to itwm two) I am afraid
I am misquoted too when I say I"just couldn't stop eating". Actually,
I put on on the blubber when I was older and in another neighborhood.
Item three: "I wanted to die" is not quite true. As I said in the interview,
I learned that something that day. The tracher had followed the comparitive
example with, "All fat boys are jolly" as I was xi laughing. What I learned
then was that even adults could be unintentionally cruel as children
might be purposefully or unintentionally.

Item four: Although this is of small consequence, I keep under
215.

Item five is embarrassing to me as this has been quoted many
times to many others. As an alleged comedian, I would have to be a
little more original than this.

Page six: Item one: While I know this makes good reading, it isn'T
quote true. Mother and Dad had an interior decorator make custom
furniture and do a complete job on the home before we moved in.

Page six: Item two: Again, to be adcurate and also to maintain
a standard. It wasn't a comic monologue. We had been asked to write
a sequel to The Last of The Mohicans. I wrote a seqqel satirizing
the style of writing of that period and put the story into mddern dress
and vernacular.

Page seven: Item one: Her name was Jaqueline Friebelman.

Item: Two: I spent but one year in private school. I
was in the public school while dad still had money. He did go bankrupt
when I was sixteen. The private school did not give me prestige. I
never told the children at school I had been there. I felt that it
might work the other way. By the time I was sixteen, I was completely
slimmed back from tennis and football.(Item two) My mother may have
said "My own son, a King". BUt I didn't hear it and if she did, I hope
no one else did, either.

Item three: I received seven scholarships in all.
Harold Van Kirk is the person most repponsible for my being in the
business today. I didn't have savings for the dramatic school. I was
there, too, on scholarship. I had also a box of Nestle instant chocolate
packages. I think it might be of some interest that both parents always
came regularly and always looked cheerful as though things were just great.
Neither had any money and my mothet used to borrow busfare to see me but
she would always look neat and affluent when she came in. So would dad.
Later in Jersey, my mother hitch-hiked to visit me. My father drove out
after working till eleven o'clock at night. He'd tap on my window and
I'd talk with him. (I was on the ground floor then)(naturally). (This
is in reference to page six, also) It is not true that I didn't believe
in formal religion. I had been raised a Catholic at that time and the
fam befor e going away , quite frequently went to church. But you really
learn to pray in a hospital.
Page nine " item one: Just for techincal reasons, this is still a fluoroscope
not an X-ray.

Item two: Pleurisy and pneumonia are not psychosomatic.
Item three: 18 months

page three

Page ten: Sorry, but to this day I have strong feelings about women paying
for things like this, Outside of that, it's true.
Psge 11: "Agreed" makes it seem as if I coaxed her. She volunteered frequently and I accepted.
        Item two; It wasn't a starved , emotional state. I had to eat it
as part of the program. The stuff was great, cooked in wine etc. The whole
crew got fat.
        Page welve item one: I had started my divorce. It wasn't final
at that point. It hadn't been litigated. I didn't feel that my personal
life had come to an end. I was thoroughly disillusioned about women
but I wasn't a basket case.
        Page thirteen: Item one: I ran like HELL. A year and a half (item two)
after I kz had been granted custody.

        Item three: Edie and I were working together
daily, rather than seeing each other. This is too much in the social
sense and not fair to Edith. The chornolpgy and fact on the abductuion
of the children is quite confused and equally confusing in trying to
striaghten it out. With the xception of the marriage, I would suggest
you eliminate beginning on page thirteen at the bottom, sentence beginning:
"A year and a half after Kovacs"---All references to the children. E cepting
to say, that one the second day when the four of us were living together,
the children asked if they could call Edie "Mother". It was actually on
the second day, not as the article has it. They ioldize Edie so much,
they actually wanted the school children to call them Edie and asked
us if we would call them Edie when the school children were around.Their
rleationship with Edie is one of the most beauti beautiful thihgs I've ever
seen.They would rather spend a day shopping with her than go to a birthday
party. Factually, it might be pointed out that I was awarded custody by
the court. Full and permanent, I believe is the phrasing although this is
a legal term again.
        Page fifteen: Supe-Clod...Cloudy Faire is done by my wife
as a takeoff on weather girls. It is "Leena," queen of the Jungle.
The other is a lawsuit. Edie has done almost everything but a few lines
of dialogue on her Maf8lyn Monroe bit, herself.
        Page sixteen: this is a little prissy and will make a million and
a half parents who vacation alone angry with me.(item one)
        item two; Antique furniture is almost always secpnd hand
unless you get there pretty darned early, about two hundred to four hundred
years early.
        Page 17- (the books) Camille (a cough is heard), Digging the Panama
Canal (shovels and mosquitoes) and The Life of Thomas Edison,(photflood
inside book when it opened)...Other titles wrong.
        last dine has been attributed to me, but I never said it. It has
appeared a few times elsewhere.
If this is of any interest: since the article, I finished a motion picture
for Columbia with Jack Lemmon,xxx Kathy Grant and Arthur O'Connel...
It is "Operation Mad Ball" and will be out in August. My book ("Zoomar")
out in October. Am writing a screenplay of it and will direct the picture.
Have been offered four broadway shows to direct, two to star in. xxxxx Four
motion picture offers. Writing a stage adaptation of a best seller.
Writing a xxxxx musical spectacular for TV. Priducing a spec for TV
and writing an hour TV programof humorous documentary. Have offers for
Climax, PLayhouse 90, Kraft Theatre...Will probably do all three.
        If the faiixming changes I have suggested can be made, I will
be most happy to set up with you for pictures.   Sincerely,

January 16, 1961

Dear Phil:

I suppose there is no being in any business, like
being in show business. The $8,000 lawyer's fee for
Mr. Nymel's little job, and now Mr. Bender's refusal
to turn over the papers until those fees are paid.

Because I have refused to be dishonest, it seems that
I'm being penalized severely. To put it charitably,
I think I could safely say that my faith in my fellow
man has diminished considerably.

However, there is one bright side; having signed those
papers for Mr. Nymel under what would be, I guess, the
legal term of duress, it would certainly seem that the
future would not be that bleak. Added to this, is the
fact that I'm not entirely made of putty. It would be
most foolish on anyone's part to believe, even for a
moment, that Mr. Nymel has been successful in what he
thinks has been his revenge.

After Mr. Rosenfeld told me of Mr. Bender's disposition,
I was rather more than convinced of what must obviously
be done.

Best regards, and good luck,

Ernie Kovacs

EK/vc:cc

180

Hors D'Oeuvres

Shrimps LA RUE	2.50	Crepes Farcies, Colony	2.50
Prosciutto Melon	2.50	Terrine de Foie Gras Truffé	4.00
Smoked Salmon	2.75	Blue Points, Cherrystone	2.75
Escargots	2.75	Chicken Livers Maison	2.25
Lobster	2.25	Crab Meat	2.25

Cracked Crab	2.75
Coupe aux Fruits	1.75
Marinated Herrings	2.00
Shrimps	2.25
Caviar	

Potages

Soupe du jour	1.00	Consommé Double au Sherry	1.25	Soupe a l'Oignon Gratinée	1.25
Petite Marmite Henry IV	1.50	Green Turtle au Xérès	1.50	Boula Boula LA RUE	1.50
FROID: Vichyssoise	1.25	Madrilene en Gelée	1.25	Waterbury	1.25

Poissons

Dover Sole Grillée a l'Anglaise	5.00	Deviled Crab Meat, New Orleans Style	4.75
Lobster Tails Grillée au Beurre Foundu	5.50	Filets of Trout, Caprice du Chef	5.00
Filets of Boston Sole Belle Meuniere	4.75	Lake Superior White Fish	5.25
Sea Food Newburg	5.00	Shrimps a l'Indienne	5.00

Grillades

New York Steak	7.00	Filet Mignon	6.75	Minute Steak	6.75
French Minute	6.75	Royal Squab	5.00	Squab Chicken	4.50
Lamb Chops	5.25	Chicken, Cressoniere	4.50	Lamb Kidney	4.50
Calf's Liver	4.75	Cotes de Porc	4.50	Sauce Bearnaise	.60

Rotis

Faisan	Reine		Grain	Poussin	Canard
Carre d'Agneau		Pigeon	Selle d'Agneau	Rock Cornish Game Hen	

Legumes

Fresh Asparagus	1.50	Stewed Tomato	1.25	Hearts of Celery, Madere	1.75
Petits Pois Francaise	1.25	Fresh String Beans	1.25	Braised French Endives	2.00
Broccoli	1.25	Spinach en Branche	1.25	Hearts of Palm	2.00
Spinach a la Creme	1.25	Zucchini	1.50	Sauce Hollandaise	.50

POTATOES: Mousseline 1.00   Baked .90   Frites 1.00   Sautées 1.00   au Gratin 1.25

Salades PER PERSON

Romaine	1.25	Verte Melangée	1.25	Italienne	1.50
Boston Lettuce Maison	1.50	Caesar Salad	1.75	Hearts of Palm	2.00
Endives Belge	1.75	Tomato	1.25	Imported Roquefort Dressing	.60

Entrémets

Mousse au Chocolat	1.25	Zabaglione	1.75	Cheese Cake	1.25
Meringue Glacée	1.25	Dobos	1.25	Almond Cake	1.25
Crepes Suzette	2.75	Pear Hélene	1.50	Ananas	1.75
Coupe aux Marrons	1.50	Cherries Jubilées	2.25	Strawberries Flambées	2.50

ICE CREAM: Vanilla   Chocolat   Moka 1.00   SHERBET: Lemon   Pineapple   Raspberry 1.00

Coffee .50   Tea .50   Sanka .50   Postum .50   Espresso .75   Iced Tea .60   B & B .25

Four percent (4%) sales tax will be added to the above prices of all food and beverage items served at the tables in this room

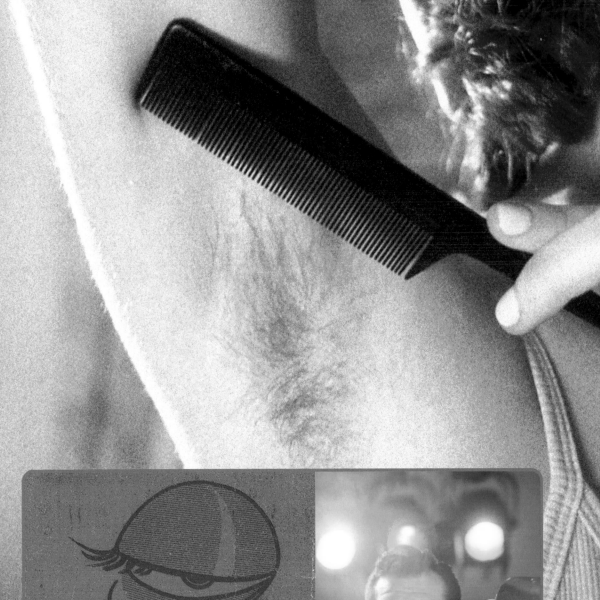

THE EARLY EYEBALL FRATERNAL AND MARCHING SOCIETY

EEFMS

1. My alarm goes off before the neighborhood rooster starts his warm-up.
2. I have an aunt named Albert.
3. I will never raise seahorses or kohlrabi for profit without permission of the president.
4. I have at least one uncle who habitually smokes a hookah.
5. My father can lick your father.
6. When in kindergarten in my youth, I received a straight "A" in "Sandpile."

(JANITOR) WCBS-TV   (MEMBER)

IF MARS INVADES, WILL OUR FIRST LINE OF DEFENSE BE NAIROBI?

EDITOR'S NOTE: Footnotes were graciously added by Ernie Kovacs after this article was written.

If you dial a certain number in North Hollywood and a woman's voice answers, "Eek," she is not calling for help. It would only be the switchboard operator at Eek Productions[1] whose whimsical name was concocted when Edie and Ernie Kovacs combined their initials when starting their own company.

Eek Productions is the focal point for the careers of two talented people: forty-two-year old Ernie Kovacs, a handsome Hungarian who spends a lot of time behind a well-trimmed[2] mustache and a big cigar and his wife, Edie Adams, who gives her birth date as April 16 and is a bright, hazel-eyed, 112-pound blonde. And so tightly scheduled are those careers it must have taken microsecond timing to get them together to sign the incorporation papers. Edie arrives home late from theatrical engagements, while Ernie, who often has an early call to a studio, has to be up and about at 5 a.m.

Once the couple arrived separately at a Bel Air charity party. The socialite hostess, who must not have been a regular television viewer, saw Ernie look up as Edie entered.

"You look interested," the hostess said. "I'll find out who she is and introduce you."

---

[1] Actually it's E. & E.K., although popular usage is making it Eek productions. It really became E. & E.K. without deliberately making it Eek because I wanted to get the corporation in a hurry one weekend and wanted to get away from Excalibur or Sloppy Enterprises, etc. Anyway, I do have a music publishing corporation which to date has published nothing. It's called Cherrystones (for clinkers or clams).—E. K.

[2] It is really impossible to have a well-trimmed mustache in a house with a wife, three daughters, and a sly cat, all of whom steal little scissors I keep buying. I shave in the steam room and try to trim it as best as possible with a razor, and some mornings when the steam is a little too heavy on the mirror it comes out pretty bad.—E. K.

THE ANNOTATED KOVACS

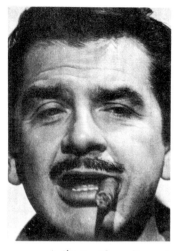

"Please do," Ernie said. "I think I may be married to her." Despite their differing schedules Edie, who is occasionally[3] away on singing assignments, tries to fly home to be with the family at their customary foregathering hour of 6 p.m., returning the same night to the city where she is appearing. The family consists of Edie, Ernie and three daughters, Mia Susan, twenty months, Kipp, eleven years old, and Betty, thirteen. On one occasion when Mia Susan was running a temperature, Edie flew in to check it herself, found it had subsided while she was en route, then flew back to New York. She had been home for all of twenty minutes.

Their home is a mansion in Beverly Hills. Built apart from the main house is Ernie's huge den, which would, if it were not so well organized, look like a film studio prop room. It contains, for instance, a priceless collection of guns[4] on which Kovacs is an authority, and a collection of rare first editions, on which Kovacs is also an authority. There are pieces of art, such as the brass leopard from India, on which Kovacs admits to being merely an expert. This rating of "authority" or "expert" is genuine.[5] When you check with those who know him, you find that out.

This somewhat contradicts his raucous television personality, and it should, because what appears on the screen is entirely the creation of a talented actor. In person, Kovacs is a tall man (six feet, two inches)

weighing 185 pounds with cigars . . . which he is never without. He has a healthy, pink complexion that the orthicon tube fails to transmit, and an exceptionally resonant voice which loses tonal qualities filtered through a mike. He's a man with great enthusiasm for whatever he is doing at the moment.

The Kovacs charm, complemented by Edie's, has broken down such well-known Hollywood barriers to the good life as back-stabbing, the caste and status system, and Hollywood clannishness *vis a vis* "foreigners" who have made their mark on the East coast. The Kovacses (the odd-sounding, but correct, plural of Kovacs)[6] conquered these problems simply by being the Kovacses. Socially, people found them completely informal and spontaneous.

Edie, for instance, is a graduate of Juillard School of Music, but is equally pleased with being an alumna of the Broadway hit *Li'l Abner*. She is also proud of her talent for mimicry.

At one party, Kovacs was entertaining with a monologue (he has a bottomless well[7] of stories that he tells with gusto) when Edie began imitating him. He caught sight of her in a mirror and immediately began an imitation of Edie's imitation of him. It was a moot point for a while which would break up first, but Edie eventually did. Ernie always breaks Edie up; for example she still howls at repeats of the "Nairobi Trio," an act that has become a comedy classic and which once

---

[3]Very occasionally these days. Less occasionally in the future, too.—E. K.

[4]Western guns as well as matchlocks, wheel-locks, flintlocks, dating back a few hundred years, from all countries.—E. K.

[5]You said it; I didn't.—E. K.

---

[6]For some reason most people spell it with an apostrophe, "Kovac's." Even T.V. networks have done it, for many years on various networks. They always say "The Ernie Kovac's Show" on scenery. At CBS I used to pick out the apostrophe on the directory on the wall near the elevators; on Monday it was always back.—E. K.

[7]I'm glad you mentioned "well" in connection with my parties. I need the water because I drink twice as much as anyone else. That's the only performance I was aware of giving. A T.V. camera brings out the ham in me. But I didn't realize that I told *that* many stories.—E. K.

caused the Pentagon quite a bit of concern.

Seems that a multi-starred general from Vandenberg Air Force Base was addressing the Hollywood Chamber of Commerce when a questioner demanded to know how he would go about winning a war with Russia.

His answer: "Why I'd have our propaganda people release films that Kovacs fellow does on the martini-drinking poet. I'd bill him as the typical American. Give 'em over-confidence."

Then, when asked, "What'd you do if there was an invasion from Mars?" the general was moved by the laugh he got on the first question to try the Kovacs gambit again.

"I'd use the same tactics. Let 'em get a look at the 'Nairobi Trio' that this same Kovacs does. They'd either laugh themselves to death or get the hell back from where they came from."

This got a laugh too, but a public relations captain noticed reporters making frenzied use of their pencils. He telephone-relayed his worries to Washington. In seconds the word made like an astronaut, going way-high up and then coming back down.

The captain whispered to the general, and the general, looking sheepish, rose and said, "Those remarks I made about that Kovacs fellow might give the wrong impression and I must ask the press to consider them off the record. What I really meant to say was . . . well, when you ask a silly question, you get a silly answer."

Letters of apology are still probably going out to the prominent Hollywoodian who asked the "silly question." The p. r. captain nearly dissolved on the spot in his embarrassment.

So much for the havoc Kovacs can cause at a distance. As for the havoc created around him by his Hollywood barrier-breaking, this has earned him surprisingly little enmity. On any production lot the star of the show usually has detractors; some have a great many. If not, one is led to suspect the existence of a press agent who knows where bodies are buried and perhaps has interred

a few himself. But not even grips will gripe about Kovacs, and it's a real challenge to find at least one person whose opinion about him is negative.

There are, of course, denizens of Hollywood whose taste is so conditioned by the endless stream of lowest-common-denominator movie and T.V. productions they've worked on that they admit to finding Ernie's humor "real curious," and hold that he "comes up with some real wild curves" (like smoking a cigar under water). But not even these simple folk have anything to say against the man or his wife.

Kovacs has come a long way from the days when he was a radio announcer in Trenton, New Jersey, a part time entertainer, part time drugstore clerk who had to put up with being introduced occasionally as "Mrs. Adams" at the time Edie's rocket was rising faster than his. Meeting him now, one realizes that here is a payload of talent that—giving off surprising sparks like his lusty novel *Zoomar* as it goes up—has yet to reach the top of its trajectory. With Edie orbiting close by, with Eek Productions a sort of second stage, one cannot predict where Ernie will eventually land. One can only, with awe and anticipation, watch him go.[8]

_____

[8]Who? Me?—E. K.

Kovacs Cult May Be in Making

Talkathon in 5th Day

Trenton, N. J., Sept. 29—(INS) —Ernest Kovacs is bent on becoming the talking-est man in the world.

The 29-year-old Trenton radio man today began his fifth consecutive day of sleepless, bathless, and weight-losing broadcasting at the New Jersey state fair.

Kovacs, who shed ten pounds since he began his talkathon last Sunday, hopes to stay awake until the fair closes Sunday. His routine includes an all-night disc jockey session, half-hour comments on the news and interviews with the visitors.

DISCUSSING PLOT AND ACTION. M— of the play, "Backstage Mystery," to be present Players, are shown talking over details of prepare for the date of their footlight app

LAZY D

And
Summ
relaxe
with
music.
on WT
to di
air-conditioned features every day

6-7
A. M.
"CHUCK WAGON
Fred-the-Fiddler wa
music of the hills a

7-8
A. M.
"???????" Ernie K
to think up a name
'n'-shine show, so
for the best suggesti
for full details.

1-2
P.M.
"NAME IT AND P
A brand new idea in
Hopkins interviews
around town and le
their favorite tunes.

WTT

'PFLAP!'

xclaimed Henry, * our 15 month old on. TRANSLATION: "I think CHICK-NFOOT JUNCTION, broadcast daily rom 7 to 8 A. M. is a delightful program. rnest Kovacs is the master of ceremonies and he's very droll. Get the habit of istening regularly for music, weather eports, time signals and jokes. It's worth getting up to hear."

W M

920

March 17, in the educational auditorium of the Prospect Street Presbyterian Church. Left to right are Eleanor Morton, Betty Ivins, Verda Cole, Ed Sutterly, William Tallon, Kermit Clegg, Ernie Kovacs, Cecil Fell, Betty Yates, and centre, back to camera, A. Jay Hudnut.

? Photo
cast
pect
they
sday,

Ernest Kovacs, 1104½ Parkway Avenue, winner of a Summer scholarship to the Easthampton School of Acting, Long Island, reportedly "brought down the house" with a skit he presented recently at a stunt night performance of the students. Kovacs portrayed a "Jersey Family and a Tramp."

Harold Van Kirk, teacher o drama at Trenton High School is a director of the Easthampton School.

here.
ds for
ening
at on
e beat
a note
these
. . . . . .

p with
as.

o lazy
w rise-
g $15.
VTTM

s, Wes
ans all
nounce

W   20   Your Dial

<u>"TAKE A GOOD LOOK"</u>

starring

ERNIE KOVACS

Jack Tester

Pre-Tape: October 11, 1959 - 8:00 P. M.
ABC - TV Center - 4151 Prospect, Hlyd.28

Studio "E"

Release Date: October 22, 1959

<u>Panel</u>:

       Janet Leigh

       Cesar Romero

       Hans Conried

<u>Producer</u>: Joe Landis

<u>Director</u>: Barry Shear

<u>Continuity</u>:Rex Lardner
           Jerry Payne

AN IMPA PRODUCTION
IRVING MANSFIELD-PETER ARNELL

jt

ANNCR:

(OFF - AS TEASER CLUE IS PRESENTED)

What you're watching is a clue to
the identity of one of our guests,
for you at home and the panel to
identify.

MUSIC: ("CHARLESTON" E.T.) (15 SECS.)	TWO CHARLESTON DANCERS IN OUTFITS OF MID-TWENTIES CHARLESTON ACROSS STAGE TO EXIT
SOUND: 1922-23 AUTO HORNS E.T.	DISSOLVE TO FILM OF 1922-23 AUTOMOBILES IN TRAFFIC
	DISSOLVE TO ATTRACTIVE GIRL IN BATHING BEAUTY OUTFIT OF 1922-23 PRANCING ACROSS STAGE

(EXPLANATION: INDICATES THE
TWENTIES WHEN OUR GANG FILMS
WERE FIRST MADE)

ANNCR: (CONTD)
(AFTER CLUE HAS BEEN PRESENTED)

And here's our panel.

MUSIC: (THEME)(1:07)
(FILM SOUND TRACK ONLY)

ANNCR: (CONTD)

Take A Good Look ...	CU ROMERO'S MOUTH
	CU ROMERO'S EAR
	MS ROMERO AND SUPER NAME: "CESAR"
(APPLAUSE)	
	OVERHEAD SHOT OF JANET LEIGH
	EXTREME CU JANET'S LEFT EYE
	EXTREME CU OF HER MOUTH
	MED. CLOSE JANET & SUPER NAME: "JANET"
(APPLAUSE	
	OVERHEAD SHOT OF HANS CONRIED PROFILE OF HANS CONRIED MED. CLOSE CONRIED AND SUPER NAME: "HANS"
(APPLAUSE) (APPLAUSE)	THREE SHOT PANEL

(handwritten annotations): 2 he's word snuging her? 3 - Long 2 - Up cut Audio

.jt

Exterior door to club room -
door knot exchange

Eugene B't -
insert: when drop cymbals.
~~no~~ tiny tingle

— OTHER INSERTS —

Mechanical Pencils
Bell, Points
Fountain Pens
Running: Counting Beans
Piano
followed by symphony:
dough in tympani
cymbals - open doors in
autumn - customers
rush for food
people come out from
space movie - same
sound with shoes -
crowd scatters

has head with cymbal,
in water idly waving
in water, starts gesult;
waves, conne with Edge
+ action of violently
shaking it

next scene shows him
being ushered out of park,
shoes thrown after him,
pigeons flock over selves -
he chases them away with
cymbal crash — c.v.
screen man —

| Cymbal crash — | |
| leaves fall off trees | |

then in to going down street
to club —

she walks on sits again,
couple run out from behind
bushes - the tenor cymbal
is left on bench, as he
goes to pick up - some
cop - he shows ownership
by showing LEFT ON one
he has say right on other

194

also you to sound technician
again - c.u. w/ earphone.
you to movie camera - Edie
& guy in camera as take -
director "cut" - during cop
bit. He walks into lake
a little bit, gets out
shoes squeaky - sound
man c.u., takes off shoes,
drying bit, sits on bench,
I tell him to move,
less scene — cuts section, pop,
walk him sit down —
at dryer as shoes ——, scene
resumes — he decides to
sit bench - starts
to open bench box - c.u.
technician - closes box again
so stops him.
sits on seat
put Ⓔ on opposite side
of lake -

he holds bar across
glass - walks in letting
door goes with him (that
one, that is)

he leans it against regular
door - which someone pulls
open - ——— inside
Barrat figure, 2nd door
closes and walks
to revolving door, looks
at other door, walks
through revolving door
with hand out as
though pushing.

Ⓔ goes into park —
but cymbals on bench

cymbal sticks to
her sporfy - she stands
up to put pigeon -
sits down with big
cymbal crash - pigeons
fly — he cannot understand
no reaction from her -
sees her hearing aid wire
is broken — does take
realizing she did not hear. -

opens bench box - all
pigeons fly to him all
over him - he reaches
hand out, lifts her
by elbow, drops her,
pigeons fly away. ——

She gets up, walks away,
sits down away from him,
(he is pouring) all ducks
in park fly away)

Ⓔ looks about to see
who she is smiling at - realizes
it's him - smiles but -
people are crossing in
front of her -
assistant director sees
him heads for him -
he leaves. —
Bus goes past with basketball
team - ball falls out -
they tell her to throw -
he throws awkwardly
over shoulder - goes into
camel sign -
goes to men's club to eat
bench - as he crosses
explicit street
cleaning water wagon passes
he walks into it -

AN ELECTRONIC COMIC AND HIS TV TRICKS

Ernie Kovacs is funnyman with ideas in national drought of mirth

The cigar-chewer below sighting down an electronic hole he has bored through the head of his lady assistant is Ernie Kovacs (*see cover*), whom many critics see as the man most likely to rouse TV comedy out of its present unamusing rut. An inventive, uneven but frequently inspired entertainer, Kovacs has had no regular TV program of his own for a while but his guest appearances have been hilarious and his one full-length show was the funniest program of the season. His talents stand out all the more in the present crisis in comedy (*pp. 176-179*) which is cutting down both the audiences and appearances of such high-rating stars as Gleason, Caesar and Gobel. Kovacs uses the tools of television for his own comic ends. Taking advantage of the enormous flexibility of the TV camera, he puts together gags and situations so outrageous yet so skillfully done that his nonsense takes on its own logic. How he applies his comic philosophy is explained on these pages in a picture compendium of Kovacs.

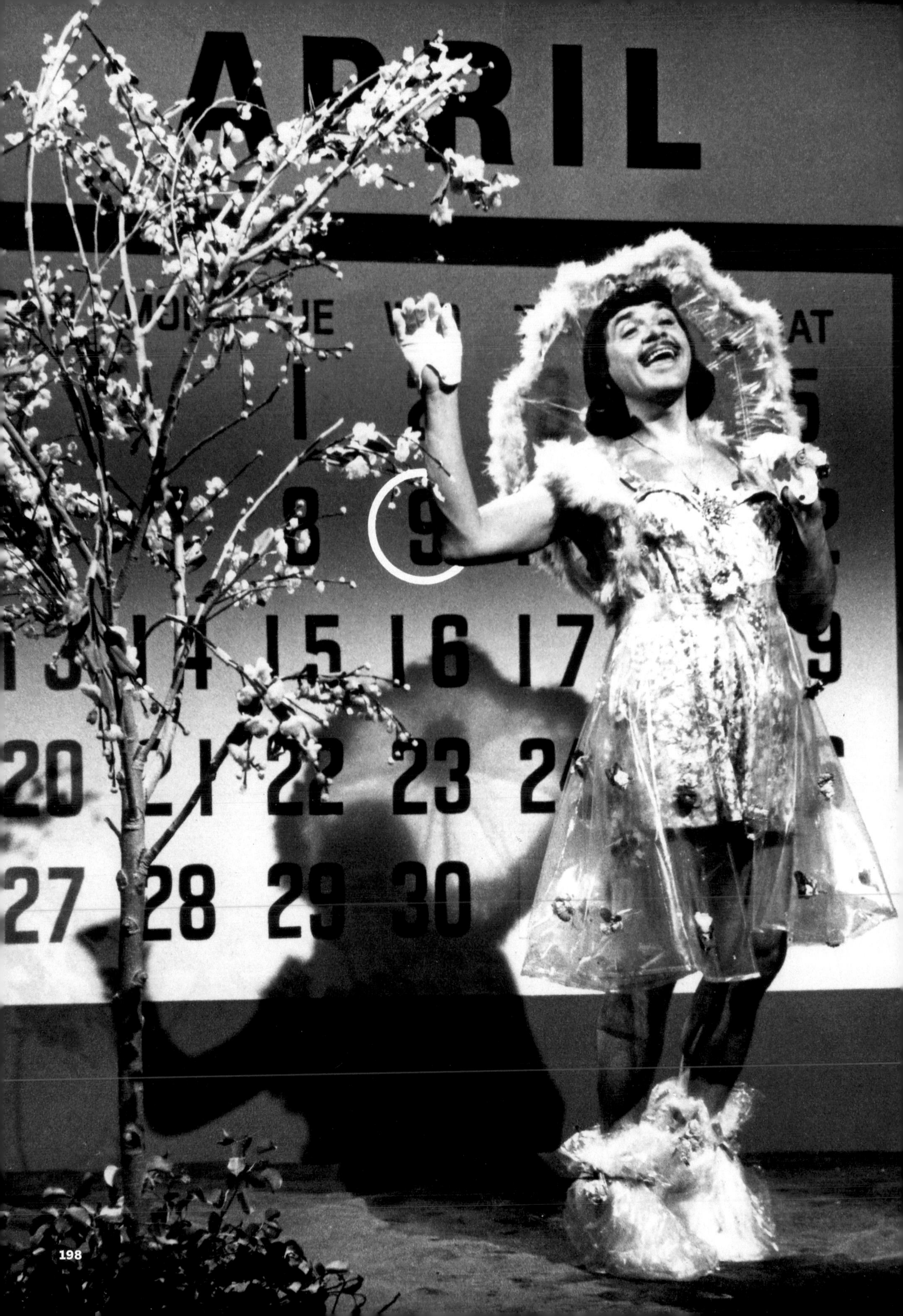
APRIL

1

Maggie rolled over on the warm, stale sheet like a slow loaf of uncooked bread.

~~The berry-sized drop of xxx~~ The berry-sized drop of perspiration re-began its

tired descent , hunching itself thinner to ride the narrow crease between the

rolls of ~~xxxxxxxxx~~ stomach fat , gaining speed on the damp places,losing on

the dry areas. It has been methodicallly ping-ponging its way from side to side

with each restless roll of Maggie's body. Maggie wasn't really that fat. She just

                                         placed
slept~~xxx~~ with her knees doubled up,/vertically it was the ~~xxxx~~ position of an amateur

diver.The man lay awake, his hands behind him ~~xxxxxx~~ each holding one of ~~xx~~ brass

runners of the ~~xxxx~~ head board watching a fly circling lazily until it laned

on her abdomen, its multi-prismed eyes seeing thousands of thighs, chins and~~xxx~~

                                         the
~~xxxxxx xxxxxx~~ breasts. It walked throuhg valley toward her chin and the man

thought of newsreels of mountain climbers. ~~Thenxx Itxxlxxrptlyxtxxnedx~~ It abrputly made

an L-turn and ~~xxxxx~~ walked up upon one breast. It was didiculous, the man thoughtm

                                    to the base of
that a fly would ~~xxxxxxxxx~~ know these things. It walked/~~xxxx~~ the nipple and the

man turned his face away, remembering other times, ~~thxxxxxxx~~ now unpleasant through

the distortion of ~~xxxxx~~ their relationship now.

. (net...raquets...balls)...Hanover was a town where "I can't tell

Pullman porters apart" was funny.

Mildred turned her/head, lifiting it a little
dark-rooted

to avoid the pressure of the/~~wire curler,~~ and her hopeless blue eyes

sent a shuffling gaze through the bedroom door, the dim, tired hall

and into the kitchen.Her lassitude was so profound, she had to look
her eyes would be on them   a

above things so that/~~xxxxxxxxxxxxxxxxxxxxx~~ after/~~the~~ drop in the

trajectory. In her terrycloth state of mind, Mildred fuzzily ~~xxx~~
free   from the insurance

passed the spot where the ~~xxxxxxxxxxxxxxxxx~~/calendar/~~xxxxxxxx~~
company hung with

the encircled date...that mystic yet mundane ~~xxx~~ eternal symbol of the

methodical female whose life consisted of twenty-eight day cycles...

her gender linked thusly with the fraternaltality of the B.P.O.E.

and their everlasting elks' teeth. The encricled date meant, in the

plodding patois of the universal kaffe-klatch, that she was due. Pausing

only briefly over the petty satisfaction that she could legitimately

put a halt to her husband's perfunctory fumbling for three days, she

turned back into the room and her focal point followed behind the
a

sweep of her gaze.~~xxxx~~ like/~~xxxxxxxx~~ recalcitrant caboose on a ~~xxx~~

slow curve.

Facing another day in Hanover was a third helping
a

of tapioca ~~in~~/plastic bowl. If there had been ~~x~~ even a Schrafft's

in Hanover, it would have come off like the Stork Club. In fact, it

was the devouted wish of the Wednesday night bridge group that, indeed,

~~xxxxxxx~~ Schrafft's ~~xxxxxxxxxxx~~ escutcheon of creamed spinach and

Helen Hokinson hostesses would grace Hanover.

Listlessly pressing down the corner of the 40% down

pillow, she looked through the window, a functional rectangle with

~~xxx~~ curtains from Montgomery Ward's. The window was an extension of

the ~~xxxxx~~ prosaic architecture of the house and through it, families

before, the same tree had been seen by other unseeing eyes...It was a window through which Wives of Cod Liver Oil employees might watch for their ~~homemanythex~~ piscatorially slippery mates.

The tree was a maple tree. It had always been there. ~~Amex~~ Among trees, it was one behind which even Joyce Kilmer might only relieve himself functionally.(Afterwards, thoughtfully rewording his line about only God making such a tree). It even lacked the distinction of blight. The tree had the/faithfulness of a girl with
unreciprocated
prominent upper teeth for the college football star. There are dogs like this who lay their heads in unresponsive laps and who are never petted. A tree which, or perhaps almost "who", would plod along on flat, sloppy roots if the residents moved to another house and would ~~nexxten~~ settle outside another similar window with the resigned patience of the
the dim, glimmering promise of
~~unxxixexxex~~ eternally constipated with/~~xxxxxxxx~~ Phillips Milk of
had been
Magnesia.~~xxxxxxxxxxxxxxx~~ If it/~~were~~ human, it would ~~park~~ have
~~its hairxin the mi~~ worn a part in the middle of its hair, voted against parking meters as being Communistic and have a sister who was a waitress at Howard Johnson's. On alighting in its branches, disconsolate woodpeckers closed their eyes and thought of happier times. Migrating starlings avoided its haven.

From this angle, Mildred couldn't see the lawn but it wasn't necessary. It was grass. As distilled water is/water/~~xxxx~~ by definition and boiled spinach is vegetable, this was grass. It was
here
a Saturday Evening Post cover and the boy who mowed/ it was/by ~~Norman~~
norman
Rockwell ~~Kent~~.Its function was to grow tall enough to be cut. It grew with a resolute lack of joy and its green was more chlorophyl than color.

Mildred closed her eyes and saw her house. It was done in wall-to-wall dull. A reading room for Mongoloids would have been/ carousel in comparison. Its indistructibility lay not in its construction but rather in motif. If there would be fire, the flames would not consume its flagrant,contemporaneous, face in the crowd. The flames would only superimose themselves palpably fraudulent as in a cheap movies disaster scene...The rugs were Bigelow losers...the kind of carpeting that factories sent out by separate exits with the trade name misspelled. The lamps were copies of those possessed by women who watched ~~daytin~~ television in the morning.

~~In this atmosphere of chenille from Sears Roebuck~~

It was possible only to compound this felony of living in Hanover in one way and that was to be there on Sunday. And Sunday it was and Mildred Henderson was suffocating.

(5)

(ITALICIZED INSERT BETWEEN CHAPTERS I AND II) (ALL ITALICS)

IT CONTRACTED SPASMODICALLY IN THE HOT, MOIST DARK. AND YET, THERE WAS NO DARK FOR TO KNOW THE DARK WAS TO KNOW THE LIGHT...TO KNOW HEAT WAS TO KNOW, TOO, COLD...MOISTURE, TO KNOW ARIDITY.

THERE IS NO UNBORN INFANT...THERE IS ONLY THE UNBORN UNBORN...UNTIL THE RUSH FROM THE WOMB, ONLY A SUSPENSION OF BEING...(THERE IS NO MUSICAL NOTE, THERE IS ONLY A COMPRESSION OF AIR WHICH ONLY ON ESCAPING FROM THE BELL OF THE HORN, BECOMES A NOTE)...

THE ONLY TANGIBLE IS NATIVITY...THERE IS NOTHING BEFORE IT AND ONLY ITS EXTENSION AFTER IT... THERE IS NO LIFE UNTIL BIRTH. LIFE BEFORE BIRTH IS A CONVENIENCE OF MEDICAL EXPRESSION. THERE CANNOT BE KNOWLEDGE WITH THE UNBORN...AND ANY PRE*NATAL INTUITIVISM IS ALL HYPOTHESIS, ALL APRIORITY.

THE UNBORN POSSESSES AN ORGAN BUT NOT THE GENDER... PARENTS BUT NOT MOTHER NOR FATHER.

THE MIRACLE OF BIRTH, PER SE, BEGAN ITS DEAPPRECIATION OF BIOLOGICAL AND METAPHYSICAL ASTONISHMENT WITH THE COMING OF ABEL, AFTER CAIN, THERE WAS "THE SECOND CHILD" SANS THE SNAKE*APPLE CATALYST...CAIN WAS BEGOT, ABEL WAS BORN...AND WHILE THE APPLE HAS NOT REMAINED SYNONOMOUS WITH INTERCOURSE, THERE MUST HAVE BEEN SUSPICIOUS MOMENTS WHEN A HALF*EATEN CORE WAS DISCOVERED.

BUT LEST, THROUGH THE SATURATION OF ITS OMNIPRESENCE, WE FORGET THAT IS IS A MIRACLE, IT IS PRESENTED EACH OF ITS MANY TIMES WITH THE AWESOME OVERTURE OF ITS PURGATORY OF SPASM, PAIN AND BLOOD. AND SO, TOO, ON JANUARY 13, 1916, WAS THE BIRTH OF MILDRED SZABO.

Mildred Henderson (née Szabo) lay suffocating and humming "Dardenella". Gray breath flowed sluggishly into her unreceptive lung cavities as the inexorable function of ooze fills the footprint of the swamp animal.

She had been breathing for forty-seven years as of that morning. Lifetimes are composed of breathing, as was Mildred's...The first slap-induced gasp at birth...the smothered breathing of suckling...the staccato intakes of roller-skating... the complete exhalations of love...the puppy-panting of death and our one, last sostenuto (so much like that of love that writers can say we die a little every time we do it).

Today was the breath of $30.95 Ladies' Elgin wristwatches...expansion bands...pot holders decorated with "Mammies"...Girl Scout cookies...serviettes with funny sayings on them...McKittrick patterns...Bon Ami...Betty Crocker prize-winning recipes....quilted housecoats...salt and pepper shakers in the shape of little owls with utile holes in the head (two extra for the salt or two less for the pepper, depending upon the point of view)....Mother's Oats, vaginal jelly, Johnson's Wax and Cokes in the Handy-Six-Pack. Mildred was suffocating in THE clitorisless, born-lived-died existence in Hanover, New Jersey.

Hanover was an inhabited cliche'. Its hackneyed residents filled each God's day with twenty-four hours of consistent platitude. Hanover was a bromide from its fat, cigar-chewing mayor through to the country club with its groping extra-curricular infideli- ties, the 50 X 20 swimming pool (with diving board, NO RUNNING sign and a gallon of chlorine added daily by the life guard whose name was Chuck and who was going to college in the fall), red clay tennis court,

OZALID PTS (4 TIMES)

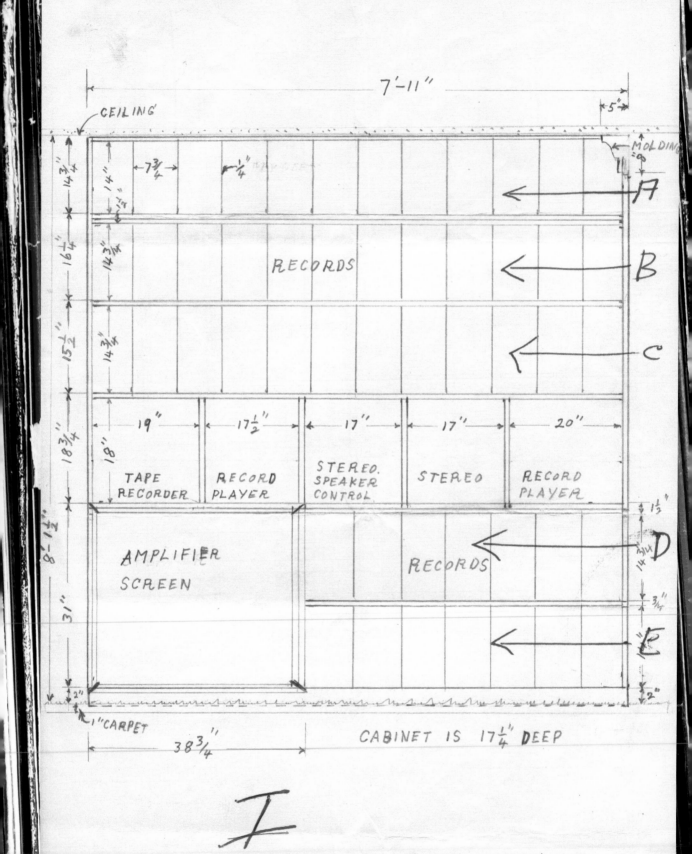

7'-11"

5"

CEILING

MOLDING

14 3/4"

7 3/4"

1 1/4"

14"

1 1/2"

A

16 1/4"

14 3/4"

RECORDS

B

15 1/2"

14 3/4"

C

18 3/4"

19"

17 1/2"

17"

17"

20"

18"

TAPE
RECORDER

RECORD
PLAYER

STEREO.
SPEAKER
CONTROL

STEREO

RECORD
PLAYER

8'-1 1/2"

1 1/2"

AMPLIFIER
SCREEN

RECORDS

3/4"

14"

D

31"

3/4"

E

2"

2"

1" CARPET

38 3/4"

CABINET IS 17 1/4" DEEP

I

Attached are two sheets of paper showing drawings of the record bin
collections. Please turn over sheet #2 to get the location of the two
new sections.

There is a flat rolodex that I want to use for the filing of the titles,
etc. We can get this from the Beverly Stationers. I would get a fairly
large one (this is not the round one but a flat one - that lies flat
and you turn the sections over). The filing system in the rolodex should
be done in sections: There should be a classical section, a classical
artist section and an operatic section, jazz section, pop vocals,
pop general, narrative, Relgious-Christmas, etc., but each one should
be under its own heading rather than a mass filing all together.
The classical music should be listed by composer. There should also
be an artist listing. Operas should be a separate section and listed
as they are in the bins by titles with the composer also but not as
a separate listing; that is, the composer is not cross-filed, just the
title of the opera. In this file the synthesis of the opera will also
be included. We will file the other stuff as we have mentioned in
classifications, also.

We will not have to file any of the pop stuff by title. On the card
if it is a Glen Miller album, underneath that, on the card, it should
have the nature of the album. On these things I would have to have
the title; for instance, on a June Christy album, I would like the titles
of the selections underneath that -- or Bing Crosby or Frank Sinatra.
It is not enough to have Swinging Session-Frank Sinatra. You'd have
to list the titles on the cards. But I do not need a cross-filing;
for instance, I don't have to have a card that says "Lonely Town" and
look it up by how many artists have done it. This would be nice to
have, but I think asking for a little too much.

Looking at Section #1, shelves A, B & C will be used for classical
music and the classical solo artists. In grouping the music of one
composer, going from left to right on the shelf (for instance, in
taking the music of Tchaikovsky) the six symphonies of Tchaikovsky
will be first. The next grouping will be ballets; then the Octets,
sextets, quartets, trios, duos and finally the soloists. In other
words, the heavest grouping of instrumentation begins at the left
and goes down. It will not be necessary to put anything underneath,
that is in the way of printed matter, except for Tchaikovsky, the
name. There will not have to be any listing underneath of instrumentation.

On Shelves D and E, beginning with the Operas and the condensed Operas
(the condensed version would be immediately adjacent to the full
version) and it will be listed alphabetically by titles. On shelf E
I think we can get the Broadway Shows, then the movies and, finally,
the Mood Music.

On drawing #2 we have that big shelf that goes across the two main
speakers in the room, labelled Section #F. In F I think we can get the
pop, the vocal groups and the jazz. Now, the pop will have the vocal
groups but not as a separate grouping but will be listed alphabetically
within the pop records. In other words, you might have a Glen Miller
album next to the Mills Bros. Jazz should be a separate section; it
will still be located on shelf F, but in its own grouping.

On Drawing #3, which is on the other side of drawing #2, we have shelves G and H. Shelf H hasn't been built yet but should be done by the time you're ready for it. On Shelf G, I think we can put our pop vocal solos and on shelf H, we can have the religious, the foreign, narrative and miscellaneous.

We'll use a temporary marking, such as I have at present, up there for Brahms and Beethoven. When we finally put everything in its proper position, then I'll get some permanent tags made.

I would suggest, as each section is completed, to take a string and stretch it all the way across that bin - across the center - so no one will take any records out until you have them in the rolodex. After you have them recorded in the rolodex it won't matter because then we'll have the positions and everything in the rolodex.

There are a lot of loose records, whose albums jackets will have to be found within the bins. Some of the maids have put the records in without putting them back in the bins. On these records, it would be most appreciated if they are wiped first, as they will probably be dusty before putting them in. Incidentally, there is one opera record in my record player, which is located in my study in the bottom right hand drawer -- the album cover for it and some other albums are in back of the television set in that room. There are also quite a few albums in my dressing room which all have to go into this plus a couple of scattered albums in Edie's dressing room downstairs. The albums that she has upstairs will not go into the main grouping because she wants to keep these with her.

I have laid these out with, in most cases, ample space. In putting the albums into the bins and listing them it will be wise to put them in as loosely as possible inasmuch as there is a steady pile of albums arriving periodically. For instance, I have an additional 100 classical albums coming from Angel Recordings this year, which is an addition to the regular Angel recording albums which I received. There are also quite a few from RCA that I am expecting this year and Columbia. Consequently they should be put in as loosely as possible. If someplace I have been wrong in these groupings, in that they do not fit into the section and it is necessary to move them, try to move the whole section, rather than spliting them from one side of the room to the other. In other words, all of the records of one kind should be in one section always.

This project is to be billed as follows: Billing for alphabetizing and cross-filing reference music for E. & E. K.

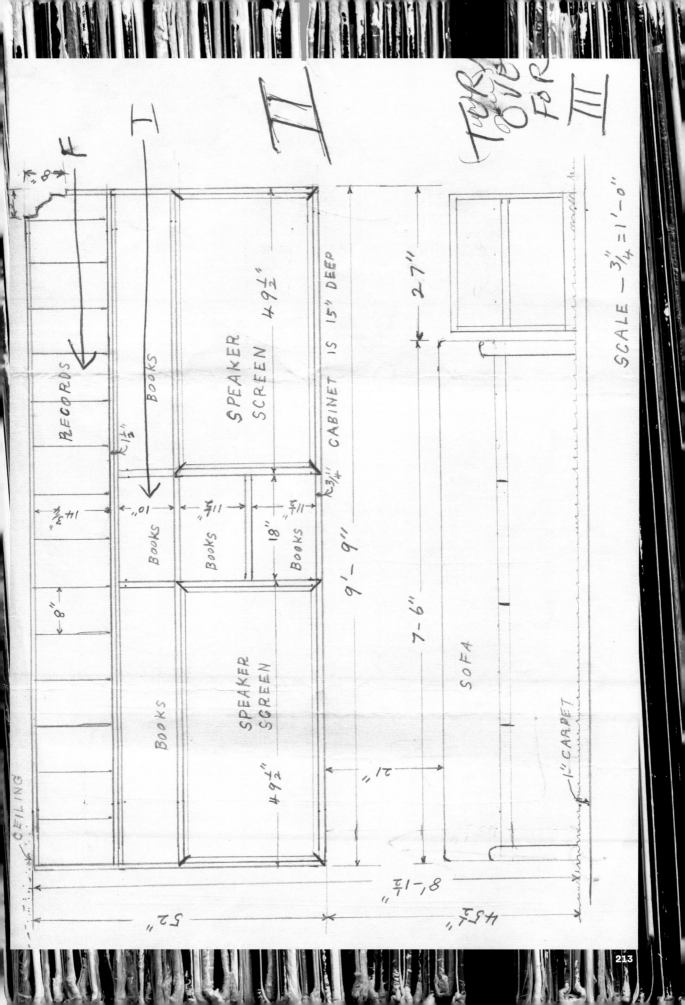

Kovacs Says Cigar Bill Tops $8,000

HOLLYWOOD (UPI) — Comedian Ernie Kovacs estimates his yearly cigar bill is somewhere between $8,760 and $13,140.

He smokes 12 and 18 cigars a day at $2 each. Kovacs believes this should qualify him as something as an expert on high class cigars.

"The cigar smoker," said the [?]-year-old performer, "is the kind of man who usually spends a little [?] time choosing his brandy or wine. He may not have as many [cigars] as other men, but he shops [more] carefully for them and enjoys them more."

Good Cigars for Enjoyment

Kovacs, who is currently appearing in the film "Bell, Book and Candle," added:

certain people that I prefer going out with, not because of their personal qualifications but because of their attitude toward cigars.

"For instance, Betty (Lauren) Bacall is the greatest about cigars. Billy Wilder and his wife are [?]

"I'm not talking about just any cigar smoker, like the guy the who grabs a cigar and sticks it in his mouth and chews on it. I mean the man who smokes a good cigar. The man who smokes good cigars wants a more solid, fuller enjoyment of life and gets more out of it." [?]

Sitting in the den of his Coldwater Canyon home, the comedian said that he smokes more at home than when he goes out.

"Socially," he said, "there are

others. David Niven's wife hates cigars, but she's real nice.

"Tony Curtis and Janet Leigh are very nice and polite. I've never found out, but I have the feeling that they air out the house when I leave. Frank Sinatra never says a word. He just lights incense when I start smoking, which ruins the cigar."

Kovac's wife, singer-comedienne Edie Adams, loves his cigars.

"In fact," he said, "she buys them for me."

It is Kovacs' belief that women who object to cigars usually have been exposed only to bad ones.

"It's like the women who sit down in restaurants and slip the silverware under the table to wipe it," he said. "You know they've been eating in beaneries. Women who complain about cigars before they smell them betray their own backgrounds."

Saturday, February 28, 1959

Cigar - Short Kovacs Rifles Letter to Castro

By JOE FINNIGAN

HOLLYWOOD (UPI) — Comedian Ernie Kovacs is having trouble getting his favorite Havana cigars, so he's written Cuban leader [Fidel] Castro a letter complaining about it.

"I hope he's got a sense of humor," the big funnyman says, "because I'm on my way to Cuba to make a picture."

A press agent sitting by cautioned Ernie, saying: "Don't let them book you into the Sports Palace down there" — referring to the arena where former Cuban Army officers were sentenced to be shot.

Ernie wrote a letter to Castro saying he wasn't satisfied with the cigar situation since the government changed.

"I didn't get an answer to the letter," he said, "but shortly afterwards I received a box of cigars with no return address and I haven't any idea who sent them.

Beard Conscious

And, speaking of Castro, Ernie is getting beard conscious these days.

In fact, he traveled cross-country to take a whiskers role on TV.

"I had this offer to do a Western for the Schlitz show and I had a chance to wear a beard. You know, I haven't worn one since 1936," the mustachioed Ernie said.

"But when I came out to the Coast from New York, they said I

SIZE - VITOLAS	Cigars per Box	Price per 100 Cigars
PARTAGAS		
Coronas Inmensas	25	$45.00*
Partagás de Partagás 1.........	25	37.00*
Coronas de Luxe	25	31.00*
Obsequios	25	29.00*
Fancy Tales	25	30.00*
Emboquillados No. 1	25	25.00*
Emboquillados No. 2	25	22.00*
Selección Extra	25	20.00*
Nacionales	25	22.00x
Club Coronas	25	21.00*
Coronas Extra Tubes	25	33.00
Coronas Senior Tubes	25	27.00
Coronas Junior Tubes	25	23.00
Petit Coronas	25	22.00*
RAMON ALLONES		
Coronas Inmensas	25	45.00*
Selección de Luxe No. 1.......	25	33.00*
Selección de Luxe No. 2.......	25	30.00*
Coronas	25	31.00*
Private Stock No. 1...........	25	30.00*
Obsequios	25	26.00*
Fancy Tales of Smoke	25	30.00*
Club Coronas	25	21.00*
Selección Extra	25	20.00*
Trumps	25	20.00x*
Real Perfectos	25	20.00*
Petit Coronas	25	22.00*
HOYO DE MONTERREY		
Monterreyes No. 1	25	37.00x
Monterreyes No. 2	25	31.00x
Coronas	25	31.00*
Cetros	25	35.00*
Coronas Grandes	25	34.00*
Super Hoyos	25	22.00x
Hoyos	50	18.00x
Empires	25	22.00*
Empires No. 2	25	19.00*

(*) Cellophane wrapped
(x) Only in English claro
(B.N.) Natural Wooden boxes

please note..

When ordering
brand name, size,

Duties: Every
exactly what yo

10% ad valore
plus $1.50 per
plus $2.00 per

To save you m
pack all our An
in Havana, send
to our brokers in
take the shipmen
by Railway Expr
all without red-ta
the value of your
invoice must be i
are $2.50 per inv

We can ship

Orders for 100
treatment as larg
cigars is paying
handling, freight,
fee for clearing 1
is $2.00, while c
whose value may
50 cents per 100

We send cigar
world. We will b
for friends, relativ
where—and the

We hope you
our appreciation
good will.

lease specify the exact
llophane wrappers, etc.

to pay them. Here is
pay:

of cigars.
weight of tobacco.
s internal revenue tax.

hipping your cigars, we
rders individually here
consolidated shipment
air-freight. They then
Customs and send them
to your home or office,
oblems for you. When
ver $500.00 a Consular
vith the shipment. Fees

parcel post also.

reive the same expedient
, but the buyer of 100
ore proportionately for
are the facts: Broker's
valued not over $25.00
r clearing 1,000 cigars
$500.00 are $5.00, or

st every country in the
handle your gift orders
usiness associates—any-
fully insured.

data useful and extend
ontinued friendship and

ES Y HERMANO.

LORES Y HERMAN

ESTABLISHED 1920

MANZANA DE GOMEZ
SALON -H-
HAVANA, CUBA

CABLES: LORESNO, HAVANA

PHONE: A-4352

FINE CIGARS

PRICE LIST
APRIL 1955

WE SHIP CIGARS TO MOST OF
THE COUNTRIES OF THE WORLD

PRICES ARE NET F. O. B. HAVANA
SUBJECT TO CHANGE WITHOUT NOTICE

THE KINSEY REPORT

or

BEHIND THE IRON KOVACS

or

WHY I LIKE ERNIE

by

OSCAR KINOOTZ

(A#1 Fan of Ernie Kovacs)

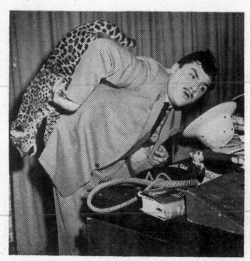

Kovacs is a real animal lover. The wilder the animal, the wilder his love.

No! Ernie Kovacs is not taking a drink with the beautiful blonde on his show. This is just one of his fans.

The lady hanging by her knees is unidentified. Standing by her side, however, is
Ernie Kovacs.

I never saw Ernie Kovacs look like this.

Well, as far as I am concerned, Ernie
Kovacs may not be as pretty as Dagmar,
and his clothes aren't as interesting as
Faye Emerson's, but I like him. He's not
as funny as Bob Hope (or maybe he is.
Sometimes I can't tell) and he can't play
the violin like Jack Benny. He's not as
fat as Jack Leonard, and he probably
hasn't got as much money as Arthur
Godfrey. But, I like him. Now as to why
—that's going to be a problem. Sure, he's
a nice enough guy, but he never makes
off-color jokes like the rest of the TV
comedians, and maybe he's not in their
class.

He doesn't go around all the time like
he was reading a script written on a
cardboard in front of him like the others
on TV. You can understand all the words
he says (most of the time) but I suppose
that's because he was an announcer, and
learned how to speak correctly.

When most of the comedians on TV
come out to say jokes, they act like they
are doing a chore, but this guy Kovacs
seems to amuse even himself. Can that
be right?

He doesn't act like he owned TV all
the time, and that may not be in the
proper atmosphere for TV. Of course,
he can't talk about family life like Sam
Levenson, but maybe they're different
type comedians.

I guess the thing I like most about
Ernie Kobacs (I never can get his name
straight) is the easy way he's got of going about things. And the screwest things
he goes about!

That girl on his show—wowee. I wish
sometimes the Rochester TV Guide would
run a picture of her. She's real pretty.
I wish I could think of her name right
off hand—she's blond, though. So, as I
was saying about Ernie Kolacs, you'd
think that coming from a town like Philadelphia (home of the Liberty Bell) he'd
be stuffy, and high-hat. Not at all. A
friend of mine saw him walking in
Philly one time, and he was using the
sidewalk just the same as other people.
Well, I tell you—this guy Kovacs is a
type, he certainly is.

(Continued on Page 21)

"Can fried chicken be eaten with the fingers?"

"No. Fried chicken should be eaten by itself. The fingers can be eaten separately."

Sing a Pretty Song…

The "Offbeat" Life of Edie Adams Including the Kovacs Years

By Edie Adams & Robert Windeler

I SETTLED MYSELF ON THE TRAIN GOING TO PHILADELPHIA AND IN MY NEW purse-size diary carefully wrote down my expenses for the day: subway to Penn Station-five cents, one-way trip New York to Philly, eighty-seven cents plus thirteen cents tax-and put the receipts in a separate envelope. My father had just started to take over as my "manager." He had driven me to the subway station for this important occasion. He had just started to drill into me the importance of what I was going to have to do, keeping records for my income tax, now that I was a national contest winner and on my way to becoming a big "star." Even Mother was softening and began to read Variety reviews of other potential "stars." This was an important audition. If I got it, I would be seen daily on the full network clear to Chicago. I just had to get it. I tried to vocalize, humming scales under my breath, trying to keep the sound under that of the noisy train as I looked out of the window at nothing.

As I got out of the cab at WPTZ at 1619 Walnut, I was more concerned about my appearance, my voice, and writing the cab fare in my new expense book than I was about what was waiting for me. When Joe Behar first introduced me to Ernie Kofax (did I hear him right?), he was much taller than I'd expected. I'd seen pictures of him, and he looked short. Even with his slouch and my three-inch heels, I could see that he was at least six feet two inches, maybe taller. He bad on a rumpled brown suit and a wrinkled shirt with the neck button opened and the tie pulled down. He had on glasses and a hat with the brim turned up (he looked like a sketch rendition of an overworked reporter from The Front Page. All he needed was a bent card saying "Press" stuck in his hatband). He had a fuller-than-leading-man mustache and was smoking the biggest cigar I'd ever seen. When he took off his hat as we met, I saw a full head of tousled dark brown hair. He had tired, soft brown eyes topped by thick, shaggy eyebrows. He had big, warm hands and a smooth olive skin. When he smiled, an enigmatic half-smile, his eyes twinkled like those of a child who's just gotten his first puppy. In fact, he looked like a big, overgrown puppy you wanted to pat, coddle, and snuggle down to bed with.

In my whole life I had never before met anyone who affected me like this. While we were still shaking hands and saying our initial how-do-you-dos, I was completely non-plussed. I had these tiny electric shock feelings traveling up and down inside. I'd felt that delicious feeling only when I'd waken from those unexplained dreams and try desperately to go back to sleep again so that I could experience some more of whatever that strange feeling was that was running from my brain to my toes. For the rest of the day just being in his presence, without even touching, brought on this cold sweat, producing feelings from somewhere buried deep beneath a whole lifetime of trying to bury my true feelings. If this was what I was missing by trying to stuff my true feelings down deep, I wasn't going to do that anymore. Here was a living, breathing way out. From that moment on Ernie could get me with a look, a word, or even just his presence. He simply became the most important thing in life, even though I subsequently tried to talk myself out of him. From then on, as long as he lived, he was it. Here he was, tall, dark, mustached, with a hat, cigar, and a foreign name. He was separated, not divorced. He looked dangerous but spoke softly. Who could have resisted?

The show was to be Ernie's first in prime time on a network. *Ernie in Kovacsland* was to be a summer replacement for Burr Tillstrom's *Kukla, Fran & Ollie* puppet show on NBC, Monday through Friday evenings from seven to seven-thirty eastern time.

I sang the only two pop songs I knew well. I was asked what other songs I could sing since I would have to do a rhythm song and a ballad each half hour we were on the air. I lied and said, "Oh, I can sing anything." So I was called back the following Tuesday, June 26, to sing two more songs, which I had to learn fast the night before. Ernie hired me on the spot to do the summer program, on each segment of which I would sing the two songs and do sketches with him. My first live show was the next Monday, July 2. On that program I sang "If I Were a Bell" from Guys and Dolls as my up-tempo song and "Don't Take Your Love from Me" as my ballad:

That finished the songs I knew. Because I was nearsighted and refused to wear the outsize whole-eye contact lenses that were popular then, I was always desperately trying to memorize new music and lyrics. After all, this was live and on the Cull network. Ernie said the first thing he remembered about me was my standing behind a set, frantically trying to learn the day's lyrics.

To my parents, and to most people, Ernie would seem too foreign. Everybody in show business then changed their ethnic names to Davis, Thomas, or other white-bread-sounding names. Nobody much wore a mustache then, except the bad guys in movies. Nobody smoked a cigar except gangsters, but Ernie wore his handkerchief in his sleeve so that he wouldn't crush the cigars in his breast pocket. He didn't give a "hoot in hell" what anyone thought of that. For me, Ernie was the "Mephisto Waltz," a Lorelei siren, the wolf call of the wild -irresistible. Everything about him seemed to fill some deep psychological lack in me. What I wasn't, he was. What he wasn't, I was. He fitted the odd-shaped pegs in my personality to a T. In 1989 Norman Knight, our former boss at the Dumont Network, said that when he first met the two of us, he'd never met anyone quite as naive as I, or anyone quite so street-smart as Ernie. Norman said we were "a colorful couple."

At first l didn't understand Ernie at all. I studied him, never having met anybody like him in my sheltered Presbyterian life. Though he seemed everything dangerous, he was always funny. He expressed himself colorfully. His language was so bad that it sounded all right to me. Sometimes, when he got mad, he would yell at the top of his voice, but always at things, never at people; if there was too much starch in the collar or the store forgot to deliver something, he swore in two languages. Like my father, Ernie never raised his voice to me. When I started to use some of the words in his vocabulary, particularly the current "army expressions," he had to explain them to me. (I thought "p.o.'d" meant "put out" and started to use it freely until Ernie said, "What are you saying?") They turned out to be even more colorful than I had thought. I didn't understand his French cunt green beans joke at all, but I laughed as though I did, so he thought I was sophisticated.

I moved into the Bellrich Apartments, a safe haven for young ladies from good families, at 301 South Fifteenth Street. He lived in Joe Babar's old bachelor pad on Sansom Street, behind the station and later moved to his own lavish apartment on Philadelphia's posh Rittenhouse Square. Coming from my frugal family, I couldn't understand his extravagance. Yet we connected right away. I never thought of him as a "date"; he was always special, because of his unique physical effect on me, even just standing close together. We started going out immediately and never stopped. After our first evening together, Ernie and I went back to his apartment to play George Shearing's recording of "The Nearness of You." We held hands, and I saw tears come out of his closed eyes. Despite his obvious larger-than-life appearance, Ernie had a soft core that not only was apparent to me, one-on-one in my living room, but came over on TV in everybody's living room. Chevy Chase remembers watching Ernie on television, fascinated by his imposing personality but knowing, "even as a kid, he wasn't ever going to hurt you."

For our first big dinner, outside at a fancy restaurant on the Delaware River, he showed up in a low-slung white convertible Cad-Allard sports car. He had just bought it with his life savings of thirty-five hundred dollars, "so you won't have to take a cab." I knew he wasn't making that much money and had a mother and two children to support, so I was terribly impressed that he would go out and spend his last dollar to live it up, especially for me. The word "extravagance" hadn't existed in my vocabulary until I met Ernie. In my family we used to have a board meeting just to cross the street on a yellow light. We had to account for every penny. As a child I split a percentage of my meager allowance into Sunday school envelopes; it was five cents for the church fund here, two cents for missionaries overseas. No wonder I just used to follow Ernie around. I was utterly taken with his live-for-today attitude; it unlocked another long-forbidden psychological door for me. From him I learned to spend money whenever I had it and sometimes when I didn't. He filled in all my blank checks.

In August 1951, while we were still doing the daily network show, I opened in the Celebrity Room, a mob-owned club down the street from the station. The owner told Ernie that I had "a great leg." Ernie wanted to know, "What's wrong with the other one?" During the week I worked there, Ernie did stand-up mob takeoffs. He could get away with it because one of his best friends from Trenton was Charlie Costello, a cousin to Frank Costello. Charlie, who raised Doberman attack dogs, took us to a

fabulous Italian restaraunt in Trenton, Chick and Nello's, commonly known as the Homestead Inn, where we ate in the kitchen. Ernie stayed friends with Charlie, who was one of the first people to call me after Ernie's death, asking, "Is there anything you need? If anybody gives you any trouble, just call me." Ernie always told me, "You do favors for the boys, but never let them do favors for you."

While we were visiting Charlie in Trenton, Ernie took me to his house at 61 Vincent Avenue, to meet his infamous mother, Mary, who was living there with his two daughters, Betty and Kippie, who were then four and two.

With Ernie, for the first time in my life I was able to be a kid. He taught me how to play. He was a big kid and proud of it. He talked outrageous baby talk; I loved it. For a long time I couldn't tell anybody because it wasn't done then. (Our matched wedding rings are engraved "Swees [sweethearts] forever.") He was not afraid to cry and met life straight on with humor. For once I could talk to someone about my deepest feelings. He was bright, witty, intelligent, funny, and sophisticated. Ever since Blithe Spirit during my drama stint at Columbia University, I had yearned to be urbane, Noel Cowardy, and all of the above. Ernie wasn't all those things then, but I thought he was. At a restaurant he could order all the things I'd never had and the proper wines to go with them. I'd always been taught that such excess was sinful, but that's the way he lived. I couldn't wait to learn how he got that way.

Ernie Kovacs was born in Trenton, New Jersey, on January 19, 1919. His father, Andrew, bad been born in a village outside Budapest, on May 1, 1890. Andrew's mother died when he was five, and he lived with his father and uncles, who were all priests, next door to the Catholic church. Andrew was an altar boy because he had to be, but he had a wild streak and no maternal supervision. The uncles were constantly admonishing him, so one day, instead of lighting the candles as an altar boy, he just blew them out and "ran like hell." At age fourteen, in 1904, Andrew arrived in New York with a name tag sending him to Trenton to visit relatives. At age seventeen Andrew married Helen Tomko. They had two children, who died, along with their mother, in the flu epidemic of 1917, and a son, Tom, born in 1911, who survived.

In 1918 Andrew married Mary Cherbonic, a professional Hungarian with piercing dark eyes and high Mongol cheek-bones, who laughed a lot. Tommy, by then seven, lived with them. Mary was a seamstress and a pistol; Mama Rose in Gypsy was an hors d'oeuvre compared to her. She tried to run everything and even then terrorized everyone she was around. She loved a fight. Andrew "Pop" Kovacs had worked at the Roehling steel mill but was a cop when Ernie was born.

During Prohibition, in the 1920's, Andrew got into the "beverage business"-making bootleg liquor in his own still, hidden away in the woods outside Trenton. He used to say, in his thick accent, of the television program The Untouchables, "This is sissy stuff. I go to still, cops say, 'Put hands up,' I put hands up, grab ice pick I have over door shade. I go boom on hand, they yell and scream, and I drive off."

Pop also owned a waterfront dive in South Trenton, the Union Street Bar. Tom Kovacs quit school al age fourteen to tend the bar for his father and do the heavy work. If any of the guys in the bar were rowdy, Andrew would get two heads and clunk them together, then throw the guys out. One time he hit one of the boisterous drunks and hung him by his collar on a coat hook, leaving him dangling for some time as a lesson to other potential troublemakers.

Andrew branched out from making booze for his own place and suddenly made lots of money. In 1928 the family went from near poverty to a twenty-room mansion, on Parkway Avenue in Trenton. They even had horse stables and clog kennels. They held lavish parties and bought a velvet suit and pony for Ernie, who was by then nine. As Ernie said, "I had to be tough dressed like that." His retreat was to go into his room and read all the Tom Swift books, on which he later did takeoffs. It was the beginning of his self-education. From then on, wherever he lived, Ernie always bad a desk, and his main occupation was reading and writing, even as a kid. For someone with only a high school education, he was one of the most well-read people I'd ever met. He'd read the classics just because he wanted to, not because he had to take a course.

One guest at a Kovacs dinner party during this affluent period remembered Mary's buffet table decorated in the colors of the Hungarian flag, red and green: all new green twenty-dollar bills under the red paprikas and stuffed cabbage.

By 1935 Andrew had advanced to owning a posh three-story restaurant, the Palms, on North Broad Street. A dumb-waiter took the food from the kitchen in the basement up to the third floor, by which time it was always cold.

In high school Ernie acted in plays, in part to escape from his family situation, like somebody else I knew. Eddie Hatrack, Ernie's high school friend who later did our music in New York, recalled their days together at Trenton High. "My first experience was when I shook hands with him and he had one of those hand buzzers on. He was always putting matches in the soles of people's shoes and lighting them, things like that. In those days Ernie and I were involved in anything and everything musical, particularly the shows. In *Pirates of Penzance* Ernie played the Pirate King; I remember our dramatics leacher, Mr. Van Kirk, a wonderful guy, reprimanding Ernie and laughing at the same time when he took too many liberties with the lines. It was a constant joke with Ernie. Everything he said, it seemed, was funny. He just turned everything into being funny." Ernie always said that it bad been his high school teacher and director Harold Van Kirk "who started the whole thing."

In 1936, the same year that Ernie's brother, Tom, got married to Mabel, Ernie's grammar school classmate, the Kovacses bought a Packard town car. All seemed to be going well. However, in 1937 Andrew's business, the Palms, went bankrupt, and he lost everything, $750,000. The year Ernie graduated from high school, 1938, his mother and father divorced. Ernie went to live with his mother, having testified in court on her behalf. Mary always maintained that Ernie and his father weren't speaking for several years afterward, but I have lovely letters from Ernie to Andrew during this period. They were very close and definitely cut from the same cloth.

After the divorce Pop inherited a bar that was losing money in the basement of the Hungarian Catholic church. The church asked Andy to turn it into a moneymaking proposition. He added live music, a cimbalom and a balalaika, and soon the church elders were asking him to suspend bar service at least until the first mass on Sunday was over. The bar flourished.

For a while after his high school graduation, Ernie taught drama in a girls' high school in Trenton, while taking post-graduate courses. He ad-libbed his own transformation in the second act of Dr. Jekyll and Mr. Hyde depending on the size of the audience. One day he

planned an elaborate second act change, with an added scene and dry ice for smoke to give the audience a real show. The curtain opened, and there were three old ladies out there.

"Van" took Ernie off to a summer stock season at the John Drew Theatre in East Hampton, Long Island, where Van Kirk was directing. Ernie played a cowboy in Green Grow the Lilacs, the play that became the musical Oklahoma! A critic wrote of Ernie's performance as the major in Shaw's Arms and the Man, "He had great vitality but overacted badly." Van Kirk, in a newspaper interview years later, said, "He didn't ... Ernie never overacted, but his personality was so that he simply overpowered everybody, even in a small part. He couldn't have played it down. It wouldn't have been Ernie."

Van Kirk's assistants in East Hampton included Martin Manulis and Henry Levin, both later successful producers in Hollywood. The three men believed in Ernie enough to help him get a scholarship to the New York School of the Theatre.

Away from Trenton, Ernie found out what poverty was really like. He was the typical small-town kid, subsisting on hopes and dreams and little more. In New York he lived in a run-down four-dollar-a-week rooming house on West Seventy-fourth Street. He was still naive enough to be pleasantly surprised when the police raided his house one day and arrested his landlady and several of her attractive "daughters" who had been operating their own rental business in the basement. He ate at the Automat for less than a dollar a week, on seven-cent cups of coffee, ten-cent plates of baked beans, and homemade gruel. On Saturdays he lived it up with a beef pie-a Horn & Hardart fifteen-cent special.

Ernie told me a funny but pathetic story of his hunger driving him to the brink of desperation. One day, as he was eating his daily ration of beans, a woman sat down at his table with her tray. He looked longingly at her roast beef dinner with candied sweet potatoes and other goodies. The woman had barely touched her food when she suddenly leapt up and left the Automat. Ernie watched to be sure that she had left, then started to take her plate-only to be beaten to it by the eager hands of a busboy. Ernie said it was the closest be had ever come to committing mayhem. I think his tremendous drive, his capacity for work, and his hunger for success and money can be traced to this period of his life.

During one vacation from drama school, Ernie went to work in another summer theater, in Brattleboro, Vermont, where Fred Clark was one of the actors and Robert Whitehead was an apprentice. Ernie and his troupe would work on the sets all day, act in the play that night, take their bows, say, "Whose deal?"-then gamble into the wee hours. Gambling was an obsession he had picked up in school, playing cards with the kids on his block, shooting craps in the street and betting on just about anything.

In his second year of drama school Ernie collapsed from pleural pneumonia, a near-fatal disease in 1940. Instead of returning to either half of his broken home in Trenton, Ernie spent the next eighteen months shuttling from hospital to hospital as a charity patient. His first stay was at what had formerly been a prison, on Welfare Island. Roaches infested the wards, and mental patients were mixed in with the physically ill. Needing his sense of humor to survive, Ernie used the doctors for straight men and played all kinds of practical jokes. He wrote a daily newspaper, the Lavabo Tribune, satirizing medicine, doctors, and illness. He also ran a card game in the men's lavatory after lights out.

Once a week he had a date for fluoroscopy, a "living X ray" hat permits observation of infected lungs. This provided great sport for Ernie, who prepared for these sessions by taping tinfoil letters on his chest. When he was called in for his exam, he'd remove his pajama top in the dark and step in front of the machine, flashing such messages as "Cut here," "Stop it," "Out to lunch," or "What's up, doc?" Then he'd wait for the doctors to groan.

With the help of Van Kirk. Martin Manulis, and Henry Levin, Ernie transferred to a somewhat nicer tuberculosis hospital, at Browns Mills, New Jersey, on April 25, 1940. But there the beds were always warm from the fast turnover. If people didn't eat, they died, so Ernie talked his roommate into ordering second helpings. "He looked so thin," Van Kirk remembered, "and there were holes in his shoes. I know he hadn't had enough to eat, but he never complained. We'd go to the hospital to cheer him up, but he'd cheer us up. Not only us, but all the other patients, too. Those poor, tired, sick old people, they never laughed so much in their lives. Entertain them? He convulsed them."

While at Browns Mills, Ernie, who was then a hunter, talked his father into disassembling a shotgun and bringing it to the hospital in a small package. Ernie succeeded in slipping out of the hospital with his package several times a week. He'd reassemble the gun in the woods and have his fill of shooting tin cans. This went on for several weeks. One day, after a thorough examination, a doctor told him, "You're coming along fine. If you continue this progress, you'll be able to sit out on the lawn for a few minutes a day."

"Thanks, doc, I sure could use some air," Ernie said.

Nonetheless, his illness was serious, and at times he was near death. After his recovery he said, "When you've been as close to death as I have and you're given another chance, you realize that every moment's a gift."

In 1943 Ernie left this last sanitarium without being released and, true to form, moved back in with his mother in Trenton.

At first Ernie worked in a drugstore, to help support himself and his mother. He stole the most expensive cigars from the store but refused to eat there. He would walk over to the Hildebrecht Hotel and eat the way he wanted to eat, being served properly. What little money he had he spent on his lunches. He said, "I'll starve first," rather than eat at a counter. When we were married and I wanted to eat in a drugstore because I wasn't "dressed," he'd still say, "I'll starve first." Mary described Ernie's salad days a bit differently: "We had only three dollars and Ernie went out and bought three charlotte russes. For days afterward we starved, on crackers, catsup, and water from the Automat." She sounded more as if she were romanticizing her own youth with a man of her own age. This was something I was going to have to watch.

Then Van Kirk directed Ernie to a job as a staff announcer at a local radio station, WTTM. Ernie's job was on a fifteen-minute daily program, where he began to create his unique comedy, writing and delivering "commercials" for such imaginary sponsors as Hasher's Imported Sheep Dip, interviewing anyone, including night workers at local factories, and producing such spots as reacting like a rabbit during rabbit hunting season (with bullets whizzing past his radio microphone).

Ernie's kind of comedy, which he brought to full flower on live television, survives in Monty Python, Rowan and Martin's Laugh-In, Saturday Night Live, and, most noticeably, David Letterman. (Letterman's head writer, Steve O'Donnell, and his staff spent three months at The Museum of Broadcasting in New York, studying Kovacs kinescopes, so I know they're fans.) In 1981 I was flabbergasted when, as I guested on Letterman's show, his first question was to the effect,

"Well, just what was it that Ernie Kovacs did? Could you perhaps explain his humor?" I was nonplussed, prepared for any question but that, knowing that much of the Letterman show's framework was pure Kovacs, including the broken-glass sound effects and the camera on the unknowing man-in-the-street. I tried to explain Ernie, as if to a ten-year-old. Imitation is the sincerest form of flattery, but ignorance is not. Aw, come on, David, lighten up.

In 1945 Ernie married a dancer named Bette Lee Wilcox on the spur of the moment. The famous Bluebelles, a dance troupe, were entertaining at the Hildebrecht Hotel, and Ernie had gone there for a date with a short blonde. The blonde didn't show up; but Bette said, I'm here," and that's how they met. They married shortly thereafter, and both moved in with Mary. It was a disaster from the start, with Bette and Mary, two tough cookies, arguing constantly about money. Ernie's escape was to lose himself in work, as would often be the case later in his life.

He took on a newspaper restaurant reviewing column for the *Trentonian*, then also commuted by train to announce wrestling matches in Philadelphia, bringing along his own sound effects, such as a dog's crackle bone, which he used on mike as he described a crushing hold. This twenty-four hour workday turned out not to be the solution to his bad marriage. In 1949 Bette deserted Ernie and their infant daughters, Betty Lee and Kippie Raleigh. By this lime Ernie had bought his own house in Trenton, so that his family wouldn't have to live with his mother. As soon as Bette left, Mary never missed a beat. She moved right into Ernie's house, ostensibly to help him take care of his little girls.

Ernie broke into television in 1950, when he was hired by WPTZ (later KYW), an NBC affiliate in Philadelphia. It was there that I auditioned for him. The unstructured, fly-by-the-seat-of-your-pants, this-is-your-first-and-only-take ambience of early live television was perfect for Ernie, who worked best under pressure and loved anything resembling a gamble. His crazy, hyperactive imagination enabled him to fill every second of air time he was given.

The first of his series that I was on, *Ernie in Kovacsland*, the NBC summer replacemenl for *Kukla, Fran &-Ollie*, went off the air at the end of August 1951, but Ernie still had his TV talk show, *Three to Get Ready*, live on the local station from 7:30 to 9:00 A.M. Monday through Friday. In September an extra half hour was added from 7:00 to 7:30, and I joined *Three to Get Ready* in October. This was the first morning television show anywhere in the world; everything else available at that hour was radio, and Ernie was determined that this show would not have the look of a photographed radio show. If he played a record of a popular song, he would have drawn cartoons

on a flip pad that usually had nothing to do with the song but were humorous additions to his interpretation of it. He called these "illustrated profuselys." If things were particularly dull, he'd throw eggs or other food at the drawings. All of us there were expected to come up with things to "kill three minutes" with only a fifteen-dollar weekly prop budget.

Andy McKay, our propman, had a hotel's dirty-linen cart full of items we could use. At first there were only three people in the studio crew: two on cameras and Andy McKay. When we had to move scenery, the cameraman had to get off the camera and move the set. When the newsman was on, we knew he'd be stationary for five minutes every half hour. The cameraman would lock the camera on the newsman, Norman Brooks. Then the cameraman was free to help Andy and me set up the next scene. There was only one man in the control booth, Joe Behar, and if he had to leave for any reason, one of us had to go in and cover for him.

If both cameramen were needed to move a set, I got to get on the camera, which was then manually controlled. I could put Ernie in and out of focus by changing the lenses with a lever on the side. The fisheye (wide-angle) lens was the most unflattering because it distorted features. Ernie would have the morning loosely planned, like a shopping list. [l was up to us to create mischief for most of the two hours. From the beginning, I always felt more like part of the production team than the girl singer. I started by telling Welsh jokes, which were notable for their lack of humor, then graduated to Frau Braun's histrionic Schiller recitations. Since I didn't have a writer and wasn't writing my own stuff yet, I tried the classics: Zsa Zsa Gabor reacting Shakespeare, "Out, out naughty spot." There was always room for my Juilliard party bit: Marilyn Monroe singing Schubert lieder, "Leise Flehen." It was a sure-fire laugh. Only steal from the best.

Garry Shandling's show's creator and producer, Alan Zweibel, a former writer on Saturday Night Live, said that all the writers on that show "had Kovacs at the core of everything we did; no matter what the bit, whenever there was a question, we said, 'What would Ernie have done?' It was Ernie Kovacs that we all idolized and wanted our show to be most like. We spoke to our generation; however, we prided ourselves on exploring the medium the way he did with electronics. He knew the conventional pictures but was more interested in the distortion of pictures and sound. He never spoke down to an audience."

When the large Saturday Night Live writing group won its first Emmy, in the midst of all the mayhem, Chevy Chase grabbed the mike and said a special thank-you to Ernie Kovacs. I'll never forget him for it.

When I did Garry's show in late 1989, it all came back to me, so much so that I felt the need to bring in mementos from the period to dress the set. I was playing the wife of an early TV nightclub comic, and I certainly knew the territory. I was amazed that those in Garry Shandling's group, aged about forty and under, are such cult admirers of Kovacs. I told them that although I'd been hired as the girl singer, my job was to see that the whole show, not just my part of it, was good. All of us had to keep an eye on the continuity because if Ernie was out of a job, we were, too. The sum total of the show was everybody's responsibility. For me, the object was not to be funny but to kill time. The only times I'd get outrageous was when something Ernie tried fell flat. We all had to be ready with a full-out save. That's the way I myself learned to perform comedy. On his show you played straight to him or you were full on center stage. Remember, it was two hours every day.

Doing the show with Garry Shandling recently was a real treat; it was the first time in thirty years I'd worked with anyone that open to any and all ad-lib suggestions. Garry's laid-back and underplayed style, especially when he breaks down the fourth wall and talks directly lo the audience, warmed my heart and reminded me of the way Ernie used to work. Garry should always be on TV somewhere, regardless of "numbers."

We had our own group for musical numbers, the Tony De Simone Trio, who were always the first to arrive, straight from a late-night gig at a club. I had to get three copies of sheet music and write out the chords in my key. One day near Christmas they read my markings wrong and played "Silent Night" in the key of G, instead of C, and I had to sing it five notes above a coloratura. It was done in front of a church set, so I couldn't just stop and tell them to change keys.

One day Tony and the boys were late. Ernie wrote out Tony's home phone number on his large sketch pad, put it on camera, and told the listeners to call Tony at home and wake him up. We always figured nobody was watching anyway. This time the phone company called up and said please don't ever do that again. We had flooded the switchboard. Ernie was thrilled; at least we knew people were watching.

I began several notebooks, labeled "Birthdays," "Household Hints," "Hymn Requests" (I sang one every day), "Quickies" (things I pulled out of the newspapers). "Funny Bits" (which required props), "Songs," and "Quartets" (with the newscaster, Norman Brooks).

Since this was the first TV show anywhere at this time of day, and it was only local-an experiment-we were very casual about our work habits. With the earlier starting time, 7:00 A.M., we all had trouble getting to the studio on time, especially Ernie. Sometimes the other regulars and I would sit around for as long as twenty minutes chatting on the air while awaiting our star. He would say, "I was shaving, and I heard the theme song, so I thought I'd better hurry up."

Other times I would come to the studio with my hair still in curlers, planning to fix myself up after I got there. The cameramen or Ernie would spot me and shout out of a back window and down a deserted hall, or they'd chase me all over the place with their lenses aimed. Eventually I learned to hide behind our church backdrop, figuring that they wouldn't dare get funny with that. Ernie loved to get me with my hair up, no makeup, and my glasses on. We did a lot of talking to the dead camera, lining up possible funny bits with the control room. Sometimes Joe would punch up the dead camera and show me making faces or setting up a gag.

With only black and white and manually operated cameras we were in the silent movie era of television. In my lectures to college students today, I refer to myself as the Mary Pickford of early TV. It was both more creative and more personal. There was a nice intimacy in Philadelphia; you knew that relatively few people had television sets, and those who were watching weren't expecting perfection. As an audience they were making mistakes right along with us. We could say or do whatever we wanted to. Ernie personalized everyone in the studio. We knew Tom was on camera one and Sam was on camera two; they became part of the family. Andy McKay, who started as our propman, became part of every sketch. He did the longest spiral faint and death scene in history. It took him so long to die one day that Ernie said he wasn't going to write Andy any more death scenes.

One time, with a frozen orange juice can, a child's kaleidoscope, and a flashlight taped to the front of the camera, Ernie moved the patterns and designs to the beat of the music. This thirty-nine-cent special effect is now done electronically and costs thousands of dollars.

During this period I got to know Ernie's real family. I always loved Ernie's father, Andrew. He was a great, fantastic bull of a man, who stood even taller than Ernie, although he was about two inches shorter. He reminded me of Oscar Homulka, the film actor, brusque on the outside with lots of raw edges, but always charming. He must have been a great ladies' man in his youth. Pop was proud and tough, and he danced a mean czardas. In restaurants he would request that the violinist play sad Hungarian peasant songs, and he would sing along. As the tempo picked up, Andrew would get up and dance frenetically with deep bent knees, pausing only to blow over his shoulder. As the music got faster and the dancing got wilder, Pop did more over-the-shoulder puffing. I asked him what he was doing. He said that was "to blow devil off shoulders."

Pop loved the strolling Hungarian violins and would cry freely while be sang along, blowing his nose at the end of each phrase. Ernie, on the other hand, would say, at the ap-proach of a gypsy musician, "Shit, here he comes, hold my band." Then be would say, softly, "We want to be alone," and give me a soulful look. He would slip five dollars into the violinist's hand as he backed away, smiling.

Andrew used to say of Mary, "She's a devil. She smile at you-look out! She seem mad, you okay. She laugh today, you cry tomorrow." Mary hated Ernie's first wife so much that when I showed up, agreeable to anything and everything she said, she adored me. She thought that I was like putty. All I did was agree with her; if she said, "That's green," I'd say, "Yep, that's green," and if she then said, "That's blue," I'd say, "That's right, it's greenish blue." I treated her, too, like a patient. Mary was later to mistake my acquiescence for weakness. It was the easiest way to avoid conflict, much as I had done when my own mother was difficult al home.

Mary was truly a unique person. When Ernie and I first started going together in 1951, I was singing at the Sun and Star Roof at the Senator Hotel in Atlantic City. The hotel had given me free rooms, which I turned over to Ernie, Kippie, Betty, and Marna Kovacs. God forbid I should even stay in the same hotel as Ernie, so I stayed at the Seaside Hotel. This was so that my mother and father would never suspect that Ernie and I might be alone together in a hotel room. They called me from Tenafly daily, saying whenever they finally did reach me at the Seaside, "You're never in." They were right, but I didn't notice it or care because I loved Ernie.

In Atlantic City I was introduced to Mary's odd gypsy ways. I went over to visit her the first afternoon, and she had all their clothes hanging out all over the place-on the terrace, 'opened drawers, doors, chairs, lamps. I asked her why everything was spread out, and she said she was "airing out the clothes." So I assumed she would hang them in the closet that night. But they stayed strewn about for the entire two weeks of my engagement. The closets remained empty, and if she washed anything, it was flown proudly on the balcony, which was already full of wet bathing suits and towels. In my family drying anything on a balcony was on a par with a pink flamingo or an iron deer on the front lawn; it simply wasn't done. This was a painfully accurate introduction to Mary, showing me what I was to put up with for the rest of her life.

This engagement also provided my first introduction to Ernie's phenomenal largess when it came to room service and charging things. When I finished my two weeks, the hotel was to

have paid me fifteen hundred dollars. However, Mary's room charges on my borrowed gratis suite came to two thousand dollars. She had discovered that could include much more than food: boat rides, Steel Pier, horseback rides, posh clothing, toys and other treats. The hotel offered Ernie a deal he couldn't refuse. They'd simply absorb the extra five hundred dollars as part of a promotional and not pay me. Not only did I still have to pay my hotel bill (by check) but it was Sunday and I only had two dollars in change in my purse. I had to ask Ernie for ten dollars pocket money. I was livid and mortified because I had never had to ask anyone for money before, not even my parents. I had never been without enough money. I had earned everything I needed by baby-sitting in the summers. My allowance had been planned on and given, but I had never had to ask anybody for anything. So I vividly remember this incident with Ernie. I made a pact with myself never, ever to let this happen again, where I would have to ask someone for money. Ernie, casually handing me the ten-dollar bill, was totally unaware of what was going on within me.

Money simply did not matter lo Ernie. He always over-tipped. He had not stuck me with his hotel bill maliciously or chauvinistically but thoughtlessly. Conversely, later, if he had the money, he encouraged me to spend it as lavishly as he did. And I did.

That September I also played the Steel Pier in Atlantic City, and we made some records for an outfit called Top Tunes in Ocean City. The company had Tony De Simone record Ernie's "Oriental Blues" theme song instrumentally and Ernie sing "Hotcakes and Sausage" on the B side. It was really not very good, and we kidded him about it on the air. My record's A side was called "Sailor Man." I liked the B side, "There May Be a Love," better. It was a pretty good melody and lyric and sung well, I realize now. But at the time I didn't have a sense of what would be a hit in popular music. I was and still am a singer who never had a record on the charts.

I began to see more of Ernie's family and began to get a closer look al their customs. He took me to his uncle's funeral in Trenton. Hungarians love to cry. They eat, they cry; they dance, they cry; they laugh, they cry, and when they cry, They really cry. They all must have been having a great time at the funeral because everyone was crying out loud. At one point the priest, who was wearing an elaborate black floor-length vestment with choir robe-like sleeves, interrupted the sermon to do what appeared to be (he was speaking in Hungarian) an elaborate commercial on Ernie, the new celebrity native son in the audience. He got so carried away that he raised both arms to the sky with his menacing sleeves fully spread. Mary, who bad been moaning and wailing louder than any-one, stopped, looked up at the priest, burst right out laughing, paused, cut loose with a loud witch's cackle, turned to Ernie, and, in a voice audible to all, said, "My God, he looks just like Batman!," and went right back to wailing.

Ernie's stint on *Three to Get Ready* had evolved from his cooking show, *Deadline for Dinner* (dubbed Dead lion for Dinner) which also starred a housewife and a famous chef, around whom Ernie kibbitzed. Ernie was a good cook, but on the day both the housewife and the chef didn't show up, Ernie toasted himself with the cooking sherry and started throwing eggshells into the chocolate pot. After the next sherry, he threw spinach into the pot. Out of that came his "choco-spin" bit (chocolate-covered spinach for kids who hated it) and Mikos Molnar, the melancholy Magyar chef.

By the time I got there his remaining show had nothing to do with cooking, which was a good thing. He loved to kid me about my lack of ability in that area: "The kitchen, honey, is that yellow room that you never see; you might stop by there someday and look in," or, "You remember pies; they were round." The first time I ever attempted to cook for him was when he was sick with the flu (he always cooked when it was the two of us). He asked me to make some oatmeal. I tried lo explain that I didn't have the vaguest idea how. He said. "Surely you can make that. Read the label." I did the best I could and brought him a sick tray with a little flower on it and a dish full of this lumpy mess. When I came in, he was moaning from his temperature. After one bite of my inedible putty, he moaned even louder. "Don't ever try that again." I never did.

When Ernie moved into his fancy apartment on Rittenhouse Square, I helped him decorate it in the fifties moderne stuff that is now on L.A.'s trendy Melrose Avenue and at the Disney World theme park in Florida. He loved it, I hated it.

I stayed on at the Bellrich but was definitely settling into Philly. My parents were not amused.

As we began to make more money, there were even more elaborate gifts and fancy dining. Ernie's mother and his kids spent increasing time at the Rittenhouse Square apartment, which was too small for Ernie, never mind Mary and her airing-out clothes. She was a houseful wherever she lived. Every time she moved or even visited, she went out and bought eight hundred dollars' worth of cooking pans. She did it in Philly and again in Englewood, New Jersey, New City, New York, Central Park West in Manhattan, and Bowmont Drive in Beverly Hills. After the holidays these pans would disappear, and we would have to buy more for the next holiday. One time in L.A. I saw some of them lined up across the lawn for the dogs to drink from, but otherwise I swear l don't know what she did with them. She may have thrown them out because she didn't want to clean them.

Mary would bother and embarrass Ernie by calling him up at the studio when he was on the air and all day long at the office. She would say such things as "I broke your father, and I can break you, too." She would send him desperate notes underlined on postcards, visible to all: "Ernie, they're turning off the gas, send more money ... Ernie, I'm starving, how can you do this to me? ... We're behind on the mortgage again." It got so that the switchboard or one of us would not put her through at all.

Just short of a two-year desertion period, after which Ernie would have been legally free, and right after his first network show, in 1951, Bette Lee Kovacs reappeared. She instigated a messy divorce and child custody case that took up most of Ernie's and my nonperforming time for about a year.

Bette, or Brx, as the girls called their mother (because she was always spelling things sot hey wouldn't understand) was even having me followed as the other woman in the custody case. My life was becoming a B movie, the kind I had never been allowed to see. Sally, and her questionable boyfriend went to Tenafly to my father's real estate office, Boddecker's, for money, or so my father thought. Now he was really unhappy about my involvement with Ernie. I began to notice that Ernie and I were now being followed everywhere, by a seedy man on a twenty-four-hour detail. You just feel it when you're being followed. When the private detective, if that's who he was, followed both of us, I told Ernie, "You go one way. I'll go another." The man followed me.

The court awarded Ernie custody of the children on the ground that Bette had deserted them, granting her visitation privileges to see the girls two weekends each month. I never met her or was in the courtroom, but I was brought up at the trial as the "other woman."

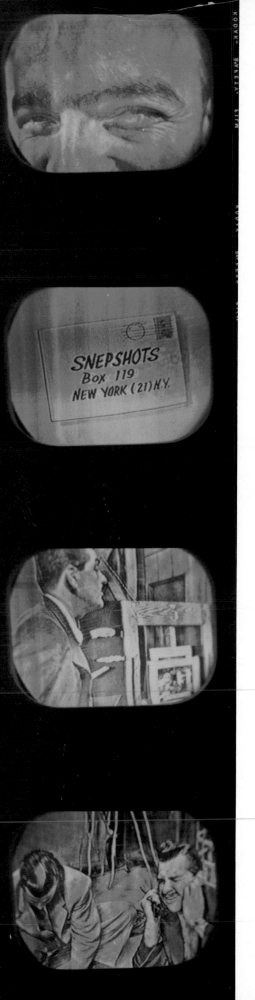

I was only upset when someone at the court proceedings said that I "looked like a Sunday school teacher." That really got me angry, I guess because I did.

For the father to be awarded custody in Pennsylvania was so unprecedented then that Judge Emanuel Belloff, who made the ruling, used it in lectures on family Law for years afterward. Belloff was considered a tough family judge, and he also ruled that Betty and Kippie were to be "removed from the care and influence of the paternal grandmother," Mary. She ignored the order, as usual, and moved into Ernie's houses from then on wherever they were.

In January 1952 the NBC network bosses in New York decided that they had something with us, but they didn't know what it was. They wanted us in the big time and foisted on us, without any consultation, network writers, performing guest stars, and a live studio audience. The only thing they asked Ernie about was what comic he admired. He said, "Oh, Fred Allen, 'Allen's Alley,'" so the New York creative types set up a show borrowed loosely from that concept, *Kovacs on the Korner*, where Kovacs indeed stood on a street corner and met up daily with a cop, a barber, and a man in a bad dog suit playing a talking dog. Neither one of us understood what we were doing in this scripted nothing. The show emanated from Philadelphia, from eleven-thirty to noon daily. Because he'd already had a radio show called *Koffee with Kovacs*, Ernie railed against the K in "Korner," so the C was quietly restored.

NBC did insist on hiring an entire new troupe to replace his regular Three to Get Ready family. I was kept on as "the singer." Ernie was forced to have on such guests as the road company "last of the red-hot mamas," who sang with Ernie standing onstage next to her, his mouth open in disbelief through the whole song. I never saw him in such pain again in all the years I worked with him. NBC also fired our beloved Tony De Simone and sent down the jazzier Dave Apple Trio from New York to glitz Ernie up.

The network also insisted on a staff of two writers, both of whom Ernie ignored and rewrote on the air. He described Kovacs on the Corner as "some of the worst moments in television history, setting back the variety format about thirty years." On the last show Ernie nailed one of the writers he least appreciated inside a trunk. She was slightly claustrophobic and, needless to say, furious.

Ernie now had to be funny for almost thirteen hours a week, plus do his own typing, weather charts, contests, and selection of musical numbers. So everything and everyone who came along became part of the humor. Some woman sent in a six-foot rag doll called Gertrude. Ernie would dance with her. If he was late, we'd aim the cameras out the window and throw Gertrude down for him to catch. She took a lot of wear and tear. When we played Johnnie Ray's "Cry," there were towels and tears all over the place. Ernie played records of pop tunes of the day in Polish. We were responsible for our own sets. I found that the cheapest one for me was to cut out my own cuculoris, a pattern set in front of a Light and projected on a scrim behind me. That way I could create my own scenery, such as an umbrella or a palm tree, and have it projected behind me on the blank wall. Or we stole sets from a soap opera that was broadcast from our studio in Philadelphia, starring Susan Peters, until their staff found us out. From then on we had to disguise their sets by throwing a drape over a chair or by pulling a picket fence off the soap's set and then putting it back before they missed it.

We never thought about overexposure in early live television; we were there to kill time. The heavy work load and virtual total creative control allowed Ernie to develop camera techniques and comedy concepts that he had begun in live radio and later refined on his network shows in New York and Hollywood.

Some things on his shows didn't work, but it was all fun in the trying, including the half-hourly newscasts. Standing on a ladder out of camera range, Ernie dropped water on either the head or the script of newscaster Norman Brooks. The viewers somehow always knew who was doing it.

The most lasting legacy of *Three to Get Ready* was Ernie's trademark phrase "It's been real," which quickly became as famous as his mustache and cigar. The slogan, which evolved mysteriously, was used on every program, usually at the end. The Early Eyeball Fraternal and Marching Society, EEFMS, was another running bit, with its own member-ship cards. "Dorf" was another non sequitur good-bye that Ernie used later, in New York.

During the early months of Ernie's divorce and child custody proceedings, the legal aspects became most bitter and public. WPTZ employees enjoyed sending Bette's process servers in search of him up blind alleys at the station. One day, to avoid being served, Ernie just didn't show up for work. We had someone behind the screening smoking a cigar to stand in for Ernie when we needed him.

Once Ernie and I were on a Philly-New York train that jolted to a sudden stop. Everybody fell down, including us. The railroad made an appointment to have an insurance inspector come see us. We set the appointment for when we were on the air, pure gold as a time killer. The man didn't know he was to be on television. I was wheeled out in a wheelchair, all bandaged up, nearly giving the inspector a heart attack. Ernie grilled the man on air for a few minutes. The inspector nervously sputtered self-consciously. After watching him suffer for what I thought was long enough, I jumped up and said, "Nothing's wrong except that I ripped a pair of stockings; buy me a new pair." Very happily, he bought me a few pairs.

Early in 1952 the Dave Garraway *Today* show had premiered on the NBC network from New York, Monday through Friday 7:00 to 9:00 A.M., the same time that we were already on in Philadelphia in *Three to Get Ready*. The network understandably wanted all its affiliates to carry this expensive project. In most cities there was nothing on at that hour, so only WPTZ in Philadelphia objected. At first the station insisted that *Today* would never be taken on in place of its most popular local show. But as NBC kept pressuring WPTZ for its lucrative market for network commercials, the station caved in. The last *Three to Get Ready* show aired on March 28, 1952. The program was uncharacteristically tearful and sentimental, including appearances by Ernie's mother and daughters.

Kovacs on the Corner mercifully was also about to be canceled, with less regret. The best way to describe Ernie's and my reaction to that show was disbelief. Ernie had offers from the other two Philadelphia television stations, but we were more than ready to move on. Dan Gallagher, a producer who worked at WCBS in New York, offered Ernie his own local show in the daily 12:45 to 1:30 P.M. time that had been formerly occupied by Steve Allen on the network. Some of the *Three to Get Ready* cast were also hired on, myself included. Peter Hanley (who was to inspire the creation of the Nairobi Trio) came along as the boy singer, as did Trygve Lund, to do sketches. Angel McGrath, who had finally been hired as Ernie's secretary, and Andy McKay, our propman turned slow dier, also moved to New York with us. Tony De Simone and his trio did not go with us; Eddie Hatrack, Ernie's high school friend, became our musical director in New York.

Before we left Philadelphia, our dear friend Merrill Panitt, who covered radio and television for the Inquirer, told us about "this new little magazine" that had offered him a job. "I don't know," he said, "I've got such a good job at the paper." Ernie said, "Take it." The magazine was *TV Guide*, and Merrill eventually became its editor in chief.

Ernie was ready for his own new challenge; he cliched, "I'm not afraid of you, New York." On April 21, 1952, *Kovacs Unlimited* made its debut on WCBS. The format was more of the same as in Philly, but this was New York City, the big time! My town! ⊙

The Night Before Christmas ... (on the east side)

'TWAS THE NIGHT BEFORE CHRISTMAS AND ALL THROUGH THE DUPLEX
JUST A VALET WAS PRESSING (A GLEN PLAID WITH FEW CHECKS).
THE MESH NYLONS WERE HUNG BY THE CHIMNEY WITH CARE.
C.O.D. FROM HELENE'S. (THE BILL WAS A BEAR!)

THE BOYS HOME FROM PREP SCHOOL WERE ALL SNUG IN THEIR BEDS
WHILE VISIONS OF MARILYN DANCED IN THEIR HEADS.
AND MATER IN HER BERGDORF AND I IN MY SAKS
LAY IN LOUIS XIV (WITH IT'S GENUINE CRACKS).

WHEN UP IN THE PENTHOUSE, THERE AROSE SUCH A CLATTER
I SUMMONED THE BUTLER TO SEE WHAT WAS THE MATTER.
HE RAN THROUGH THE ROOM IN A FORTY YARD DASH
AND PULLED THE VENETIANS I'D BOUGHT WITH COLD CASH.

THE MOON ON THE SIDEWALKS OF CHIC SUTTON PLACE
GAVE THE COLOR OF LIVER TO THE OLD DOORMAN'S FACE.
WHEN WHAT TO MY WOND'RING EYES DID APPEAR
BUT A MERCEDES BENZ PULLING UP IN HIGH GEAR!

WITH A LITTLE OLD DRIVER, SO LIVELY AND QUICK
I KNEW 'TWAS THE CHAUFFEUR OF JOLLY SAINT NICK!
MORE RAPID THAN ALLARDS, HIS CONVERTIBLE CAME
AND HE WHISTLED AND SHOUTED AND CALLED IT BY NAME.

NOW STUPID! NOW JUNK-HEAP! NOW BUCKET OF BOLTS!
ON TRASH-CAN! GO TAXIS! (THOSE DRIVERS ARE DOLTS!)
LOOK OUT FOR THE PORCH! LOOK OUT FOR THE WALL!
WE'LL GET UP THIS HILL UNLESS'N YOU STALL.

AS PEDESTRIANS THAT BEFORE TAXIS AND BUSES DO FLY,
HE HIT A POOR COP AND KNOCKED HIM SKY-HIGH.
SO UP TO THE DUPLEX, THE CONVERTIBLE FLEW
WITH A TRUNK FULL OF TOYS AND ST. NICHOLAS, TOO.

AND THEN IN A TWINKLING LIKE A FAST-DRIVING HEIRESS,
HE SLAMMED ON THE BRAKES AND CRASHED ON THE TERRACE!
AS I DREW ON MY HOMBERG AND WAS TURNING AROUND
DOWN THE FAKE FIREPLACE SANTA CAME WITH A BOUND!

HE WAS DRESSED ALL IN CASHMERE FROM HIS HEAD TO HIS FOOT.
"ABERCROMBIE AND FITCH" WAS STAMPED ON EACH BOOT.
HE HAD A HATHAWAY SHIRT — AND WAS LOOKING QUITE "DUDIE"
AS HE TOOK GENTEEL PUFFS ON A MEERSCHAUM KAYWOODIE.

HE WORE A CAVANAUGH HAT AND BRIGHT ARGYLE SOCKS
AND THE FUR ON HIS SUIT WAS ERMINE, NOT FOX.
HIS BEARD WAS WHITE MINK — A RIGHT JOLLY OLD ELF
AND I LAUGHED AT HIS SPATS, IN SPITE OF MYSELF.

BUT A LOOK AT HIS TIE (SILK SHANTUNG AND ALL RED)
MADE ME GIDDY AND I WISHED THAT I'D STAYED BACK IN BED.
HE SPOKE NOT A WORD BUT WENT STRAIGHT TO HIS WORK
AND DROVE THE CATERER FROM SARDI'S FAIRLY BERSERK.

HE ATE LIKE A DEMON AS HE TRIMMED UP THE TREE —
(CANAPES OF CAVIAR AND IMPORTED TEA!)
INTO A FINE, LINEN HANKY HE BLEW HIS NOSE,
AND SUCKED IN HIS TUMMY — AS UP THE CHIMNEY HE ROSE.

HIS CHAUFFEUR AND STENO (A LOVELY YOUNG DAME)
CAME FORTH AS HE WHISTLED AND CALLED THEM BY NAME.
"COME, THURMOND, MY CHAUFFEUR AND PAMELA, WITH BELLS!"
AND THEY PIROUETTED TO HIM LIKE TWO SADLERS WELLS.

HE SAW ME AND HOLLERED ERE HE WHIZZED OUT OF SIGHT —
"I'LL BILL YOU NEXT MONTH FOR MY LABOR TONIGHT!"

MERRY CHRISTMAS
ERNIE

how to talk at gin

ERNIE KOVACS

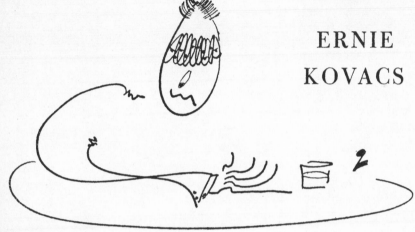

A BADLY TORN 2 OF SPADE

A 2 OF SPADES NOT AS BADLY TO

ILLUSTRATED BY THE AUTHOR IN A
MOMENT OF OVERCONFIDENCE

PLAYER MAKING FAIR ATTEMPT
GAIN SYMPATHY

6 OF CLUBS RETURNED TO DECK

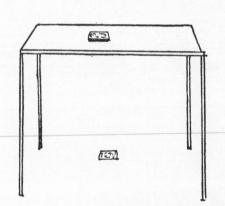

A 6 OF CLUBS DROPPED ON FLOOR

PLAYER WHO HAS BROUGHT GIRL TO GAME

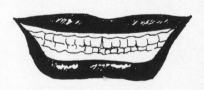

HOST'S WIFE WHO IS "ONE-OF-THE-B

"How to Talk at Gin"
by Ernie Kovacs

CHAPTER FIVE

THE EVENING PROGRESSES:
NOT GO THAT PART JUNGLE …
BWANA, SHE-DEVIL, AND SIMBA!

There now comes about, dialogue peculiar to the second hand of this round which is labeled best, **DIALOGUE FOR THE SECOND HAND**. It takes place as the cards are being dealt for the second hand. The partners who lost the first hand turn to each other like two members of a Wagnerian chorus who have just extricated themselves from a maze of backstage scenery and we hear this rather lovely aria:

All right. Let's settle down, partner." (Shoulders are bent forward.)

"They've got false confidence. Now we hit 'em hard and low and keep driving."

"They were lucky that first hand, partner."[1]

When there is less camaraderie between the partners who have lost the first round, the dialogue comes with a dillerent flavor:

"All right, Charlie, for cripe's sake, watch it this time."

"Maybe you can get your mind off'n the broads and play a little cards this hand, huh?"

"Get off my back and win one. You play like a wrinkled prostate."

Gin players who are in motion pictures are permitted an extracurricular form:

"Producer!? You couldn't produce gas pains with a pound of radishes!"

"You're supposed to be a great actor . . . how about acting like a gin player?!"

"Play a little faster. No wonder your last picture took eighteen months."

"If I put your latest album on the hi-fi, you think you might play a little better?"

"Look, the studio is closed for the night, Bridget is back home with her husband eatin' lasagna and playin' with the kids . . . you're only her big boy friend in the picture you're making with her so will you forget her and try to get your mind on the game?"[2]

The winning team, at the beginning of this second hand, counterpoints thusly:

"Well, that's a start. Now we march all the way across!"

---

[1] *That line will be used between 80 and 103 times during the evening's play. Its delivery will never diminish in ferocity and honest conviction . . . the last reading of it will be as good as the first.*

[2] *If Bridget is not Italian, goulash or corned beef and cabbage may be used here.*

"All right, Partner, get on the other two games now and we DESTROY 'em."

(Joe): "It's okay with me."

Later on, we will deal with the expressions to be used by the first player of a team to gin or knock on an opponent. His conversation is different from the winner of the latter half of that hand. One of those expressions will be put down here immediately as it is deserving of special attention. The most used of expressions designed for the situation as we have described it is:

"I got my man."

The conjecture of players who are in the entertainment business is that this line became the basis of an early hit of Fanny Brice's. Others contend the reverse and say that it was derived from the song and is connotive of humorous lament.[3]

The student of conversational gin rummy has now sufficiently progressed to take up discourse as uttered after the preliminary hand has been played.[4] Therefore, let us examine:

WHAT TO SAY ON HAVING BEEN DEALT:
I (OR A): A GOOD HAND
II (OR B): A BAD HAND

To avoid confusion, let us consider them in the order named. If the gin player should have a terribly, terribly good hand, he may wish to enjoy additional satisfaction. (A kind of "second" pin in the groin of an already mounted butterfly.) He may say:

"I'm thinking of a card."

Can the student here feel the full impact of this statement upon the other player? Can he visualize the forming of cold crystals in the bone marrow? . . . the Bela Lugosity of the atmosphere? "I AM THINKING OF A CARD" is surely indicative of the hand being 99 per cent complete with all runs already stapled neatly together ready to be laid upon the table. Other phrases to be used with a terribly, terribly good hand:

"I'm really embarrassed to do this to you,"

"You won't believe this hand."[5]

"Je suis triste pour vous."[6]

There is a point of confusion which arises here on the comments made for good hands. One school of players make no comment at all and only commit themselves to low moans of dismay. This moan of dismay is ceased abruptly to make the hearer feel that the giver of the moan let it slip out by accident.

HOW TO HOLD A GOOD HAND

A Good Hand is held quite tightly. A card to be discarded can only be dislodged by forceps designed for recalcitrant birth. The cards are held firmly so that none may fall upon the table and begin a discussion that could lead to a call for a misdeal.

HOW TO HOLD A BAD HAND

The Bad Hand is held as sloppily as possible so that a card can accidentally fall out on the table and start a discussion that could lead to a call for a misdeal.

The Good Hand is usually held so rigidly, with the cards so close together, that a hanging Mona Lisa or the player himself cannot see anything but the cards themselves. There is a little byplay here that exists between the two partners in the case of this Good Hand.

The owner of the hand will put them together, one atop the other, hand them to his partner while

---

[3] *Our researchers were unable to supply definite proof for either contention. We therefore present this interesting sidelight purely for the student's meditation.*

[4] *A review of the first three chapters is recommended.*

[5] *It is interesting that this very same phrase is also used when the player has a terribly bad hand and wishes to frighten the other player.*

[6] *This is French and is translated, I believe, "Where can I change a five-hundred franc note?"*

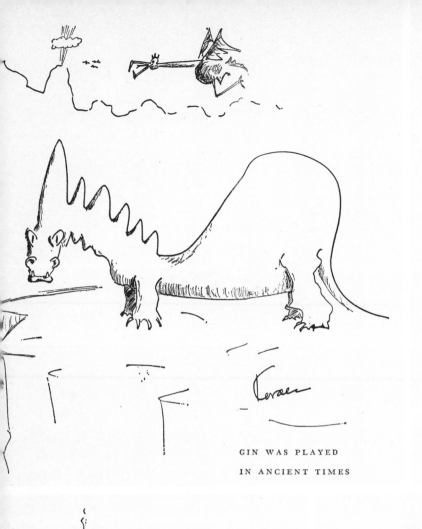

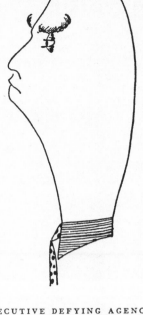

AD EXECUTIVE DEFYING AGENCY MAN
TO DECLARE GIN

GIN WAS PLAYED
IN ANCIENT TIMES

CANDLE HOOKED UP TO POWER GENER-
ATOR IN CASE OF ELECTRIC LIGHT FAILURE

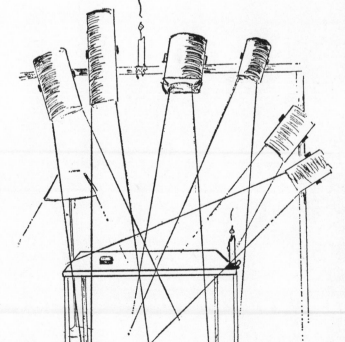

SUITABLE METHOD OF RIFFLING CARDS—
LSO EXCELLENT ILLUSTRATION DISPROVING
THEORY THAT "HANDS ARE MOST
DIFFICULT PART OF BODY TO DRAW."

TOO MUCH LIGHT

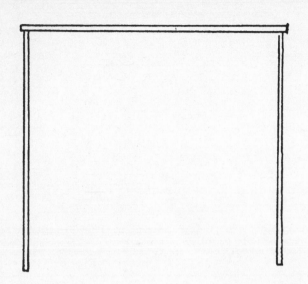

CARD TABLE UNSUITABLE FOR PLAY BE-
CAUSE OF ONE SHORT LEG (SIDE VIEW)

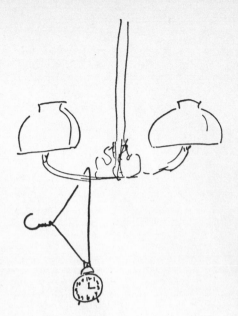

ONE METHOD OF HANGING ALARM CLOCK
FROM CHANDELIER

maintaining an expression which is a composite of Hate, Love, Fear, and Joy, shake his head with the tragic countenance of Menelaus, and say in a voice meant ostensibly to be heard only by his partner:

"Look at this."

His partner looks at the hand (which is always already a perfect gin) and says in return:

"Gee, that's rough. Hope you can make a hand out of it."

In the earlier days of gin rummy, this little playlet was accompanied by a lascivious wink and the tongue flopping up and down while hanging out of one side of the mouth. This delivery however, has become passe and is only used in some fraternal organizations. The little byplay above is considered quite in good form, but any improvement on the histrionics would put the participants in the light of being crooks. (This will be discussed later under "Coffee Housing.") (Normally, that would have been a footnote but the author wasn't quite up to a footnote at the time of this insertion.)

Some more about The Bad Hand. One or two popular expressions by players receiving bad hands:

"This ain't a hand, it's a foot."

"This hand looks like a bunch of keys."

"You gin now and you make one million points."

"Knock now and 111 punch you in the mouth."

There is byplay with The Bad Hand, too. The player folds them together and hands them to his partner, his eyebrows soliciting comment. The partner looks at the cards, refolds them, shakes his head like a Dalmatian with an infected tooth, and says, gleefully:

"He DEALT you this, Charlie? Why don't you knock right away!"

(This is to fool the others into thinking it is a great hand.)

As he returns the cards to the owner, he will portray the holding back of merriment much as Don Ameche in the role of Alexander Graham Bell surprising his wife with a blue Princess phone for her birthday. The fact that a mounted owl would not be taken in by this atrocious performance does not discourage its appearance several times during the evening.

FRESH OR FRISCH

Some players use the compatible system of throwing in freshly dealt hands if both players agree that the hand is ridiculously bad. This is usually determined by one player asking: (It is really not a question but a mumbled comment)

"Like your hand?"

If the other player does not like his hand, he will quickly throw it down face up before the other player can repudiate his comment. If he does not throw it quickly enough, the other player may add "-because I like mine." It is a happy thing for all when both players throw down their hands. It is not a happy thing when after the first player has made the comment "Like your hand?" the other player says:

"LOVE it!"

The interrogator now finds himself on a busy street comer suffering the embarrassment of an unzipped fly. He has betrayed the fact that he has a bad hand and now frantically assumes a grayish smile in a brave attempt to pass off his remark as friendly banter. He will now do all kinds of things to make the other believe the hand he really has is worth being laminated and hung in a foyer. The interrogator's partner does not go along with this shabby masquerade and gives him what might charitably be called a withering look for having exposed his bad hand. (A kind of look the bachelor gives his pregnant girl friend for fainting in front of friends.)

This little curtain raiser is only that, a curtain raiser. The real acting and choreography of the game comes about as the evening progresses. Let us put the bifocals on the situation arising over the delicate art of considering a card that has just been thrown. This cannot be too successfully done without preliminary training by the study of silent

SCORE PAD DESIGNED BY EXECUTIVE AS GIFT FOR FRIEND

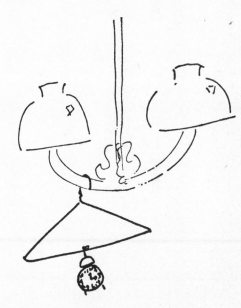

ANOTHER METHOD OF HANGING ALARM CLOCK FROM CHANDELIER

NOBLE DEALER WHO HAS THROWN CARD TO FLOOR AND IS WAITING FOR OTHER PLAYER TO PICK IT UP

films . . . an analysis of the Japanese theater ... a course in Zen Buddhism and the running off of a few stag movies just to round out the curriculum.

It is assumed by the gin matriculant that one of two things must be done with a card discarded by one player:

I-It is to be picked up.

II-It is not to be picked up.

This is as silly as the assumption that there is only one way to skin a pussycat.[7] The histrionics accompanying the meditation upon the possible selection of a discarded card are as carefully applied as a ballerina's chafing powder. This is no ponderous Polish polka . . . it is, in fact, more Tango than Cha-Cha. To illustrate, we take:

THE CASE OF THE DISCARDED KING OF HEARTS

NORTH has discarded the King of Hearts to WEST.[8] Two plays preceding this, North discarded a 5 of Diamonds. He then picked up the Deuce of Spades. To the most isolated of Alaskan Eskimos, it will be obvious that these three cards can have nothing to do with each other whatsoever.

But let us see what happens when Lester West could possibly use that King of Hearts in speculation. Lester West suddenly sees Albert North's discarded King of Hearts. He looks into his own hand and notices, let us say, the King of Spades or perhaps the Jack of Hearts. Dare he boldly speculate on this card? If he picks the King of Hearts, Albert North will not know whether he needs it for a collection of three kings or to complete his Heart run and little does Albert North know Lester West can use it either way! But wait-damme! He has tarried too long ... Albert is growing big with suspicion . . . oh to deliberate a mo' or two longer . . .

to have a few precious seconds to decide what he shall do! But he mustn't let Albert North know why he is taking this time looking at the King of Hearts. What does Lester West do? He now portrays his greatest role. He will deliberate upon the King of Hearts while delivering running dialogue cleverly phrased to throw Albert North off the scent. He will put the onus of the delay upon Albert! As the King of Hearts is a card that has been in this deck and many decks before it for years, it is not sufficiently unique so that it, by itself, can provide Lester West time in expressing awe at simply seeing the King of Hearts. The very first time, perhaps, that a King of Hearts appeared as a part of the 52 card deck, then, perhaps, this might work. But no longer. Lester West will fabricate a story line to give him time to ponder! He looks at the King of Hearts . . . cocks his head to the side like a doctor seeing a navel with a left-hand spiral and mutters:

"Discarded the 5 of Diamonds . . . then picked up the Deuce of Spades . . .

NOW he throws the King of Hearts . . . hmmmmm"

Lester West is slyly giving the impression to Albert North that he is confused because Albert is not keeping the King of Hearts with the Deuce of Spades. Now, if Albert is the player of tradition, he will fold his cards to his chest as though shielding them and perform other overt acts of na'ive camouflage. If, however, our Albert North is tired ... if this has taken place once too often in his association with Lester West, he will say in as bored a manner as possible:

"Cut out the bull . . . if you wanna speculate with the King of Hearts go ahead and speculate but don't try to make out like you're layin' plans to blow up the Kremlin.

There is another unfortunate possibility to this profound maneuver. Sometimes the Lester Wests who do this are not particularly bright or prone to quick decision. Consequently, the time begins to drag a bit and as Lester isn't really capable of weighing the possible uses of the King of Hearts with his other king and the Jack of Hearts while

---

[7] *There are two.*

[8] *The actual players are Albert North and Lester West.*

conducting the conversation of subterfuge needed, he puts his mind into neutral as he thinks and
simply does variations on his original theme which
can be annoying to the other player . . . to wit:

"Picked up the Deuce of Spades . . . PICKED
up the Deuce of Spades . . . picked UP the Deuce
of Spades . . . picked-picked up, the Deuce of
Spades . . . picked-picked up-up the Deuce of
Spades . . ." and so forth.[9]

What is the solution then to carrying out this
marvelous ruse properly?

Simply this: after exhausting the conversation
re: the Deuce of Spades, lay down the hand and
while slowly filling a large pipe bowl with a fine
grind tobacco, ask Albert North to "look at this
picture in my wallet and guess who it is . . . don't
say anything right away, think about it a couple
of minutes."[10]

If the Lester Wests of this situation are not
much on remembering dialogue, cards picked,
or if they carry no wallets, a simple but effective
measure is to lean forward a bit, look at the King
of Hearts as though it were a tremendously funny
cartoon from a popular magazine, tap it in the face
with a bent forefinger, and say "Hmmmmmm"
with as much significance as you think Albert
North will buy.

ANOTHER INTERESTING HAPPENSTANCE OF DISCARD, THE DISCARDED QUEEN OF CLUBS

Lester West has just picked the Queen of Diamonds and then discards the Queen of Clubs!
Hey? Obviously, he is not saving queens.[11] He
very probably has the Jack, Queen, and King of
Diamonds in his hand in a run. Why does he
throw the other queen so quickly, thus letting
his opponent know he does not need another
queen? Because he needs the Queen of SPADES
for another run which he is building in Spades. He
is very anxious for Albert North to notice that he
has thrown a queen back so that Albert will throw

him the Queen of Spades as quickly as possible.
So he makes little comments like:

"This ought to show you I'm honest." "Catch
on, Albert North?"

"Guess what I'm doing?"

Also, the manner in which the Queen of Clubs
is thrown is important. It is not simply discarded.
It is thrown to the table with a certain amount of
disgust, somewhat in the manner of warm camel
dung or a Communist leaflet [12] to give the impression that ALL queens from now on are undesirable.

If Albert North has some brains,[13] he will know
that Lester wants the Queen of Hearts or the Queen
of Spades or he wouldn't be giving away the Queen
of Clubs at this time. Eventually, his curiosity
will get the better of him and he will throw the
Queen of Spades anyway and when Lester West
picks it up laughing somewhat insanely, North is
obliged to say:

"Nice suck job."

---

[9] *Unless Lester West is Albert North's boss or they are both perhaps, on a small boat out at sea, it is not uncommon for Lester West to look up after all this and see that Albert North has taken his hat and gone home.*

[10] *It is a good idea to stuff several pictures into your wallet before the players arrive as you may have to do this a few times during the evening. Any old magazine shop will sell you some 5X7s of old racing car drivers, silent movie stars, or obscure automobile parts manufacturers. Each can be labeled on the back and it is an added soupcon of excitement to the evening when you say, after twenty or thirty minutes of your opponent's rapt study of the pictures: "No, you're wrong, Albert. That happens to be, believe it or not, Theobald Prawn who used to make carbureter screws in Milwaukee!"*

[11] *Or, if he is, he is not saving many.*

[12] *If the game is being played outdoors, one may also spit.*

[13] *If Albert had any brains, he would be home in bed.*

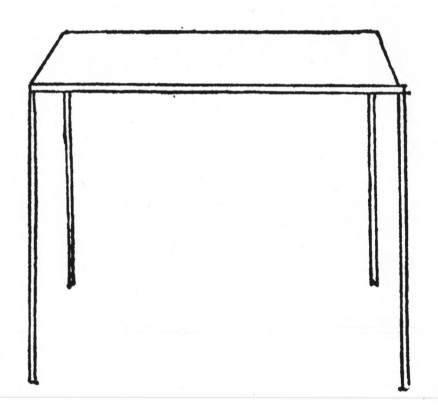

SLIPPING PHONE

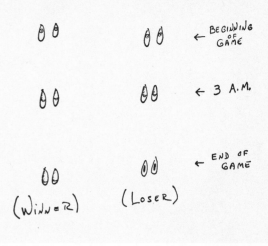

← BEGINNING OF GAME

← 3 A.M.

← END OF GAME

(WINNER)   (LOSER)

NE ANTHRAX GERM

PLAYER "FISHING"

GIN

8   4

32

26   7   6

19   12   74

49

22

16   13

11

SOME NUMBERS FREQUENTLY USED IN
KEEPING SCORE

♪

ONE OF THE NOTES USED IN
"THE MESSIAH"
(With Permission of the Publisher)

3   12

A GOOD KNOCK   A POOR KNOCK

10
40
100
───────
278

A MISTAKE IN ADDITION

Ernie Kovacs: The Last Spontaneous Man

By Frederic Morton

With his thick black hair practically shaved and his mustache whitened for a movie role, Kovacs resigns himself to his ever-present cigar.

He has no enemies—and also no sponsors. He is a once-in-our-lifetime comedian who succeeds by being simply his earthy, human self

● A famous television comedian is someone who has lost at least one big-time weekly network show. Ernie Kovacs stands out as the exception: he *never* had any. Yet he is a chronic award winner; he has summer-replaced and winter-substituted to consistent acclaim. The special half hour of pantomime he created on N.B.C. last year was the only TV film shown by the United States at the Brussels World Fair. His drainpipe-sized cigar and unlandscaped eyebrows are now a nationally recognized escutcheon whose appearance on the TV screen heralds such sights as Kovacs starting a show from inside a bottle, or "burning down" the studio at the fade-out, or philosophizing while camera-truncated to invisibility from the waist up, or unwrapping a bandage-swathed girl into raw air. The Kovacsian humor blends Puck and Peter Lorre into a style that instantly identifies our most original *jongleur* of electrons. And still, despite decent Trendex ratings, he bears the stigma (to some, the stigmata) of being "not too commercial."

Why? Possibly because Kovacs is too much of an exception. His manner is intrinsically television; it does not rise out of proved box-office veins like Milton Berle's (night clubs) or Jackie Gleason's (musical comedy), where TV, the cuckoo medium, has hatched many of its prominent performers. Furthermore, Kovacs' public image is hair-raisingly genuine. We live in an era of "personalities" no more personal than our casual clothes are casual. Both are carefully tailored, with just a bit too much Dacron. There is nothing well pressed about Kovacs' psyche. If he ever goes so far as to say, "Thank you for letting me come into your

living room," he will add, "but it's a shame you couldn't clean it up a little."

The Kovacs manner is the unreserved, sometimes uninhibited, creature of his own imagination. He is a maverick, a screwball loner, outside the great creative dynasties in which a Hemingway follows a Mark Twain, or a Sid Caesar a Charlie Chaplin. Almost untouched by the dominant traditions in comedy, he concerns himself solely in the complete, and therefore eccentric, release of his character onto his work.

"I don't like to write the first five minutes of a show," he said the other day. "I just like to get through to them out there with whatever comes into my head. Crazy stuff, noncrazy stuff, whatever. I want 'em to get to know me, really me, exactly the kind of clod I am."

Watching Kovacs "get through" at a TV show can be a fairly tempestuous experience. Earlier this year he guest-starred in and subverted a usually well-behaved musical divertissement called *The Big Record*. It was 8 P.M., a half hour before air time, and Kovacs tumbled through the high-tension, split-second mazes of the C.B.S. studio like a merry-mustached hellion. At the finale of the dress rehearsal he seized Patti Page's little finger and mimed exploring his nose with it. At 8:15, while everyone else communed with lyrics or studied lines, poker cards were flying in the wings between Kovacs and Marty Kummer, his MCA agent. At 8:25 he jumped up in apparent terror to shout at the stagehands. "No, not the campus set! They changed that to a torture chamber!" At 8:28 he did a jig in back of the flats, cigar in full eruption. He was not "on," as some comedians always have to be. Nobody had time to watch him, and he didn't even seem to be aware of himself as he hopped along the wall, puffing away, wailing a weird tune under his breath.

"I like to let go just before the show," he explains such behavior. "That's the time I don't want to suppress any impulses. It's

like revving up your personality. Then it's all there when you hit the camera."

At 8:30 he pirouetted past his personal prop bearer, tossed him four dollar bills as though they were roses, and escaped thanks with a Swan Lake leap. At 8:31, right on cue, a haphazard motion brought him into fifteen million living rooms where he said his first line with spur-of-the-moment chattiness.

At 8:35, and back to poker while three yards away Miss Page sang of sad love. 8:50: The producer called for the Nairobi Trio, the one typically Kovacsian bit in the show. Kovacs got up, but instead of putting on his costume began to play snake charmer to the electric cables, very upset that they wouldn't dance. This convulsed a script girl but tortured the stage manager. At 8:52, some forty seconds before his cue, Kovacs tossed on his ape mask and ape gloves. "You guys look like you're in show business too," he said to his fellow anthropoids, walking toward the fifteen million living rooms.

The Nairobi Trio, as almost every antenna owner must know, restates the Book of Job in terms of a nihilistic operetta. To the eerie tintinnabulation of a certain record tune three monkeys snap into unearthly motion; one at an upright, pushing down piano keys as though they were gearshifts; a second wielding xylophone hammers without benefit of xylophone; and the baton of the third presiding over the whole madness with rigid precision. At a certain recurrent phrase Kovacs, the conductor monster, is clouted on the head by his ensemble's xylophonist. The manner, nuance and mood of the clout may vary with each performance, but it always produces a drool of bottomless consternation on the conductor's snout, it always dramatizes the unfathomability of fate and the treacherousness of life, and it always has the audience in stitches over seeing someone else betrayed.

8:54: Kovacs, the chimp-in-chief, returned to the wings, arms around his two cohorts. Off went the simian apparel, up came Kovacs' shirt end with which he dried off sweat formed under the mask. Then he leaned toward a studio watchman. "Gonna loan me a comb, or are you going to be a prig?" Coiffured at 8:56, he entrechatted into the finale.

At 9:15 members of the cast sat in the Cordial Café opposite the studio, talking about Mr. K. The discussion produced an astounding fact. As of this writing, Kovacs has not only no sponsors but also no enemies.

"I don't know anybody who doesn't like the guy," said Peter Hanley, the No. 2 ape and featured singer of Kovacs' former regular series. "You never feel he's putting on all those shenanigans just to kid the tensions away. It's not calculated. He's naturally that way, and you become that way, too, when you work with him. Everybody in the show gets to be sort of a happy maniac. Nothing throws you, even if there's a foul-up."

"Like tonight there was a little boo-boo," said a script girl.

"That's right," Hanley said. "Barbra Loden—she's the girl who's usually the third ape—she couldn't make it. We had to train a third ape in a hurry, and the timing went snafu. That Nairobi thing is a bitch, you know. Well, did you see how Ernie came back from the bit with his arms around us? That meant, 'Never mind, it wasn't anybody's fault.' It's the kind of guy he is."

"Ernie's the only uncalibrated V.I.P. I know," a network press girl said. "The other big shots in this business are so damn precise with their kindnesses. I used to be a sort of column-item planter for a few N.B.C. stars, and I always got a bottle of Christmas booze each from the names I handled. One bottle of booze is what I rate. Guess how many I got from Ernie last year—and that after I stopped working for him? Five! Not a half dozen either—

it wouldn't be like him, one of those exact big kindnesses. But five bottles, that's Ernie all over."

Practically everything about Kovacs is big and inexact, including his height, nominally six feet two but slouch-reduced by a varying number of inches. Kovacs' New York abode displays similar vagaries. His apartment lies on the unfashionable West Side, a highly imprecise location to be inhabited by a celebrity. But it is a vast duplex penthouse, containing sixteen rooms, seven bathrooms, four telephone lines with countless extensions, four complete hi-fi systems, several centuries of antiques, porcelain and ivory collections, a mounted armory of guns, two giant wooden blackamoors, and a miniature Yorkshire terrier named Pamela.

Yet all these posh vistas somehow avoid the protestation of success customary in Kovacs' bracket (current motion-picture salary, $7500 a week). There is here the tropical luxuriance common to show-biz Hungarians, even second-generation ones like Kovacs. But there is also the informality of the Trenton boy who has never bothered to shake off Jersey. Amidst the rampant good taste everywhere, hangs a huge portrait of Edie Adams (Mrs. Ernie) entwined with Kovacs' two children of a previous marriage, which testifies to nothing but the pokiest sentiment. From under carpets and out of panelings, wells a certain heartwarming and irrepressible messiness. A hike through the various reaches of the penthouse is likely to turn up some jovial disorder at any time of day. The connoisseur in Kovacsian dishevelment, however, ought to take his trip across the apartment on the morning after one of the master's all-night poker games.

These revels, by the way, may take place at any of Kovacs' three homes: in Hollywood, in New York State's Rockland County, and at Central Park West. Recently, I came on the remnants of a Central Park West party still around at twenty minutes to noon. The apartment, of course, was at optimum disarray.

On the terrace with its voluptuous view across Central Park, the chaises longues lay sopping because nobody had bothered to take them in during the night's rain. In the living room a half-dead cigar had toppled from an ash tray onto a marble table. From a gold, carved knob in a hallway closet dangled a jacket even though there were hangers galore inside. Piles of television scripts in Kovacs' study were held down not by paperweights, which lay idly elsewhere, but by poker-chip containers. The solarium, an eyrie made of sky and glass, was exuberantly littered with cards.

To perfect the casual chaos of it all, Kovacs appeared walking to one of the apartment doors with his arm around Sidney Chaplin. Kovacs chugged away bouncily at his freshly lit cheroot. But young Chaplin (Charlie's son and a Broadway-musical lead) showed the effects of a fourteen-hour poker game. His countenance was a symphony in ashen gray.

"Gee, it was great," Kovacs said at the threshold. "Good night, old clod." It was 11:46 A.M.

Kovacs shuffled into his sun-filled study, greeted me, made a monstrous face into a mirror, and observed that he looked a little punchy.

"I didn't get to bed last night either," he said. "I spent it by this desk—wait a minute, that must have been night before last. Well, whatever night it was before the game, I spent it here, doing odds and ends kicking around a spectacular."

"You mean you've been up for forty-eight hours?" said agent Kummer, another walking ruin, who had just materialized from the card room.

"Why not?" Kovacs asked. I said that was remarkable.

"Not for this here clod," Kovacs said. His rather low and gentle tone, often a contrast to his burly Broadway vocabulary, became more pronounced. "I was just thinking the other day. I've been on that kind of schedule ever since I got out of Trenton High twenty years ago. And the funny thing is I sort of drifted into show business because I had nothing else to do after graduation. I didn't want to become something solid like my brother (a civilian employee of the Air Force) or my father (a restaurant owner). No plans or ambitions. I started to fool around in summer stock."

"Fooled yourself right into the hospital," Kummer growled, examining *his* post-poker face.

"Well, I wanted to fool around my own way," Kovacs said. "I couldn't get the parts I wanted. So I got my own organization. I was practically a one-clod stock company. I auditioned actors with a paint brush in my hand, and starred, produced, directed and cleaned up the john, and opening night I looked over the footlights and, by God, there were seven people in the audience."

"Bet you went on too," Kummer said bitterly.

"To me it wasn't a small audience, it was an intimate performance," Kovacs said. "For years I was Jersey's most intimate performer."

"Till you went to the hospital," Kummer said, stubbornly.

"Best rest I ever had," Kovacs said. "A year and a half. Pneumonia and pleurisy."

"Overworked?" I asked.

"Overcardplayed," said Kummer.

"The only thing I ever could relax with is cards," Kovacs said. "Tennis I love, and swimming, but I always feel I ought to be working instead. But with poker I don't feel guilty, because—well, I tried to analyze it the other day. Maybe because it's one way to catch up on my friendships. I can't be a one-cocktail-every-three-months friend. If a guy is a friend and he's around, I want to poker it out with him one or two nights a week."

At this, Kummer expired with a groan into a sofa and never stirred to life again.

After the hospital Kovacs was supposed to "rest" in radio. He went to work for WTTM in Trenton, where they made him chief announcer, director of special events, and night disc jockey. Then a Philadelphia TV station heard him broadcast a wrestling match. "So they hired me for a cooking show. And then I got my own show. Heck, I had my own station. I was on the air thirteen hours a week at WPTZ. No secretary, no typist, just a migraine headache." Kovacs demonstrated that he is the one man alive who can smile sadly with a cigar in his mouth.

"So then N.B.C. shoved me to New York to replace the hell out of guys like Steve Allen and Sid Caesar. Network's more exciting than local, but not so much fun. Your budget's bigger, network, and your headaches too. Like the pantomime show I did last year on N.B.C. Now they call it a classic, dirty names like that. The whole thing took me eighty minutes to write, not much longer than my Philly stuff. Now, there was one bit in the show with a set built at an eighteen-degree angle. The idea for that I always had—actually, that's my whole life philosophy, that the world's at an eighteen-degree angle—but it was the first time I had the money to build a big-scale set. For each fifty-second camera motion, like an olive rolling down a 'horizontal' table, we had to rehearse a whole afternoon. It's a nightmare when your dreams come true."

As if he had to fortify himself against the recollection, Kovacs bent over his table and yelled, "*Coffee, please.*" Marty Kummer on the sofa didn't stir.

"Rehearsals you can't ad-lib," Kovacs went on, more peacefully. "That's why I hate 'em. Ideas you've *got* to ad-lib, so I love 'em. Every idea I ever had is based on the fact that it's 2:30 and there's a production meeting at three. Like the Nairobi Trio. I had those ape masks lying around in the room and I was playing a record called *Solfeggio* which somebody had just sent me. Actually it's just an ear-training exercise. But when that wood-block clunk came on in the tune, I immediately had a divine revelation: One of those monkeys is getting a shot in the head! Only I wasn't sure what kind of a shot. I played it again, and this time I saw it: One monkey at the piano, one monkey conducting, one monkey braining. In fifteen minutes I was set. *Then* came the back-breaker. Working out the timing. *Doll!*"

Continued on Page 155

THE ANTIC ARTS

Continued from Page 91

Edie Adams had come in, beautiful, blond, diabolically sacked, a musical-comedy star bearing a coffee tray for her husband.

"Oh, no!" Kovacs jumped up and took the tray away from her. There followed something so tender that it imperiled the coffee and forced me to peruse my shoes.

"Look, doll," Kovacs said five little fondnesses later. He wrote a prideful figure on a sheet. "Last night."

"You won!" said Miss Adams, electrified.

"Give me a smooch," said Kovacs, and led his wife back to the corridor. There, not entirely out of eyeshot, endearments were renewed, not only without any of the "darling!" veneer customary in show business, but with a bear-hugging heartiness orchestrated by joyous smacks, a display of affection rarely found outside of boat piers and railway platforms. The spectacle reminded me of something an N.B.C. executive said recently: "There's something elemental about Kovacs. He can't be formated. He's his own format, and that's a crime these days. He's the last spontaneous man."

Kovacs returned, all element and aglow. "Isn't she incredible?" he said. "I go A.W.O.L. two nights in a row, and she comes in with the coffee! I was thinking the other day. We've been apart much too much lately. Me making movies out West, and she back East."

He sighed and played morosely with a copy of *Zoomar*, his first novel, which was recently published to favorably surprised review. "Maybe I'll just write," he said. "I can do that anywhere, wherever Edie and the kids are. I love writing, anyway. I ad-libbed that novel. I did the thing in thirty-six-hour stretches, some forty pages at a time. I remember writing the last page—and it's a fairly big book, maybe a hundred thousand words—and I was rushing down to Edie to tell her I'm finished, when I looked at the calendar. It was thirteen days after I'd written the first line. Everybody's always so surprised at that. But it's the only way for me. If I start tinkering with a thing, it sounds labored. I don't see how these other writers operate."

He warmed his hand lovingly on an Edie-brought cup.

"You think it's crazy to write a book like that, the way you're looking at me. They looked at me like that when I started my first movie last year, *Operation Mad Ball*. They said I've got to change all my TV habits. Never look into the camera, never improvise, the whole works. It's not true at all. I found you can ad-lib in pictures too. Sometimes better. In Hollywood they never tried to squeeze me into some category the way they're always trying in TV. In *Mad Ball* I played an icky Army lieutenant. I'm a supernatural Mexican in *Bell, Book and Candle*, which hasn't been released, and in *Miss Casey Jones* I'll be a weird old tycoon. Anyway, any role I play is half nuts. That's understood. And Dick Quine—he's the director in all three of them—he's a member of the fraternity. I mean he knows, too, that the world's really at an eighteen-degree angle. Dick and I play poker right on the set, even while they're putting make-up on me ——"

Suddenly he stopped. He ran over to a mantel shelf lined with a number of Chinese ivory figures. His hand held up a tiny mandarin, whose face had split off and fallen into a fold of its tunic. "*Look at that!*" Kovacs said in a flabbergasted, entirely different voice. In vain he tried to restore the face to the figurine. "The poor bastard."

There was nothing of the collector's chagrin in the phrase, but a bottomless and naïve disconcertment, as though he had a secret five-year-old cheek somewhere that had just been slapped. An apple-cheeked emotion appeared round his eyes which cigar, poker virility and heavyweight physique made all the more vivid. His stance recalled the conductor of the Nairobi Trio just after the clout. Perhaps his discomfiture

dramatized his peculiar genius: in the ability to visualize in one small outlandishness a large dilemma of life; in his capacity to be amazed by what is negligible to most, but which he can tickle the world into seeing.

He stood there, still trying to press the old mandarin's head back into place. It kept falling off, and at last he gave up and merely stroked his little Chinese. Cigar drooping, he rocked him to and fro.

Through the intercom the secretary announced that she was going out for lunch. "Good night, Lillian," Kovacs said from deep within a sad trance, standing there, gently swaying. It was 1:46 P.M. He looked like exactly what he is: a great big slob of a poet. **THE END**

NATIONAL BROADCASTING COMPANY
CORRESPONDENCE MEMO

_____ 19 ___

TONIGHT (Monday-Tuesday) KOVACS - Budget

D:

ABOVE THE LINE

Cast and Talent
Kovacs	1250	
Guests	1810	
Writers & Producer	1200	
Announcer	400	
Director	550	
Orchestra	1560	
Orchestra Conductor	600	7370

BELOW THE LINE

Technical Facilities
Engineering Personnel	1500	
Studio Usage	2970	
Sound Effects	150	
AD and SM	260	
Monitor	25	
Film	170	
HV Wipe	85	5160

Staging Services
Construction (and scenery)	350	
Props	500	
Painting	120	
Trucking	125	
Draperies	50	
Costumes	600	
Graphic Arts	110	
Set Design	160	
Stagehands	1900	
Wardrobe	120	
Special Effects	100	
Lighting Equipment	100	
Makeup	40	
Storage	50	
Contingency	200	4525

Miscellaneous
Teleprompter	200	
Travel and Entertainment	200	
Film Usage	100	
Film Print	120	
Film Editing	60	
Contingency	200	880

17,935   TOTAL

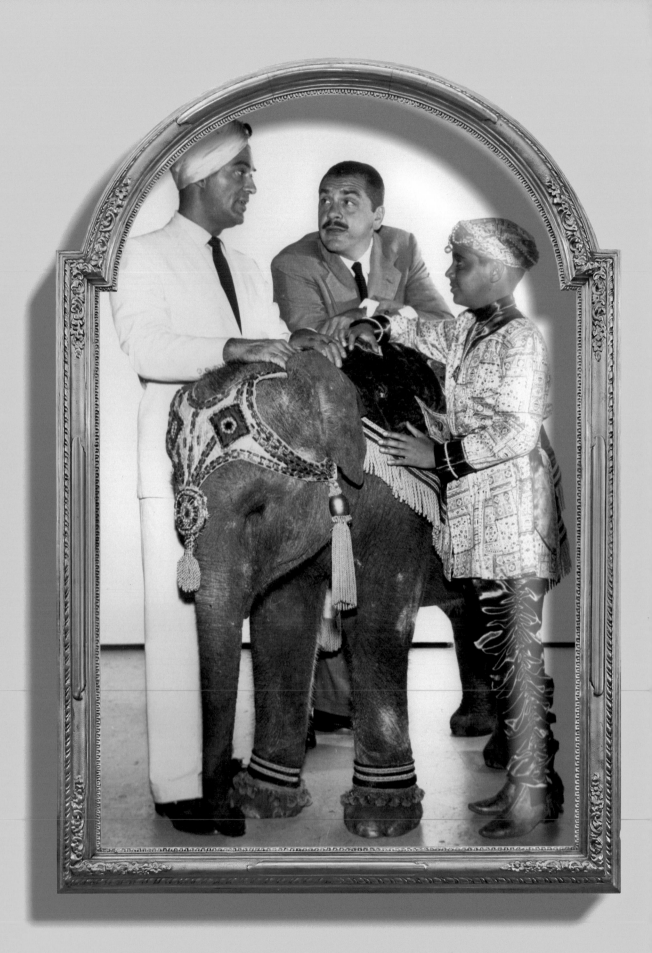

Annotations

Image annotations by Ben Model

01   *From Kovacs's cigar order, during a trip to Havana, Cuba, in April 1955.*

06   **TOP:** *See annotation for p. 183.*

07   **TOP:** *See annotation for p. 183.*

08   *Taken during the taping of the "Dinner Symphony", where people eat dinner in time to a movement from the* Seven Beauties Ballet *by Kara Karayev. Part of Kovacs special #2, taped on April 22, 1961 and aired May 18, 1961.*

10   *Ernie's "Uncle Gruesome" character, seen here mid-1950s in a photo taken off the TV screen and sent in by a fan. Kovacs encouraged viewers to do this and to mail them to him at "Snepshots" at the TV station's mailing address. Edie Adams saved several boxes of these. For some reason, Kovacs did this character as "Auntie Gruesome" in some of the video clues for* Take a Good Look *(1959-1961).*

11   **TOP:** *April 23, 1956 (NBC) Edie sings "You're the Top" in front of a faux TV set during an episode of Kovacs's daily half-hour show, and then after "...surprises Edie." At the end of the song, the puppeteer turns out to be Kovacs himself. At the beginning of the number, the puppet in the window is "O'Brian," the monkey from "The Kapusta Kid in Outer Space"; at one point in the song, the puppet is switched for this one of Ernie, and it surprises Edie. There is a piece of rubber tubing that allows cigar smoke to be puffed through it so the puppet appears to be smoking.*

11   **BOTTOM:** *The tire hanging on the set of either* Kovacs Unlimited *(1952-54, CBS) or* The Ernie Kovacs Show *(1954-55, DuMont) is seen closer here, revealing what appear to be autographs of guests who had been on the show.*

12   **BOTTOM:** *Another possibly-DuMont-show "snepshot."*

14-15   **CENTER OF SPREAD:** *Article in* Trenton Evening Times — *February 27, 1949.*

15   **CENTER:** *Article in* Trenton Evening Times — *July 1, 1951 announcing Kovacs's national summer replacement show that stood in for the popular* Kukla, Fran and Ollie; *it was for this show that Edythe Adams auditioned and was hired. Edie used the name Edythe up to 1952, then changed how her name was spelled to Edith from 1952 to 1954, and used Edie from 1955 on.*

16   *Ad for the 1968 compilation special* The Comedy of Ernie Kovacs.

18   **TOP:** *Undated photo, although likely somewhere 1954–56, of two of the three members of The Nairobi Trio. Kovacs is most probably the ape on the right, as he was usually the group's conductor. It's anybody's guess who the mallet-wielding one is, as members of the trio rotated, changed, or were occasionally celebrities at live performances whose identity was never revealed to the audience. Another inside joke on Kovacs's part.*

20   TOP: *Ernie, Edie, and Ernie's daughters Kippie and Elizabeth on vacation overseas, ca. 1954-55.*

20   CENTER: *Ernie moved to New City, NY, when he got the* CBS Kovacs Unlimited *daily show (1952-54). It was a town where a lot of musicians and other showbiz people lived then.*

20   BOTTOM: *Edie, with Ernie's daughters Kippie and Elizabeth in the background, during a vacation in Acapulco, ca. 1954-55.*

21   TOP: *Unidentified photo of young Kovacs, probably taken during one of his summer stock stints in the Hamptons.*

21   BOTTOM: *Ernie Kovacs, during his Philadelphia years (1950-52).*

22   *Undated publicity photo, although from Edie's hair and makeup and that pinky ring of Ernie's, this looks like it was taken during the NBC era, in 1956.*

24   *Ernie in New City, NY; most of "The Mysterious Knockwurst" film that Ernie made for "Unlimited" looks like it was shot in that town.*

27   *This photo is seen, used, and right-clicked a lot, but without any context. This was taken on the set of* Take a Good Look, *the bizarro panel-quiz show that Ernie hosted. This was the first regularly scheduled show either of them had done since 1956, and was done on tape with a studio audience, and aired in what would be Ernie's same time slot for the remainder of his TV career: Thursdays at 10:30 on ABC. Right after* The Untouchables.

28   *Unidentified posed photo of Ernie and Edie at home, ca. 1953-55.*

29   *Piano-conductor part for a duet to be sung by Ernie and Edie; the song is "Inch Worm" by Frank Loesser, from his score for the movie* Hans Christian Andersen; *date is probably 1956 as Peter Matz was the arranger on Kovacs's shows on NBC.*

30   *Ernie has taken the opportunity of a spread in the May 14, 1960 issue of* TV Guide *to promote* Take a Good Look *to instead pen a piece of humor and have some fun with a photo shoot to accompany it.*

31   (SEE ABOVE)

32   *Unidentified sketch from NBC Kovacs show (1956), with announcer Bill Wendell, who was also part of the sketch performers ensemble and who was later the announcer on David Letterman's late-night shows.*

35   *Main title card from the DuMont-era* The Ernie Kovacs Show *(1954-55), taken off a TV screen. A "snepshot" taken moments later, it seems, mid-dissolve into the show.*

36   TOP: *See attribution for p. 74.*

36   CENTER: *Credit title cards for the 1956 Ernie Kovacs shows on NBC. The technical crew were usually listed by name, but occasionally a joke title like this one would appear.*

36   BOTTOM: (SEE ABOVE)

38   *Kovacs often would have the director cut to extreme close-ups of parts of his face. There are a few "time-killers" that survive on kinescopes of the NBC-era shows where Kovacs needed to fill 15 seconds before going to a commercial or promo spot, and he goes to an* *extremely tight close-up of his face and moves eyebrows, earlobes, et al. in time to the show's drummer playing.*

41   **BOTTOM:** *A 1952 promotional image for use on-air for* Three to Get Ready *(1950-52) Kovacs's wake-up show on WPTZ in Philadelphia. The show's name comes from the fact that this local NBC affiliate was on Channel 3; photo gives a good look at early television production and the show's set.*

42-43   *The closing shot from "Baseball Film" (1951) which Kovacs reused a number of times on all of the 1950s-era shows.*

48   *Was your 8th birthday party written up in the local paper? And if it was, did it get this much space? The attention and money lavished on Ernie by his folks in his early years is notable in this announcement...which may not have been free considering it wasn't actually "news."*

49   *One of the more popular or oft-performed of the Percy odes. Ernie updated the cultural references in "Stanley's Pussycat" over the years he performed it. This version is probably from 1960 as it matches the text recorded for the LP.*

51   *Popular, at age four? Decades later, Kovacs would spoof bratty, spoiled kids in his sketches.*

52   **LEFT:** *Not your typical 13th birthday party, being "feted" as a surprise with an orchestra featuring vocalists and tap dancers. This was 1932, before the repeal of Prohibition the following year put an end to Kovacs's father's stint (and income) as a bootlegger.*

52   **RIGHT:** *Candid photo of Joe Mikolas as "Rancid the Devil Horse," from Ernie's send-up of westerns on TV, from ABC special #7, taped July 22, 1961 and aired Dec 12, 1961; Mikolas is wearing lederhosen from the "Einsam Aufseher" sketch.*

53   **TOP:** *Ernie had multiple duties at WPTZ as an announcer, one of which included the show* Deadline for Dinner, *during which chefs from local Philadelphia restaurants would come to the studio and cook dishes. Ernie often referred to the show as "Dead Lion for Breakfast."*

53   **BOTTOM:** *1959 newspaper story promoting* Take a Good Look *(ABC, 1959-60).*

57   **TOP:** *Kovacs was planning to make a movie called* Eugene. *While it is not known whether Kovacs saw Jacques Tati's* Monsieur Hulot's Holiday *(1953) or, more importantly,* Mon Oncle *(1958), it's not too hard to connect the dots of influence. Not just with Kovacs, but also with Jerry Lewis. The non-linear narrative comedy form Tati employed and his films' worldwide success turn up in Lewis's* The Bellboy *(1960),* The Ladies Man *(1961), and* The Errand Boy *(1961).*

60-66   *This article about Kovacs and his television comedy appeared in the magazine* After Hours, *a magazine which only published four issues — all of them during 1957. The photos look like they were taken of Ernie during his stint as host of* Tonight!, *during which Edie was appearing in* L'il Abner *on Broadway. Although this article is in issue number 2, it reads as though it had been written before* Tonight! *was cancelled on January 15, 1957. There is also mention of the NBC color* Silent Show, *which aired on January 19, 1957. Had Kovacs's regularly scheduled TV work not stopped mid-January, this would've been a nice piece of publicity for him.*

67   **CENTER TOP:** *Late night had caught on a little more by 1956, at least to the point that Kovacs wasn't having "Admit one passing stranger" printed on the tickets. He'd done that for the DuMont show in 1955, when getting a live studio audience for a live late-night show was like pulling teeth.*

67   **CENTER BOTTOM:** *November 1956 was Kovacs's second month doing tag-team hosting duties with Steve Allen on* Tonight! *The show would be cancelled during January 1957.*

68   **BOTTOM:** *Ernie and Edie played the Tropicana night club in Las Vegas in 1957.*

69   *Kovacs's notoriety as a local personality is in evidence here. This is most probably from the tail end of his days at WTTM radio in Trenton, as the Martha Vickers picture is a 1949 release, despite the A&C comedy being a 1942 film and top billed.*

70-71   *Ernie in Kovacsland title card, which would have been placed on a stand in front of a TV camera. This show was a summer replacement for* Kukla, Fran and Ollie *that ran July-August 1951, and was Ernie's first national exposure. It was also the occasion for his needing to hire a "girl singer" — Edythe Adams. Kinescopes survive for episodes of the first and last weeks of the show.*

72   **BORDER:** *The feature story heralded on the cover of this August 18, 1951 issue of a local TV guide appears on pages 218-219 of this book.*

72   **CENTER:** *A newspaper ad for* Three to Get Ready, *Ernie's daily wake-up show for WPTZ Channel 3 in Philadelphia.*

73   *First page of one of "The Kapusta Kid in Outer Space" puppet sketches that were done throughout the run of the daytime* The Ernie Kovacs Show *(NBC, 1955-56).*

74   **TOP:** *"Pathé News" was a newsreel series that ran in US theaters from the 1920s through the 1950s and whose slogan was "The Eyes and Ears of the World." The Skavocian "Pathetic News" was of course "The Eyes, Ears, Nose and Throat" of the world, and was a series of gag news stories done as blackouts of various lengths.*

74   **BOTTOM:** *Title card for the Percy Dovetonsils segments on Kovacs's shows. While this graphic does not have a date on the back, it looks like others from either the WPTZ (1951-52) or CBS (1952-54) era. For the 1955-56 NBC shows, the title read "Percy Dovetonsils: Poet Laureate." The title here spoofs a 1940s radio program called* Between the Bookends, *hosted by Ted Malone who read poetry to listeners. Percy was not a spoof of Malone himself, but of the concept of his program.*

75   *What prompted the making of this puppet is not known, although a possible clue is that its only surviving appearance is on an episode of* The Ernie Kovacs Show *on April 23, 1956 (NBC, daytime)...a date that is one week after Edie's birthday. See annotation for p. 11 (top).*

76   *The puppet show set for "The Kapusta Kid in Outer Space," Ernie's regular sketch that appealed to kids who may have been watching, as well as adults. From the NBC daytime show that aired weekdays at 10:30am Eastern. Note the "Skavoc" ("Kovacs" backwards) legend at the top. This was a brand name Ernie had been using for years for spoof commercials.*

77   *Grootz the Funnel Monster, an evil overlord of sorts, from Kapusta's adventures on The Square Planet. There is another character from The Square Planet that does not survive, Spiegel the Sponge-head. Spiegel is basically a large sponge with eyes.*

78-79   *This prop is from the workshop of Burlington Gearshift, a mealy-mouthed, nerdy character of Kovacs's who was an inventor. One surviving episode of the NBC morning show (April 30, 1956) with Edie as a reporter interviewing Gearshift in his workshop shows this prop on the set.*

80   **TOP RIGHT:** *The Kapusta Kid, from the puppet segment "The Kapusta Kid in Outer Space," which appeared two or three times a week on the NBC morning show throughout its run. The puppets were made by Larry Berthelson. Berthelson was the founder of the Pickwick Puppet Theater in NYC. "The Kapusta Kid in Outer Space" followed the terrestrial and interplanetary exploits of the Kapusta Kid (who spoke with a severe lateral lisp).*

80   **TOP LEFT:** *"The Lady Known as Lester," one of the Kapusta Kid puppets, voiced by Edie.*

80   **BOTTOM RIGHT:** *Celeste, another one of the Kapusta Kid puppets, voiced by Edie.*

80   **BOTTOM LEFT:** *O'Brian, the Sicilian Monkey, another of Kapusta's sidekicks, who spoke with a Chico Marx-type accent.*

81   *Albumen the Horse, Kapusta's sidekick and right-hand man, spoke with a dopey dumb-guy kind of voice.*

82   *Promotional photo of Ernie and Edie, for* Kovacs Unlimited *(CBS 1952-54).*

83-85   *More humor writing. Kovacs was always writing… According to Edie Adams, Kovacs would have his typewriter brought to his dressing room on movie sets so that he could write.*

86-94   *From* Sing a Pretty Song, *by Edie Adams: "In November 1956, just as I was opening in* Li'l Abner *on Broadway, not only was Ernie for the first time not doing three shows at once, he wasn't even doing one. ABC had canceled the radio show, and both NBC shows went off. He was still under contract to NBC, and the network was looking for a new format for Ernie, which he did not want. He wanted airtime and to be left alone.*

At a meeting at NBC, in a big boardroom, to determine the content of his next program, the network presented him with an appointed creative team. This strong producer, executive producer, and director, each of whom was adamant in his idea of what Ernie should do, tried to streamline "zany, wacky, unpredictable Ernie."

Each one presented, from the head of the table, his idea of what Kovacs was all about, while Ernie sat silently on the sidelines. As he told me, two or three times he tried politely to interrupt, to say that it wasn't going to work that way, but nobody paid any attention. The director was saying, "No, this is absolutely the way it's going to be done." As the director was continuing in his diatribe, Ernie raised his hand like a kid at school and said softly, "Excuse me, I have to go make a phone call," and tiptoed out of the room. Once outside, his Hungarian temper must have boiled over because instead of going to the phone, he kept right on down the hall, down the elevator, and out the Sixth Avenue entrance. He walked home, north about forty blocks, to Ninetieth Street; although it was bitter cold, he didn't seem to notice. He had left his vicuña coat, muffler, hat, and alligator briefcase behind. He walked into the apartment, still in a fury, told me the story, and sat down at his typewriter. He stayed there for nearly two weeks, having only carbon paper, food, and an occasional drink delivered. He napped on the sofa in his den whenever he was tired. Otherwise he wrote straight through.

When he handed me Zoomar, *a novel about a rising television executive in the middle of the network power structure, its fictional characters read very much like our life. The Miss Wipola sounded suspiciously like a certain Miss U.S. Television contest in which I had been very much involved. The couple had a nice country place up in New City, New York. Rereading the book recently brought back into sharp focus what day-by-day life was like in television and at home as we lived it in the 1950's, fake flip dialogue and all. After all, the leading lady was named Eileen.*

The hero of Zoomar, *Tom Moore, is an advertising account executive "at liberty" who suddenly finds himself a TV producer and an expert in a field about which he knows nothing — par for the course. As Ernie's alter ego he comes up against a host of characters who were thinly disguised real people we all knew. He even included in the novel an extramarital affair for the man, something I felt was totally unnecessary.*

When the book came out, Pete Martin of the Saturday Evening Post, *the best interviewer I ever met, asked Ernie how he could have written the book in thirteen days. Ernie told him:*

> *When you're writing about a subject you know, because it's all you've done for eight years, it's spontaneous writing. You don't even have to do research.... I wrote my book this way: I had no plot, I wrote the first line, then I wrote the second line, then I wrote the third line. I kept on that way. Some days I wrote 40 pages, some days two.... I would never revise. The TV shows I wrote went straight from my typewriter to the copy-makers. I don't change a thing. I figure the first things a man says are his spontaneous things. I know it sounds ridiculous but I looked at* The Man in the Gray Flannel Suit *and* Don't Go Near the Water *to see how long they were. They are good books, so I'd make mine the same number of pages. Then I had an even better idea, ''I'll make mine as long as* From Here to Eternity." *At that point I had six hundred pages, then I got a hurry up call to make a movie, so I made the book shorter, pages lopped off — about a hundred. It was just as well, I would have talked too much if it had run as long as I had originally planned."*

96   *While this could have been ghostwritten by one of Ernie's writers, it's certainly got his style and it's not inconceivable that he could've dashed this off himself.*

97   **UPPER LEFT:** *Kovacs directing Joe Blauner in the "Dinner Symphony" from ABC Special #2, in which a group of people eat a meal in time to a piece of music by Hungarian composer Kara Karayev.*

97   **RIGHT:** *Kovacs as "Irving Wong, Moo Goo Gai Pan Alley Song-Writer".*

98   **LEFT:** *Kovacs in one of several costumes he wore in a Dutch Masters cigar commercial from 1960; in the spot, Kovacs speaks into a mike that isn't working; he looks around and sees that everyone on the crew — all of them played by Kovacs - are too distracted by the flavor and aroma of their Dutch Masters cigars to make sure anything is plugged in.*

98   **RIGHT:** *Cover of* High *men's magazine, the April 1958 issue that includes the following chapter from Kovacs's novel* Zoomar.

99-103   *The article printed here is actually a chapter from* Zoomar *and not a piece of humor prose Kovacs wrote for the magazine.*

105-111   *This article in the March 1958 issue of* Real for Men, *a monthly whose sub-head was "The Exciting Magazine," is one of the rare instances of evidence of Ernie's working methods and demeanor. The lengthy quotes from Kovacs's NBC producer Perry Cross give a glimpse into what working on a Kovacs show would have been like. Although published in March 1958, the research and interviewing may have happened during the fall of 1957, given a reference elsewhere in the piece to Kovacs having been in the one-off "Topaze" that aired in September 1957. Kovacs did not have a weekly show from January 1957 until October 1959 and was doing guest shots and making movies during this time. A section of this part of the article in* Real for Men *covers Ernie's stint as a guest panelist on* What's My Line? *from August 11 to November 3 of 1957. The line about his possibly likely being the successor to Fred Allen's seat on the panel is interesting. This could be a clue as to the photo of Kovacs and Allen together elsewhere in this book, as well as to the conflation of the two comedians as to the origin of the medium-rare-well-done line about TV.*

111   **BOTTOM:** *Business card for the Ernie Kovacs and Edie Adams fan clubs, ca. 1990s.*

112-116   *Yet another piece of humor writing that wound up published posthumously in one of the "gentlemen's magazines" of the early 1960s.*

117   *Kovacs and Bobby Lauher, in a moment from one of the clues on* Take a Good Look *(ABC, 1959-60).*

118   *A draft of something written for Percy Dovetonsils — "file with Percy poems" — although undated, it's probable that it was written in 1956, given the references to RCA and Sarnoff. Kovacs often ribbed Sarnoff and Pat Weaver on-air in this NBC morning show.*

119   *Percy Dovetonsils poem "Ode to a Dude Ranch" in unidentified magazine.*

120   **BOTTOM LEFT:** *Ernie Kovacs has been quoted as saying, "Television is a medium, so called because it is neither rare nor well-done." Many times, over and over, and yet there is no instance of this line in print or in a recording anywhere by Ernie. Ernie and Fred Allen were both panelists on* What's My Line? *and overlapped, and there is evidence that the line was actually said by Fred Allen. It sounds more like a Fred Allen line, although it certainly fits Ernie's sensibilities and quite probably has been conflated as a Kovacs line. After all, who remembers Fred Allen?*

120   **CENTER RIGHT:** *Unidentified radio studio photo. Going by the microphone and that pinky ring, this could have been taken during the run of Kovacs's 6-9am dee-jay stint on ABC radio in New York (May 1955-August 1956).*

120   **BOTTOM RIGHT:** *Production photo taken during the taping of Ernie's first special for ABC. The ballerina is Muriel Landers; the spinning cow head from the 1812 Overture sound-into-sight music piece is visible.*

121   *On-set photo during an episode of* The Ernie Kovacs Show *(NBC 1955-56) of Kovacs, Edie as Marilyn Monroe, and singer-songwriter Matt Dennis. See annotation for p. 120, above, regarding the Kovacs quote seen here.*

122   *Ernie's Percy Dovetonsils character was created during the WPTZ era, most probably in 1951. There was less than no budget, and the show's props — if there were any — came from the local 5¢ & 10¢ store. These were novelty glasses that made it look like you were awake, so you could sleep during class. Clearly someone (Ernie?) has drawn the eyelids at half-mast with grease pencil.*

124   *Ernie recorded an album for Warner Bros. in 1960 entitled* Percy Dovetonsils....Thpeakth *that was never released, due to creative interference from the label and Ernie's staunch resistance to that interference. Rights for the project went to Vanguard, and then to Cedars-Sinai, and eventually years later back to Edie. Tracks from this were included on* The Ernie Kovacs Record Album *— released by Columbia in 1975 and reissued by Omnivore Recordings in 2019 — including one that ends with Percy saying, "Ready for side two...?" This, and Kovacs's mentioning the record in his 1961 CBC interview, prompted Kovacs archivist Ben Model's search for the elements for the album — and a eureka moment happened when going through the Ediad collection's holdings.*

127   *Typed script for the introduction to side one of* Percy Dovetonsils....Thpeakth. *It differs only slightly from the recording.*

128   *Script for the band (which is what "tracks" were called on LPs) that would be the end of side one, cueing the listener to turn the record over. That track ends side one of* The Ernie Kovacs Album, *released by Columbia Records in 1975, the first time the recording had ever been heard, as the Percy record languished in vaults for 52 years before finally getting released by Omnivore Recordings.*

129   *This poem was written and performed as both "Ode to a Bookworm" and as "Happy Birthday to a Bookworm." The latter has a slightly different ending, where, rather than the worm's demise because the cats had hidden his Alka Seltzer, Percy the birthday well-wisher has enrolled him in "Book-of-the-Month."*

130   *Typed script pages for "Black Day at White Rock" show detail of Kovacs's writing of the sketch. Of note here is the cinematic style in Kovacs's vision, which is more so than typical sketches.* Caesar's Hour *on NBC from 1954-1957 overlapped Kovacs's tenure at NBC; Kovacs was given the summer replacement slot for Caesar's show in 1956.*

131   *There is no date attributed to the "Black Day...," sketch unfortunately, and so we do not know if it was written before or after Kovacs's summer replacement, which aired in Caesar's time slot Monday evenings from July through September 1956. The MGM movie,* Bad Day at Black Rock, *was released in early 1955.*

132   *Kovacs did a spoof of the famous-at-the-time commercial for White Rock beverages on the summer replacement show on July 30, 1956. The "White Rock Girl" logo depicted the goddess "Psyche" perched on a rock surrounded by water. In Kovacs's takeoff, he stamps his foot and the woman on the rock slips and slides into the water. The following week, claiming they'd heard from the White Rock people, Kovacs showed a kinescope film of the bit...running backwards.*

133   *Handwritten script page for "Black Day at White Rock," which appears to be a sketch Kovacs was proposing or writing (on spec?) for* Caesar's Hour, *the show Sid Caesar did following the run of* Your Show of Shows, *which had run on NBC from 1950-1954.*

134-135   *It's unclear as to what this what written or intended for, but it's possible Kovacs's jumping-off point may have been the Tennyson poem, "The Lotos-Eaters."*

136   *Screen grabs of Kovacs from the beginning of "Eugene" (ABC special #6, November 1961.)*

137-139   *Kovacs hinted at his interest in making a "Eugene" movie in an interview on the CBC in the summer of 1961 on the program* The Lively Arts. *He describes the film's opening sequence, down to what kind of lens was to be used. He also talks about the idea of Alec Guinness, whom he'd met and worked with on* Our Man in Havana *(1959), portraying Eugene. These details match what is in these typed proposal pages.*

   Kovacs had spent three years playing meanies in light comedy features for Columbia, and did not have the creative outlet doing a TV show would have offered. The panel-quiz show Take a Good Look *(1959-1961) was a close second. Lewis's* The Bellboy *was released in the summer of 1960, and it's conceivable that Kovacs had the idea somewhere in 1959 or 1960 to revisit the character and sketches that were his ticket to the "big time."*

   In 1961, following the filming of the CBC interview, Kovacs appears to have bumped the 6th ABC special, already taped in July and intended for air in November, according to the show's opening slate, to the #7 slot in December. Kovacs wrote, produced, and shot a remake of the "Eugene" show for air in November, and instead of the usual 3rd-Thursday-of-the-month-at-10:30pm slot, got the Friday of Thanksgiving weekend for the "Eugene" special, pre-empting The Flintstones *(ABC, 1960-1966), then in its second season. Was this Kovacs's way of doing a pilot for his intended feature film? We'll never know, although it seems likely.*

141   *This Percy ode was originally written back in the WPTZ era in the early 1950s.*

142-144   *A handful of Kovacs's humor pieces were published in men's magazines, posthumously, in 1962 and 1963. This one is from the magazine* Cavalier, *launched by Fawcett Publications in 1952. Per the attribution at the bottom, this is from Kovacs's unpublished manuscript* Please Excusa Da Pencil. *What is remarkable is that during a time of extraordinary amounts of activity — the ABC shows, acting in Hollywood movies, plus the endless gambling and card games — Kovacs still had the energy and focus to write these pieces. That is, unless he'd written them earlier, and the luck he had getting them in print is evidenced by these publishings after his untimely death.*

145   *Promotional photo of Kovacs in costume for one of the Dutch Masters commercials he wrote and directed for* Take a Good Look *(1960).*

147-151   *Another selection from* Please Excusa Da Pencil *in an issue of* Cavalier *magazine.*

152-157   *Yet another selection from* Please Excusa Da Pencil *in an issue of* Cavalier *magazine.*

161   *This article in* Focus, *a digest-sized men's magazine, was published in May 1953, to promote Ernie's Tuesday night show on CBS. Considering he was up against Milton Berle and Bishop Sheen, it only ran for 4 months and actually had been cancelled by the time "Kovacs Hates TV" was published.*

162-163   *Captain role number three, in* Wake Me When It's Over *(1960), starring Dick Shawn, Jack Warden, and Margo Moore. Kovacs got tired of playing the same role as the one he'd been cast in for* Operation Mad Ball *(1957), that of the buzz-kill military officer in command. Kovacs took out a full-page ad in* Variety *that read simply, in his own handwriting: "PLEASE NO MORE @%*%!!!! CAPTAINS!" Despite his comedic abilities, Hollywood casting just saw him as an imposing 6' 4" Hungarian with a moustache.*

164   *Publicity photo for the unaired pilot* Medicine Man *(1962), which co-starred Buster Keaton.*

165   *Promotional poster for* Five Golden Hours *(1961), one of the rare films where Kovacs has the lead role and is not the meanie ruining the fun for the main characters.*

172-173   *Budget breakdowns for episodes of* Tonight! *during Kovacs's 4-month stint hosting the iconic late-night show on Mondays and Tuesdays. Steve Allen hosted the other nights of the week.*

175   *The date on this, the note about editing a show on the upcoming Sunday and Ernie's handwritten "tell Joe Mikolas" would indicate this was referencing the third* Ernie Kovacs Special *for ABC, taped May 28, 1961 for air on June 15, 1961.*

176   *Kovacs's den, where he did a lot of his writing, card-playing, and steam-bath-taking. It was intact when Josh Mills was a kid and growing up in that house on Bowmont Drive. This unidentified color photo looks like it was meant as promotion for the show* Silents, Please, *produced by Paul Killiam. Kovacs taped all his wraparounds in his den, and a few surviving kinescopes of those are the only footage of that room. Note the 8x10 of Kovacs as "Charlie Clod," his sendup of "Charlie Chan," in sketches in the mid-1950s.*

177-179   *Ernie's attention to detail and desire for creative control is evident in his writing this detailed fact-checking response to Robert Stein of* Redbook *for a profile on Ernie in June 1957. There don't appear to be any 1957 issues of* Redbook *that contain this article, unfortunately. Kovacs's own writing style and personality is evident here as well. No business-like language, or terse editorial comments like "cut this" etc. The reference mid-way the first page shown here to another comedian and the line not being Kovacs's own style is of interest. Could this be the infamous "medium-rare-well done" line that has long been attributed to Kovacs but is most probably a line from comedian Fred Allen?*

182   **BOTTOM LEFT:** *The EEFMS, pronounced "EE-fuhms", was the Kovacs shows' fan club. Originally launched in 1950 or 1951 when Ernie was doing the* Three to Get Ready *wake-up show on WPTZ and continued into his CBS era (1952-54) as seen here. There are fans who still have their membership cards.*

182   **RIGHT:** *Ernie on the cover of* Life *magazine. This followed the breakout success of the* Silent Show *that aired on NBC's Color Spectacular in January 1957. The articles and photo spread about Kovacs and his style of TV comedy considered the fact that his style might be the next direction in small-screen humor, given that so many of the sketch-and-monolog comedians were starting to run out of steam, producing weekly live shows.*

183   *There were EEFMS ties, and lyrics were written that were sung to the tune of "Alma Mater."*

190   **TOP LEFT:** *Kovacs did one broadcast live, non-stop on WTTM radio, for 24 hours a day all week long.*

192   *Front page of a typed script for an early episode of Kovacs' bizarro panel-quiz show* Take a Good Look *(ABC, 1959-1961).*

193   *Although the rest of the script is pretty conventional and straightforward, this "cold open" page is all Kovacs, and shows Ernie's surreal/visual ideas about opening a panel-quiz show.*

194-195   *These pages of handwritten notes indicate a wide variety of ideas for sequences for the film version of "Eugene" Kovacs was working on in 1961. The "E" in a circle is Eugene; the "she" in these pages refers to Edie, who is mentioned by name in other pages of handwritten notes. This tells us Kovacs was writing a part for his wife Edie Adams in the film. These notes match Kovacs's description of the opening sequence to the film Kovacs describes in his interview on the CBC show* The Lively Arts. *Eugene — to be played by Alec Guinness, in Kovacs's mind — is a cymbal player in a symphony. The opening gag is at a concert and, as the camera pushes in on Eugene, he strikes the cymbals together in an upward motion, propelling him through the floor of the stage.*

196   *The headline and first two paragraphs of the* Life *magazine feature story published on (of all dates!) April 15, 1957, interestingly, poses the question as to whether Kovacs's unique, visually oriented style that wasn't rooted in nightclub or theatrical performance might be the new trend or way forward for TV comedy. Considering the creative burnout cited by other star performers discussed in the article, it was a question on performers' and producers' minds. Mel Brooks has mentioned in interviews that he and the others on Sid Caesar's shows knew something was up around this time when they were getting beat in the ratings by Lawrence Welk's polka show. Ultimately, TV comedy continued with variety shows and, especially, canned-laughter filmed sitcoms, while Kovacs finally got a break from the daily grind he'd been on since entering radio in 1940 and enjoyed the Hollywood lifestyle of a movie actor and doing occasional guest-shots on other performer's variety shows.*

197   *The infamous tilted-table set, seen here in a production photo taken for Kovacs's* Silent Show, *a Color Spectacular broadcast live on NBC on January 19, 1957. Henry Lascoe, who had appeared in* Wonderful Town *with Edie, is at the right.*

198   *One of the secret guests on* Take a Good Look *was the artist who drew the pin-up girls for G.I. magazines during WWII. One of the clue videos has Ernie in a few different outfits and settings like this. Another clue shows Dracula bowling and at the last minute, after his opponent has bowled, Dracula makes the pin rise in the air and ball goes by. Get it? Pin...up...? If you didn't know who the guest was, none of this made any sense. Just ask the panelists on the show that night.*

199   **TOP RIGHT, BOTTOM LEFT, BOTTOM RIGHT:** *Three iterations of Ernie seen in one of the Dutch Masters commercials where all the TV crew members making the commercial were Ernie; the 4th image is of his Luigi character, who spoke with a Chico Marx Italian accent and turned up in loads of* TaGL *clues.*

199   **TOP LEFT:** *Kovacs and Andy McKay in either a sketch or posed photo for* Three to Get Ready *(1950-52); McKay was the all-hands-on-deck production assistant and on-camera performer for the WPTZ show.*

200   **TOP:** *Photo of baseball team sponsored by Toots Shor's; undated but most probably from 1956 as that was the year Al "Double-Talk" Kelly was on the Kovacs shows.*

200   **BOTTOM:** *Group photo of performers who appeared on the short-lived* The Walter Winchell Show *(NBC, 1956) that includes Joe DiMaggio, George Raft, Dorothy Kilgallen, Martha Raye, and Winchell (center, in fedora).*

200   **CENTER:** *Candid production photo of Joe Mikolas and Jolene Brand from closing credits blackouts taped for ABC special #7, aired Dec 1961; at right of the photo are prop birds from the "Story of a Drop of Water" music video piece.*

201   *Publicity photo of Kovacs and Ronnie Burns (son of George) for "The World's Greatest Quarterback" (1959), an episode of* The General Electric Theater. *Kovacs's hair was still growing back after his head was shaved for his role in* It Happened to Jane *(1959).*

202-207   *Manuscript pages for* Mildred Szabo, *an unfinished novel by Kovacs, a send-up of* Mildred Pierce.

209   *"Bridge" is a term for a brief musical segue. This is from the 1958 NBC special* Kovacs on Music, *for which André Previn served as musical director.*

210-213   *Ernie's record collection. He appears to have had not only a hand in the design of the shelving but also in the meticulous notes on how its construction was to be carried out.*

216   *From Kovacs's cigar order, during a trip to Havana, Cuba, in April 1955.*

217   *From Kovacs's cigar order, during a trip to Havana, Cuba, in April 1955.*

218-219   *Feature story on Kovacs, clearly written by Kovacs, in the August 18-25, 1951 issue of the TV listings magazine whose cover is on p. 75 of this book. This was the final week of* Ernie in Kovacsland, *which aired July-August 1951 nationally on NBC. Oscar Kinootz is a very Kovacsian-sounding name, and from the writing style of this piece it's pretty clear that Kovacs wrote it himself. Match it to any of the excerpts from his writings for* The Trentonian *that are in the book by David Walley,* The Ernie Kovacs Phile.

221   *A question and response from Ernie's 1956 recurring sketch "Mr. Question Man."*

222   *Publicity photo for* Private Eye, Private Eye *(1959), a sketch/variety special that was produced by Max Liebman, of* Your Show of Shows *and* Caesar's Hour *fame; L to R Hans Conried, Edie, Ernie; Conried would become one of the regular panelists on* Take a Good Look *(1959-60).*

228   *Cartoon inspired by and inscribed to Kovacs by Milton Caniff, whose strip "Steve Canyon" was very popular during this era.*

235   *Ernie and Edie seen in candid photos taken on the set of* Kovacs Unlimited *(1952-54, CBS).*

241   **TOP:** *Promotional photo for Ernie's daytime variety show* Kovacs Unlimited *(CBS, 1952-54); Trig Lund, Edie Adams, Ernie, Eddie Hatrak, and Andy McKay; from the way Edie and Ernie look, this could be from the beginning of the run, in 1952.*

241   **BOTTOM:** Kovacs Unlimited *(CBS, 1952-54): Andy McKay, Eddie Hatrak, Edie, Ernie.*

242   *Edie with baby Mia Kovacs in late 1959.*

243   *From Kovacs special #8, with Ernie as sculptor Miklos Molnar, and Maggie Brown as the artist's model. From a sequence of sketches about modern art and poetry.*

244   *This Percy poem was recorded for the unreleased* Percy Dovetonsils…Thpeakth *album in 1960, and appeared in the December 1961 issue of* Playboy.

245   **BOTTOM:** *Candid production photo of Kovacs and unidentified actor as Santa Claus between takes on a Dutch Masters cigar commercial taped for the holiday season.*

245   **TOP:** *Candid production photo of Kovacs between takes on a Dutch Masters cigar commercial taped for the holiday season.*

256-259   Holiday *was a travel magazine, originally published from 1946-1977 by the Curtis Publishing Company. Far from the kind of article one might find in an Amtrak or in-flight magazine today, this piece is a much more in-depth look at Kovacs's working method and attitude, and a sense of that manic energy Kovacs possessed. This article is the source of the quote about having an hour before a production meeting as creative inspiration, as well as the telling of the origin of The Nairobi Trio.*

260   *Publicity photo taken during the taping of ABC Special #6, also known as "Eugene." Bobby Lauher does not appear in this outfit in the final edit of this episode.*

262   *Publicity photo for "I Was a Bloodhound," an episode of* The General Electric Theater *(1959).*

269   **CENTER LEFT:** *Production photo of* Firebird Suite *sound-into-sight piece with Frances McHale, Jolene Brand, Joe Mikolas, Maggie Brown, and Bobby Lauher, in which surgeons operate on what turns out to be a Thanksgiving turkey; for ABC special #6 taped June 24, 1961 and aired Oct 26, 1961.*

269   **BOTTOM RIGHT:** *Candid production photo taken during taping of "Eugene" ABC special (aired Nov 24, 1961; Maggie Brown is in costume for statue that taps Eugene on shoulder and then disintegrates when he kisses her.*

274   *Promotional cartoon to promote* Take a Good Look, *Ernie's panel-quiz show (ABC 1959-1961); depicted are panelists Hans Conried, Edie Adams, and Cesar Romero as well as Kovacs and a burglar who appears in a Dutch Masters commercial from the run of this show.*

278   **BOTTOM:** *Edie with a bust of Ernie, presented at a ceremony in Trenton, NJ, in 1994.*

279   *People who were Kovacs fans felt a bond with him that was personal. People who remember hearing the news of his death have vivid and emotional memories of the event, as if it were a close relative or friend who'd suddenly died. This tribute to Kovacs was written and read by news broadcaster Harry Reasoner on the night of the accident.*

280   *Photo is of Kovacs as "Kenneth Mockridge, Philosophical Cab Driver," a character he did on his mid-1950s shows.*

281   *Although Edie was never known as Edie Kovacs, their company name bore the initials E&EK Productions.*

284   *Candid production photo of Kovacs, during the taping of one of his commercials for Dutch Masters cigars.*

ERNIE KOVACS

An inspiration to generations of comedians, including Johnny Carson, Chevy Chase, David Letterman, and Jimmy Kimmel, Kovacs was a comedian, actor, and writer known for his visually experimental and often spontaneous comedic style. Some of his quirky behaviors included having pet marmosets, wrestling a jaguar on his live Philadelphia television show, and hiring a taxi cab driver to enter his apartment with his own key, cook the two of them breakfast, and then drive Kovacs to the WABC studios so that he didn't have to eat breakfast alone. While he received Emmy nominations during his lifetime, it wasn't until after his tragic death in a car accident that he was formally recognized – the 1962 Emmy for Outstanding Electronic Camera Work and the Directors Guild Award came shortly after. Kovacs was inducted posthumously into the Academy of Television Arts & Sciences Hall of Fame and awarded a star on the Hollywood Walk of Fame for his work in television.

ERNIE KOVACS

1919-1962

Born in Trenton, New Jersey

Presented with admiration on the occasion of
Ernie's 75th birthday, January 23, 1994

SCULPTOR HAS ANOTHER COPY
OF THIS KOVACS BUST ~ SHE WILL DONATE
IT - TO ANY ORGANIZATION I'D LIKE !!
TRENTON PBS HAS ONE AFTRA MN. HOOD
HAS ANOTHER ~

On THE LATE NEWS,
Saturday, January 13, 1962,
Harry Reasoner broadcast
words he had put on paper
immediately after the
death of Ernie Kovacs.
A large number of viewers
were so moved that they
wrote to Mr. Reasoner and
to WCBS-TV asking for
the text. To those viewers,
and to others, we are
sending this reprint of
what has come to be called
"A Shiver in the Sunlight."

NORMAN E. WALT, JR.
Vice President & General Manager
WCBS-TV, New York

A SHIVER IN THE SUNLIGHT

ERNIE KOVACS *died in a car accident in Hollywood this morning and the guess has to be it was the most widely discussed news event of the day—one man's death in a world where everybody dies. This always happens when a man who belongs to the public, a man whom everyone knows, comes to a sudden end: the sense of loss and tragedy is heavy and immediate.*

The trite but probably true thought is that an event like this hits us wherever we are on a Saturday morning—in a supermarket, on a skating rink, self-satisfied in a late bed—with the old promissory note of our own mortality in a way that generalized warnings from the National Safety Council never could.

All prayer books ask for protection from <u>sudden</u> death: it is nice to think we will have a warning, time to think things out and go in bed, in honor and in love. Somebody dies in an unprepared hurry and you are touched with a dozen quick and recent memories: the sweetness of last evening, the uselessness of a mean word or an undone promise. It could be you, with all those untidy memories of recent days never to be straightened out.

There's a shiver in the sunlight, touching the warmth of life that you've been reminded you hold only for a moment.

Harry Reasoner on "The Late News," Saturday, January 13, 1962, WCBS-TV New York

E. & E. K. ENTERPRISES, (INC)

2301 Bowmont Drive, Beverly Hills, California

Date _____

Editors: Josh Mills, Ben Model, Pat Thomas

Designers: Jacob Covey and Kayla E.

Production: Kevin Uehlein, Jon Klages

Copy Editor: J. Michael Catron

Associate Publisher: Eric Reynolds

Publisher: Gary Groth

Fantagraphics Books, Inc.
7563 Lake City Way NE
Seattle, WA 98115
www.fantagraphics.com
facebook.com/fantagraphics
@fantagraphics

ISBN: 978-1-68396-667-8
Library of Congress Control Number: 2022936603
First Fantagraphics Books edition: April 2023
Printed in China

Acknowledgments

JOSH MILLS SAYS:

This book is dedicated to Ernie Kovacs for making all this great work and to Edie Adams for preserving it.

First and foremost, I'd like to thank my wife Jennifer for respecting my mom's and Ernie's life and career together and not insisting I throw all this stuff away as most partners would have. (And that's on top of all the other collections I have of my own including CDs, LPs, DVDs, books, baseball cards, my dad's massive photo archive et al.) They broke the mold when they made you; you found out you were pregnant while we were cleaning out my mom's house and still insisted I keep everything.

Secondly, I want to thank my daughter Madeline for being such a bright light in my life. Just looking at you, Madeline, I see my mom, my sister Mia, myself, and my wife in you. Your grandmother left you an amazing legacy and your constant curiosity to learn more about Grandma Edie fills me with pride. I only wish you got to meet her.

Thanks to the following people:

Pat Thomas for taking a very unselfish step into the world of Ernie and Edie with no clue as to what awaited him and digging in with both hands to help me form this book and connect me to Fantagraphics.

Ben Model, the official Ernie and Edie archivist since 2008, who has been nothing short of a savior. You truly know this archive better than anyone.

To Kevin Uehlein for his Herculean scanning and archiving abilities with this project as well as creating a template for this book via his book map.

To Jason Sundberg for his on-point scanning abilities as well. See you at the Pie & Burger.

Gary Groth at Fantagraphics who wanted to do this book. It takes a fan(ta) to make this happen.

To the good folks at Comedy Dynamics, Shout! Factory, MVD & Omnivore Recordings who are keeping the visual and audio works of Ernie Kovacs alive.

To Rob Stone, Alexis Ainsworth, Cary O'Dell, and Mike Mashon at the Library of Congress for preserving Ernie and Edie's visual history.

To the UCLA Film & Television Archive's Mark Quigley and former archivist Dan Einstein for always having my mom's (and my) back. That means a lot.

Joel Hodgson, the first Ernie Kovacs Award winner at the Dallas VideoFest, who has always been a huge Kovacs fan, supporter, and friend.

To ex-CBS Videotape Archival Services' Bob Haxby who my mom trusted like few others and passed that trust along to me.

To Gordon Smith who has been there for us with every major deal we've had — since the Reagan administration.

To Jeff Briggs for all your hard legal work with all matters Ernie and Edie through the years. A huge thank-you for all your time, effort, and friendship.

Posthumous thanks to Ernie and Edie's publicist, Henri Bollinger (and family). Henri was there with Ernie in 1957 when *Take a Good Look* started, worked with Edie for approximately 40 more years and was there for me in 2008 when I really needed help and guidance at one of the lowest points of my life. You helped me in more ways than I could thank you for.

Posthumous thank-yous to all these folks who I know would have loved this book: Mia Kovacs, Becky Greenlaw, Lynne Honus, Hal Prince, Lenita Law, Nan Burris, my dad Marty Mills, and Hal Willner.

Additional thanks to everyone who graciously has given their time to help publicize the Kovacs name whenever we have asked: Charlie Tabesh at TCM, Paul Malcolm at the UCLA Film & Television Archive, Cole Stratton at Sketchfest, Laura LaPlaca & Journey Gunderson at the National Comedy Center, Jack Vaughn at Sirius XM Comedy, Chris Strouth, Dick Fiddy at the BFI, Bart Weiss and Kelly Kitchens at Videofest, Raquel Chapa, Ron Simon at The Paley Center for Media, Museum of the Moving Image, Adrienn Dorsanszki, Shawn Yanez, Marc Walker, Steve Gorelick at the New Jersey Motion Picture Commission, Leah Churner, Stan Taffel at Kinecon, Jed Rapfogel at Anthology Film Archive, Lynne Sheridan at the Grammy Museum, Jessica Paxton at the Parkway Theater, Brent Kado at Chicago Comedy Film Festival, Dan Schlissel at Stand Up! Records, Robert Klein, George Schlatter, Jolene Brand Schlatter, Bob Odenkirk, Jim Hodgson, Dan Pasternack, Jeff Abraham, Kevin McDonald, Dave Foley, Gerald Casale, Dana Gould, Chris Stein, Debbie Harry, Wayne Federman, Merill Markoe, Jeff Garlin, Harry Shearer, Chris Elliott, Bob Elliott, Martin Mull, John Cleese, Terry Gilliam, Paul Reubens, Mike Judge, Amy Sedaris, Robert Smigel, Michael Nesmith, Al Franken, and everyone who bought this book.

For more information:

www.erniekovacs.com

Twitter/IG/Facebook: Realerniekovacs

BEN MODEL THANKS:
Alexis Ainsworth, Mana Allen, Steve Friedman, Eric Grayson, Jane Klain, John Lollos, Alan and Alice Model, Al Quagliata, Rob Stone, Seth B. Winner

PAT THOMAS DEDICATES:
This book to Hal Willner; we had a wonderful long lunch at Canter's as I embarked on this journey — I'm sad he's not here to enjoy it. And to Eddie Schmidt — the only person I trust in Hollywood. And to Gary Groth, just cause he's Gary.

This book was proofread by Jon Klages and facilitated by Kristian St. Clair.